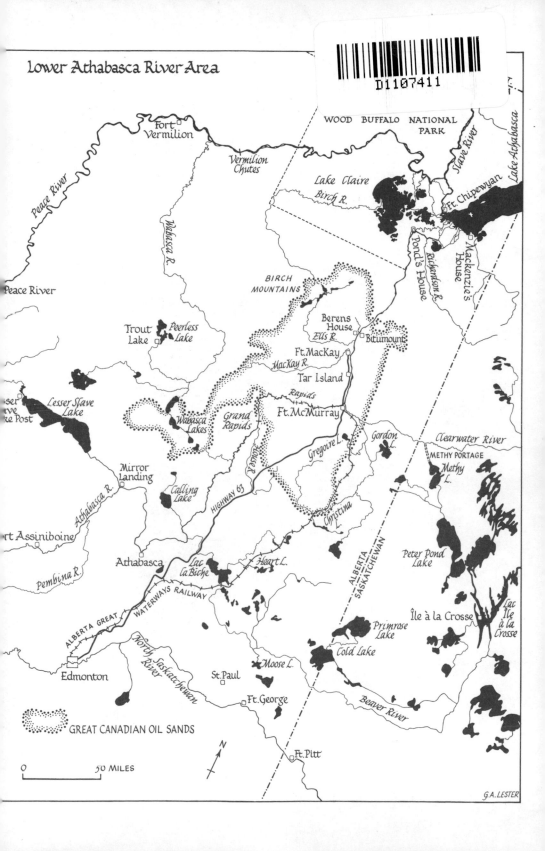

Lower Athabasca River Area

D1107411

Peace River

Fort Vermilion

Vermilion Chutes

WOOD BUFFALO NATIONAL PARK

Slave River

Lake Claire

Birch R.

Ft. Chipewyan

Lake Athabasca

Wabasca R.

Peace River

BIRCH MOUNTAINS

Pond's House

Richardson R.

Mackenzie's House

Trout Lake

Peerless Lake

Berens House

Ells R.

Bitumount

Ft. MacKay

MacKay R.

Tar Island

Lesser Slave Lake Post

Lesser Slave Lake

Wabasca Lakes

Grand Rapids

Rapids

Ft. McMurray

Clearwater River

Gregoire L.

Gordon L.

METHY PORTAGE

Methy L.

Mirror Landing

Athabasca R.

La Biche

HIGHWAY 63

Calling Lake

Christina L.

Peter Pond Lake

Fort Assiniboine

Pembina R.

Athabasca

Lac la Biche

Heart L.

ALBERTA
SASKATCHEWAN

Île à la Crosse

Lac Île à la Crosse

ALBERTA GREAT

WATERWAYS RAILWAY

North Saskatchewan River

St. Paul

Moose L.

Primrose Lake

Cold Lake

Edmonton

Ft. George

Beaver River

:::: GREAT CANADIAN OIL SANDS

0   50 MILES

N

Ft. Pitt

G.A. LESTER

Paddle Wheels to Bucket-Wheels
on the Athabasca

Paddle Wheels
to
Bucket-Wheels
on the
Athabasca

J. G. MacGregor

McClelland and Stewart Limited

© 1974 J. G. MacGregor

All rights reserved

0-7710-5450-5

The Canadian Publishers
McClelland and Stewart Limited
25 Hollinger Road, Toronto

Printed and bound in Canada

Contents

Acknowledgements

In a book of an historical nature an author is always under a heavy obligation to many persons who helped him and to many institutions and libraries which placed their collections and records at his disposal. Foremost amongst these in the present case is the Hudson's Bay Company; all the many quotations from its fur-trade records and from the invaluable publications of the Hudson's Bay Record Society have been used by the kind permission of that company.

Through the kindness and assistance of the Public Archives of Canada, the Alberta Provincial Library and the University of Alberta's Cameron Library, I have obtained a great deal of information. I am also indebted to Rev. Father E. O. Drouin, OMI, Edmonton, Archivist of the Order of Mary Immaculate, for allowing me access to his priceless records. Amongst the material made available to me by the Provincial Archives of Alberta were the records of the Anglican diocese of Athabasca, and from them I obtained the story of the tragedy at Trout Lake.

Amongst the many local authorities and old-timers who have been exceptionally helpful, Walter H. Hill, whose half-century in Fort McMurray has made him an amiable encyclopaedia of the region's history; Julian Mills, the steamboat captain of wisdom and renown; Bob Duncan, a northerner to the roots of his white hairs; Mrs. Ashacker, who allowed me to study the diaries and photographs of her father, Sergeant "Nitchie" Thorne; Raynor Whitley, who chuckles as he relates tales of the early days along the Athabasca Trail; and that typical, generous priest, Rev. Father Queff of the Nativity Mission at Fort Chipewyan have all been most kind and helpful.

Dealing with more modern times and with the development of the oil sands, I am indebted to Russell A. Patrick, one-time Minister of Mines for Alberta, for much interesting information, as well as to Mr. L. J. Bland of Great Canadian Oil Sands, who kindly read and commented on the part of the manuscript dealing with his company's activities.

Once more I am grateful that Geoffrey Lester has drawn the fine maps that help to elucidate the text.

In the matter of pictures, as usual, I have leaned heavily on a number of sources which invariably have been helpful and to which I am very grateful: *The Beaver Magazine*, the Public Archives of Canada, the Provincial Archives of Alberta, the Geological Survey of Canada, Great Canadian Oil Sands Ltd., the Alberta Film and Photographic Branch, the Research Council of Alberta and R. E. Duncan.

Introduction

Until recent years the mighty Athabasca River formed the sole link which led from civilization to all the mysteries of the remote North. For a hundred years only canoes and York boats plied its waters. Then for nearly another century sternwheelers carried its commerce to the faraway places dotted so sparingly along the chain of magnificent rivers leading to the Arctic Ocean eighteen hundred miles downstream. Those days are gone, but even though planes, trucks and locomotives have superseded the old-time canoes, scows and steamboats, the romance of the old days lingers.

It is with that romance that this book deals. From the days thousands of years ago when the first Indians explored this northeast quarter of Alberta extending from Athabasca Landing to the Fort Smith rapids, until the days when they guided William Stewart, the first white man to tread in the Mackenzie watershed, it remained a vast, empty land. Empty it still is, but its rustling forests, tinkling streams and roaring rapids are filled with tales of the heroic or desperate deeds of Indians, fur traders, voyageurs, priests, scowmen, sternwheeler captains and the sturdy folk who finally won the battle to unlock the secrets of the region's vast deposit of oil sands.

Unfortunately of the multitude of tales not even the few which have come down to us can be compressed into the limits of one book. As a result, we have had to pick and choose and in doing so have decided to tell the tales of the area's early days in far greater detail than those of its more modern times which began in 1926 when the Alberta and Great Waterways Railway reached Fort McMurray.

But the fascination of this far-flung land lies not alone in these tales of its early days. Much of it lies in the remoteness and loneliness of the lower Athabasca watershed. This quarter of the province is some sixty thousand square miles of almost continuous forest, silent, mysterious and seemingly boundless. The modern traveller flying low in a small plane sees a deep, blue-green carpet of conifers stretching away for scores of miles on all sides till it loses itself in the dark blue of the distant hills—the endless boreal forest. Through that forest for hundreds of miles flows the broad Athabasca.

Rising in Jasper Park's mountain glaciers, the river flows some eight hundred miles to the meandering and muddy channels that build up the vast marshes of the delta at the Alberta end of huge Lake Athabasca. Near its mid point is the flourishing town of Athabasca and from there down to the majestic lake lies its historic navigable portion. Once it sweeps around its wide bend at Athabasca town and disappears into the protection of the woods, it heads generally north for 165 miles to Grand Rapids. Along that course for the most part it glides placidly but determinedly, 250 to 400 yards wide flowing in a valley some 300 to 400 feet deep.

The Grand Rapids, however, are a different story, for in descending them the river roars. There, as it divides into two channels to gallop down amidst boulders on each side of an island, the Athabasca drops thirty-two feet in less than half a mile and twice that much before reaching the end of the rough water. The left hand passage is a raging torrent which no craft could navigate, while the right one is a calmer chute down which empty boats and scows could be lowered. Steamboats, however, found the Grand Rapids an impracticable barrier.

While these rapids ruled out through steamboat navigation all the way from the Landing, the remaining eighty-seven miles to Fort McMurray tested the scows' mettle to the utmost. In that stretch where the Athabasca flows practically straight east through a deep rift in the hills it drops almost four hundred feet in a series of vicious rapids: the Brule, Boiler (where the steamboat boiler was lost), Middle, Long and Crooked (where the river makes a spectacular hairpin turn), Rock, Little Cascade, Cascade, Mountain and Moberly. A mile or so below the Moberly Rapids and passing high banks saturated with oil sands, the river saunters innocently into Fort McMurray. There, almost head-on, it collides with its largest and historically most important tributary, the Clearwater River.

Augmented now by the Clearwater, the Athabasca resumes its northerly course for 120 miles until it enters the western end of Lake Athabasca, where it loses its identity in the confusion of the Peace-Athabasca Delta. Mingling its waters with those of the Peace River and with those originating in the Fond du Lac River of eastern Saskatchewan, and wandering in the immense marshes of its own making, it splits into a maze of channels. Some of them wind their way into the Delta; the Embarras, the Fletcher and Goose Island channels. Others wander forlornly seeking their way out the northern end of the delta flats; the Chenal des Quatre Fourches (the river where the four forks intersect at one place at right angles to each other), the Revillon Coupe and the Rivière des Rochers. Note these names bestowed by the voyageurs.

In loops and ox-bows other lesser streams, flowing this way and that, criss-crossing like the veins on the back of a hand, trickle their way through this marsh labyrinth. On their way they connect many a minor lake with the larger shallow bodies of water—Lakes Baril, Hilda, Mamawi, and Claire. Lake Claire alone covers nearly six hundred square miles, and even it, as big as it is, occupies little more than one-quarter of the huge 2,300-square-mile Delta, which is larger than the province of Prince Edward Island and whose east-west axis extends nearly sixty-five miles. The Delta's length equals the distance from Toronto to Trenton, Ontario. If it were located near Edmonton it would reach from there as far south as Lacombe and would spread out to touch Pigeon Lake on the west and Camrose on the east. And over this vast area the waters of the Athabasca River wander back and forth.

This huge delta is one of nature's fascinating creations. Every spring, before the building of the Bennett Dam hundreds of miles away in British Columbia, the mighty Peace River overflowed its levees and poured its surplus waters and their silt into the marshy delta. When it did the channels which usually flowed north, the Claire and Rocher rivers, the Revillon Coupe and the Quatre Fourches backed up and allowed Peace River waters to enter the Delta marshes, reinvigorating them and raising the levels of Lakes Baril, Mamawi and Claire. Then when the spring flood subsided and the level of the Slave River dropped, the water began to leave the Delta and the Revillon Coupe and the Rocher River once more flowed north. Out of all the confusion and the complexity of floods and reversing flows, this annual inundation fostered a unique and healthy ecology of plants, fish and fur-bearers.

Although the Athabasca River loses itself in the expansive marshes, its waters, sweeping around the corner near Fort Chipewyan to form the Rivière des Rochers or Rocher River, then unite with the Peace to make up the Slave, allowing steamboats to navigate all the way from Fort McMurray to the rapids starting one hundred miles down the Slave at old Fitzgerald. These waters leave the Athabasca behind, marching on to Fort Smith, to Great Slave Lake and on into the mighty Mackenzie River to debouch at last into the Arctic Ocean some 1,400 miles from Lake Athabasca. Except for the interruption of the Grand Rapids and those of the Slave River, they form the 1,800 miles of navigable waterway reaching from Athabasca town, the northern edge of Canada's prairies, to the iceberg-strewn Arctic.

Throughout its whole length one of the waterway's characteristics is the almost total absence of people dwelling more than a mile back from its shores. On the stretch of the river downstream from Athabasca, for instance, the only town is Fort McMurray (population 8,000), a near city built to service the extraction of the oil sands but some 180 road miles from its nearest incorporated neighbour, Lac La Biche. Except for the occupants of a shack or two at the mouths of its main tributary streams, a few trappers and occasionally one or two Indian families, no one lives along its bush-lined banks from the Landing to the oil sands town. On reserves, usually well back from the river and clustered around such bodies of water as Gregoire and Heart lakes in the Athabasca's watershed, or else actually on its banks as at Fort Mackay, live some 750 treaty Indians. As well as these, a number of non-treaty Indians and Métis eke out a slender existence throughout the area. Few wildernesses on earth have less people per square mile and, except for the focal points of Fort McMurray and Fort Chipewyan, the situation is not changing.

When, however, the first men, the ancestors of our Indians, came to hunt along its shores or to light their little campfires on its banks, they discovered it to be part of one of the continent's greatest waterways. Before long the red men's canoes had followed it to the junction point of western Canada, Lake Athabasca, the cross-roads, the marshalling yard of the North, receiving from three rivers and feeding to a fourth, each mighty in its own right. The Peace, 900 miles long, bears tidings from the continental divide to the west; the Fond du Lac brings the drainage from Lake Wollaston near the Manitoba border, some 350 miles away; our Athabasca, 780 miles long, points the way out to the prairies; and finally the outflow from the lake, the Slave-Mackenzie stream, heads north along the 1,400 miles to the Arctic Ocean.

Though these great waterways leading east, south, west and north have been destined to remain remote from the echoes of civilization, each is of the utmost importance to man, Indian or white, and each has contributed its share of romance to Canada's lore. Of them all, however, the lower 437-mile stretch of the river from Athabasca is perhaps the most fabulous. As its waters lap against the now empty waterfront at Athabasca town—the

Landing—and finally flow around the point to disappear into the mysterious fastnesses of Alberta's northern forest, ghosts of its former glories call back and forth over the crescent basin below the town. For they are the ghosts of French, Scottish and Métis voyageurs, the spirits of mixed-blood pilots, river captains, solitary adventurers and the shades of a horde of Klondikers pushing off towards the romantic places. Their old-time destinations were Fort Chipewyan and Fort Smith, Fort Simpson and Arctic Red River, for they were headed for the land of the faraway people, the Yellowknives, Dogribs and Eskimos. They were bound north to the haunts of the polar bear and the pastures of caribou herds and muskox. And as the shadows lengthen and the mists of evening rise to hide the once lively basin, well may their spirits whisper, chuckle or sing in the twilight.

It is of these men we propose to tell. For in their day they were mighty adventurers.

Paddle Wheels to Bucket-Wheels
on the Athabasca

CHAPTER ONE

Native Peoples and Samuel Hearne

Who was the first man to discover the Athabasca River, to marvel at its size and to venture down it on a log or raft or in a canoe? We can never know, but he was some ancestor of our Indians and he did so many thousands of years ago. Then as one generation followed another pressing ever farther north as the glacier retreated, his kin also discovered the magnificent lake as well as the Peace and Slave rivers.

That they did so during the millennia before any man anywhere had invented the art of record-keeping by writing is perhaps neither important nor unfortunate. What is unfortunate, however, is that even as late as the time when white men arrived to "discover" the Athabasca River the Indian people, pursuing their civilization along its banks, still kept no written records. As a result, the only information about the races that lived in northeastern Alberta 250 years ago is that recorded by white men and viewed from the white man's point of view. True enough the Indians have their traditions. Since, however, their contents are susceptible to elaboration, contraction or distortion with each mouth-to-ear transmission, they offer no reliable substitute for the written word. Consequently, except for some fascinating hints provided by archaeological research, all we know of the Indians' past is what tribes inhabited the general Athabasca River area when the great explorers Samuel Hearne and Alexander Mackenzie visited them and wrote about them towards the close of our 18th century.

At that time, according to Alexander Mackenzie, four tribes lived in our particular section of the Mackenzie watershed; the Slaves, Beavers and Chipewyans, all of Athabaskan stock, and the Crees of the Algonkian language group. Undoubtedly down through the ages they had shifted their relative positions as frictions developed between them or with other tribes which they had driven out. For wherever he goes, fighting and warfare accompany man, red, white or of any other colour.

The Slaves were the most northerly and extended along the gigantic

1

watercourse from Great Slave Lake to Fort Norman. Their name, like the names by which we know most Indian tribes, was of course not what they called themselves but that which their native enemies who were armed with the white man's guns called these defenceless people whom they drove north and west. The Beavers lived in the lower basin of the Peace River and in a tract stretching from Lake Athabasca upstream as far as Fort McMurray and also up the Clearwater River as far as the Methy Portage. Their name, also assigned to them by their neighbours, is derived from what they called their magnificent Peace River, *tsades*, the river abounding in beavers. The Chipewyans ranged over a vast rectangular area bounded approximately by the Slave and Athabasca rivers on the west, the Churchill (whose waters rise near Lac La Biche) on the south, the shores of Hudson Bay on the east and extending far enough north into the Barren Lands so that they came into sporadic conflict with their neighbours, the Eskimos. They received their name from the Crees who, finding their most distinguishing characteristic to be the pointed design of their reindeer tunics, called them *chipwayanawok*, or pointed skins.

The Crees, whom we know by a contraction of the French form of a name of unknown meaning which a portion of that tribe applied to itself, *kristineaux*, also laid successful claim to an immense region. At the time of their first dealings with white men they ranged from James Bay west through northern Ontario, most of Manitoba and on into northern Saskatchewan, where along their northern frontier, the Churchill River, they came into conflict with the Chipewyans. Enjoying a slightly gentler climate than their northern neighbours, more aggressive and able to obtain guns from the French and Hudson's Bay Company fur traders, the Crees soon set about enlarging their territory by warring first on the Chipewyans and later turning their smoking guns on the Beavers and Slaves and seizing much of these tribes' one-time homelands.

The Crees, living on the shores of Hudson Bay and within reach of the St. Lawrence River, were amongst the first Indians to get the white man's goods and guns. Being somewhat merchant-minded, they soon became middlemen making their profit by passing European goods on to the tribes of the West and taking furs in exchange. It was but a step from that to carrying their gunfire beyond their territorial boundaries. By 1680 they had passed west of Lake Winnipeg and shortly after that they drove the Chipewyans farther west and north from their former homeland. Ever as they progressed west, the Chipewyans, Beavers and Slaves backed up before them.

At the end of the ice age primitive men had followed the retreating glaciers northward and the farther north they went the harsher the country became. When Stewart, Hearne and others first saw them, the Chipewyans appeared to the white man to be the most primitive natives in Canada—those who had been thrust ever farther north into a land whose climate and resources enabled only a scanty population to eke out a meagre existence in a vast region remote from the centres of more advanced Indian culture. Moreover, the conditions of life in their inhospitable land were such as to preclude the Chipewyans from developing a higher plane of social life. Even oratory, such a noticeable achievement of tribes farther south, failed to evolve and eloquence counted for little. Because their struggle for existence was so constant and their political organization so tenuous, prestige and authority came only from outstanding personality combined with physical prowess, success in hunting or accredited influence over the spirit world.

Yet harsh though their land may have been, it was the Chipewyans' native land and in spite of its austerity they came to understand it and to love it. Moose, caribou, wildfowl and fish were of necessity the mainstays of their diet, although the smaller mammals—rabbits, for instance—were of course not ignored. In that land the natives' life revolved about the cyclical nature of the caribou migration and therefore was itself migratory. In the spring the Chipewyans followed the caribou out into the Barren Lands; in the fall, led by the caribou, they retreated south into wooded regions. During the winter they impounded the larger game in enclosures of saplings and brush, while in the summer they would drive them towards a line of concealed archers or would force parts of the vast herds into lakes or rivers where they speared them from canoes.

Because they led such a migratory life the Indians in the northern woods or the Barren Lands did not build any sort of permanent house. Their dwellings, usually teepees but sometimes only brush shelters, provided little more than the minimum requirements of keeping out the snow and breaking the force of the wind; their function was not to provide comfort. As anthropologist Douglas Leechman wrote:

> The natives often performed most of their tasks, and ate their meals, outside their houses, if the weather permitted; and their dwellings were not so much homes in our conception of that term, as indispensable shelters against the elements.

Living under such conditions their lives were far from idyllic and they had little opportunity to advance along the road towards any higher social organization. Owing to their extreme hardihood, however, they continued to exist in an environment where their only luxury came in the form of days of feasting idleness when the caribou were plentiful and where their only tools and conveniences were those which with exhaustive patience and effort they contrived from materials at hand. Their axes, knives and scrapers were chipped from stones or shaped from beaver teeth or caribou antler, their clothing was fashioned from caribou hides and their fishing nets from thongs or roots.

Improvements in the tools, clothing or fishing gear of all the Indians of northern Alberta, and their ability to cope more successfully with their environment had to await the appearance of white men's goods manufactured in Europe. Passing west from band to band from Hudson Bay to Great Slave Lake, the first of these goods began trickling through to our Indians about the year 1700. Few possessions could have raised the women's spirits or eased their drudgery as much as steel needles, awls, knives or copper cooking pots to replace their horn, bone or stone household tools and few better gifts could have been put into the men's hands than sharp axes, hunting knives or guns. We have to think long before we

3

can appreciate the hours of painstaking toil these saved the women, how they eased the labours of the hunters and how much they contributed to raising their standard of living. To the white men they were the incidental products of their factories; to the northern natives they were veritable godsends.

In 1715 the Hudson's Bay Company operating out of York Factory sent out the first white man ever to tread in the Mackenzie watershed, a Scot named William Stewart. He walked hundreds of miles west to the vicinity of Great Slave Lake to get acquainted with the country and its natives, to patch up a peace between the Crees and their neighbours and to induce the Chipewyans to descend the Churchill River to Hudson Bay. In 1717, after the company established Fort Churchill to accommodate them, they began going there and securing guns of their own and were able to prevent the Crees from making further serious inroads into their territory. At the same time, unfortunately, they waged their own war of expansion, clearing the defenceless Eskimos out of the southwestern edge of the Barren Lands and driving the Yellowknives and Dogribs farther north and west. Following the continent-wide pattern the Chipewyans denied these two tribes access to the white traders and, acting as middlemen in their turn, forced the tribes of the lower Mackenzie watershed to exchange their furs for European goods at an exorbitant profit.

But Stewart's peace was a frail thing and ignoring it one branch of the Crees carried on their western expansion, this time invading the lands of the Beavers and the Slaves. They drove the Beavers out of the Clearwater River region and forced them back to the banks of the Peace. The Slaves fled farther north down the Slave River to the great lake at its mouth, the lake that ever since has borne their name. The Crees' expansion was still under way when in 1778 Peter Pond arrived to trade on the lower Athabasca.

Back at Hudson Bay about 1717 when the English company's Governor James Knight, worrying about the effect of Indian warfare on the firm's business, held a council with the aggressive Crees and tried to dissuade them from persecuting the Beaver and Chipewyan tribes, they gave him a rough idea of the geography of the land beyond the headwaters of the Churchill River. They told him of the great Athabasca River and of the sea-like Lake Athabasca. The most promising Cree convert to Knight's peaceful policy was an Indian by the name of The Swan, one of the many merchant types among the Crees whose interests were better served by peace than war. The Swan undertook to have a try at this business of bringing about a peace and disappeared up the Churchill River.

Ultimately he returned to the Bay and reported that the natives of the lower Athabasca valley (doubtless Beaver Indians) had welcomed his peace overtures. Almost immediately The Swan set off on his second trip and two years later, after wintering along the Athabasca River, possibly near our Fort McMurray, he returned to Fort Churchill. He brought not only the first report of the Athabasca oil sands ever to reach white man's ears, but true to his merchandising proclivities brought back a sample of "that Gum or pitch that flows out of the Banks of that River." After that this merchant who over-leapt tribal passions in the pursuit of profit continued to trade

4

with the Beaver Indians. Having The Swan and several other native traders like him to bring northeastern Alberta's furs down the Churchill River and later on the Chipewyans themselves coming to the Bay, it was many years before the company had occasion to send any other men into the area.

Meanwhile, the Cree ascendancy over the Beavers and Slaves, with its resulting clashes, continued unchecked until about 1760 when another fragile armistice was concluded. Shortly after this, about 1781, a devastating epidemic of smallpox decimated the Crees in the Lake Athabasca area. About the same time, probably because of the resultant relaxation of Cree vigilance and partly because Peter Pond had established a post in the area, the Beaver Indians themselves obtained guns. With them they began to even the score but within a year or so at a gathering at the white man's urging, they concluded what became almost a lasting peace. Ever since, the scene of that gathering has been known as *Unchaga* or Peace Point. From it the mighty river marching northeast across Alberta derived its name—Peace River.

This peace, however, came into being some seventy years after William Stewart had tramped his difficult way across the seven hundred airline miles from Hudson Bay to the Mackenzie River watershed. Like all white explorers, Stewart was led and instructed in the method of living off the Barren Lands by an Indian—in this case a Chipewyan, and, even more remarkably, a woman. In the records her name is not given and she is known to us only as the "slave woman," but she had been a victim of one of the numerous Cree attacks and had been kept as a prisoner. When she escaped, she made her way to York Factory on Hudson Bay, where, using the Cree tongue, she explained to Governor James Knight much of the geography of the vast land lying north and west and then undertook to guide Stewart and a few dubiously peaceful Crees on their remarkable trip towards Great Slave Lake.

Leaving York Factory on June 27, 1715, the little band set out on foot on the round-trip which was to take them until May 7 the following year. All summer long the courageous and capable "slave woman" guided the party and then, urging them over the snowy waste, finally brought them safely to a gathering of her people in the vicinity of Great Slave Lake. There she not only explained the advantages that would accrue to the Chipewyans if they took their furs to the Hudson's Bay Company but also showed them how to prepare their skins for market and induced two youths of the tribe to return with Stewart and herself to the Bay. With the aid of the Slave woman the Chipewyans had been brought into contact with the fur company and the first white man had put in a winter in the Mackenzie watershed.

The next European to enter that area did so in 1771. He was Samuel Hearne, who, by leaving Fort Churchill and travelling far out into the lands to the north and west until the winter's snows gave way before the vibrant spring of the Barren Lands, reached the mouth of the Coppermine River in July 1771. Not only was he the first white man to travel overland to reach the rim of the Arctic Ocean, but his trip finally proved that the long-sought Northwest Passage, a mythical sea lane through northern Canada, did not exist. His notes enabled the Hudson's Bay Company to produce the first reasonably accurate map of the territory through which he had walked. On that map the huge body of water which he called Athapuscow, but which we know as Great Slave Lake, was shown for the first time.

Hearne's trip established him as one of the great explorers of Canada, but his fame rests on an even broader foundation. First of all, like Anthony Henday and many another Hudson's Bay explorer before or after his time, he was an exponent of living off the land. Later generations of explorers, not Hudson's Bay Company men, could not believe that they could do this and burdened themselves by carrying with them supplies sufficient for months and as a result often sacrificed the extent of their surveys by their solicitude for security. Secondly, he was a careful observer of the mammals, birds and fish he encountered. Finally, and perhaps most importantly, Hearne's carefully prepared journal gives us the first clear insight into the lives of the tribes of Indians he travelled with or met and is one of the best sources of information we have on the Chipewyans' manner of life. Moreover, he was the first to give a good description of muskox—a description based on seeing them killed and eating their flesh. Rumours of such animals had reached white men previously but Hearne's was the earliest first-hand account. In like manner, he was the first white man to see and describe the wood bison which his party began killing when they entered the valley of the Slave River.

After being an unwilling and helpless witness to his Chipewyan friends' massacre of a few harmless Eskimo families at what we still call Bloody Falls, near the mouth of the Coppermine River, Hearne turned south and on December 24, 1771, reached the north shore of Great Slave Lake to spend his second Christmas in the wilds. From there he crossed the lake and after ascending much of the Slave River struck off east and, probably by way of the Taltson and Thoa rivers, made his way to Labyrinth Lake, passing some thirty miles north of Alberta's northeast corner. In due course he followed his outbound track east until on June 30, 1772 he returned to Fort Churchill.

The details of his outstanding trip do not concern us so much as the mine of information about the Chipewyans he left us in his journal. On their trips with people of this tribe many later white travellers made various comments which in the main confirm his conclusions but their notes were never as complete as his. Moreover, few of these men were as tolerant as he was. It is inevitable that when men of two races as completely different as the individualistic, hard-pressed primitive Chipewyan and the somewhat cultured Englishman were thrown into rather intimate contact each should come away with an incomplete assessment of the other's culture. The difference in their everyday life, in their discipline or lack of it, their religious outlook and social structure and their whole philosophy, simply would not allow one to see with the other's eyes. Keeping that in mind, however, we will probably not go far astray if we accept Hearne's appraisal of the Chipewyans with relatively minor reservations.

Fortunately Hearne was led and cared for by a man called Matonabbee, who appears to have been the outstanding individual of the whole tribe. By his dominant personality and his leadership, he alone made Hearne's trip possible and on top of this tutored the European in the ways of the Barren Lands and of its peoples. The first thing he did was to make it clear to

Hearne that no man, either red or white, could live or travel in that harsh country without the support and faithful service of women,

"for," said he, "when all the men are heavy laden, they can neither hunt nor travel to any considerable distance; and in case they meet with success in hunting, who is to carry the produce of their labour? Women," added he, "were made for labour; one of them can carry, or haul, as much as two men can do. They also pitch our tents, make and mend our clothing, keep us warm at night; and, in fact, there is no such thing as travelling any considerable distance, or for any length of time, in this country, without their assistance. Women," said he again, "though they do every thing, are maintained at a trifling expense; for as they always stand cook, the very licking of their fingers in scarce times, is sufficient for their subsistence."

Hearne's journal provides ample confirmation of this, as well as the best illustration of what a harsh and brutal life the Chipewyans led. In addition to many other facets of their life it shows how necessary it was for a man to have several wives to do all the work that had to be done in their wandering existence and how the stronger men simply took wives away from the weaker. Hearne's comments deal with the philosophy underlying their improvident slaughter of game animals and many of their other practices, such as their abandoning the sick or the aged, which seem harsh when seen through our eyes.

One of the many stories which Hearne passed along to us is that of a young woman the party encountered when it was approaching our Fort Smith area. On January 11 someone discovered a young Dogrib woman hiding in a brush shelter. A year and a half previously she had been captured by some of her tribe's enemies but had escaped from them about seven months before Hearne's companions found her. When her captors had attacked her band at night they killed her father, mother and husband and everyone else except herself and three other young women. In the dark she managed to hide her five months' old baby in her clothing. When, however, she was taken back to her enemy's camp one of the women there discovered her infant and "killed it on the spot." After she finally ran away she lived alone and had

supported herself very well by snaring partridges, rabbits, and squirrels; she had also killed two or three beaver, and some porcupines. That she did not seem to have been in want is evident, as she had a small stock of provisions by her when she was discovered. . . . When the few deer-sinews that she had an opportunity of taking with her were all expended in making snares, and sewing her clothing, she had nothing to supply their place but the sinews of the rabbits legs and feet; these she twisted together for that purpose with great dexterity and success. The rabbits, &c. which she caught in those snares, not only furnished her with a comfortable subsistence, but of the skins she made a suit of neat and warm clothing for the Winter. . . .

Her leisure hours from hunting had been employed in twisting the inner rind or bark of willows into small lines, like net-twine, of which she had some hundred fathoms by her; with this she intended to make a fishing net as soon as the Spring advanced. . . .Five or six inches of an iron hoop, made into a knife, and the shank of an arrow-head of iron, which served her as an awl, were all the metal this poor woman had with her when she eloped; and with these implements she had made herself complete snow-shoes, and several other useful articles.

She had kept herself warm by making a fire using two stones which

by long friction and hard knocking, produced a few sparks, which at length communicated to some touchwood; but as this method was attended with great trouble, and not always with success, she did not suffer her fire to go out all the Winter.

The sight of her set Matonabbee's blood tingling. When several of Hearne's party contended for her hand "the poor girl was actually won and lost at wrestling by near half a score different men the same evening." Matonabbee was only prevented from entering the contest because one of his seven wives shamed him out of it "by telling him that he had already more wives than he could properly attend." Unfortunately, at this slur to his virility, he attacked this wife "and bruised her to such a degree, that after lingering some time she died."

We are fortunate that through Hearne's *Journey* we can not only trace the wanderings of one of the hardiest explorers who ever ventured to cross the Barren Lands and who became the second white man to enter the Lake Athabasca area, but can also glimpse the life style of the Chipewyans at the time of one of their earliest contacts with white men. We are fortunate too that a man so observing as Hearne and one who viewed his native companions with some measure of understanding and compassion took the trouble to write his journal.

CHAPTER TWO
Peter Pond and Alexander Mackenzie

While Hearne had been on his trip various independent traders from Montreal, who eventually were to form the North West Company, had been providing stiff competition for the Hudson's Bay Company in the region north and west of Lake Winnipeg. In 1774, shortly after he returned from his Coppermine journey, the company sent Hearne to try to offset their efforts by building Cumberland House in the watershed of the lower Saskatchewan River and at a point where streams provided access to the waterways leading to the Churchill River.

Trade rivalry soon forced the traders to move much farther up the Saskatchewan River. Involved in these moves were two men who were soon to play their part on the Lake Athabasca stage, Philip Turnor and Peter Pond. In 1776 Pond built a post some four miles upstream from modern Prince Albert, while Turnor of the Hudson's Bay Company went farther up the river to build his Hudson House. At the same time, Thomas Frobisher, another of the independents, established himself on Lake Ile-à-la-Crosse. The commercial approach to the Athabasca River watershed had begun and Beavers, Crees and Chipewyans of the Lake Athabasca basin began pouring furs into Frobisher's fort.

At one time Alexander Henry, Thomas Frobisher and others had considered going back towards the Lake Athabasca area with the Chipewyans who traded at Ile-à-la-Crosse. When, in 1778, these associates finally decided to extend their trading area by the relatively unspectacular feat of crossing the height of land leading to the Athabasca River, they selected Peter Pond to take charge of their venture. Guided by Indians who had been trading at Frobisher's post, he spent about three weeks making the trip of 350 miles to where, near the Embarras River, he decided to set up shop.

His partners could not have placed the venture in more capable hands. Born at Milford, Connecticut, in 1740, when the region was still a British colony, Pond had served as a soldier for a time but soon went on to find his life's work as a fur trader. After spending several years trading near Detroit and on the headwaters of the Mississippi, he set out in 1775 for what was then the northwest frontier of Canada. A year later he operated his post near modern Prince Albert. By that time he had gained the respect of his fellow traders for his ability, aggressiveness and integrity.

Pond, then, was the first white person to cross the famous Methy Portage and thereby to take the route which was to give his fellows ready access from the Saskatchewan and Churchill rivers to the Athabasca River and from there to all the northland. Except for the fact that his four canoes and all his supplies had to be carried over the twelve-mile portage, the 350-mile water route he took was neither particularly difficult nor dangerous. Since, however, for over a hundred years after Pond's time this route which crossed the Methy Portage was the only practical way to the North, perhaps we should examine it in detail.

Leaving Ile-à-la-Crosse, Pond's canoes headed north up one of the twenty-mile-long arms of the lake and at its end paddled up the Churchill River until they could skirt the south shore of Churchill Lake. Then by way of Buffalo Narrows they crossed over to another large body of water which required some thirty-five miles of paddling to its northwest end where the mouth of the small Methy River appeared. Before long that lake had come to be called Peter Pond Lake. Another twenty miles or so up the swift but shallow and therefore difficult Methy River, brought Pond and his voyageurs to Methy Lake, where, after another fifteen miles of paddling, they

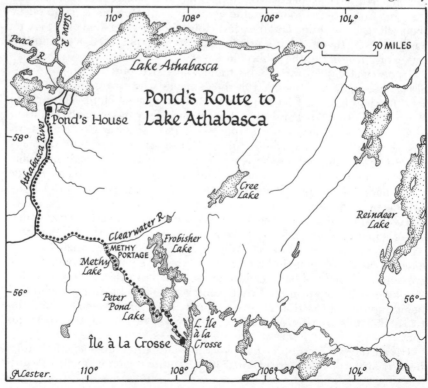

came to the end of water transit and had to start carrying their canoes. For there the twelve-mile portage commenced—the back-breaking Methy Portage over to the Clearwater River.

Fortunately the whole twelve miles did not have to be taken in one gruelling stretch. When Pond's people set out along the low ridge with their canoes and equipment, the first eight miles brought them to one of the clear, little, mile-long, sandy-beached lakes so typical of this area of sparse spruce and jackpine. From this, the Rendezvous, the portage trail started a gentle climb but now, as the Indians said, Pond's people were only four miles from the Clearwater River and most of that distance was downhill. Before long the crews reached the point whence they could look far out over the valley of the Clearwater whose waters were some seven hundred feet below them. Even though it was all downhill from there, the steepness of the grade made carrying their gear very difficult and Pond and all his crew were heartily glad when at last they eased their canoes into the water and could start loading them for the quick seventy-mile trip down to the Athabasca River.

This stage of the trip was not all clear sailing because the Clearwater drops rapidly and one awkward waterfall and six treacherous rapids tested the voyageurs' skill. Before long, however, Pond found himself in the slack water of the flat on which much later Fort McMurray was to be built. There at last his canoes glided into the magnificent Athabasca or Elk River, which, sweeping in from the west, changed direction and headed north. They had reached the great waterway which was to lead them and their successors deeper into the unknown and mysterious northland.

Four days' easy paddling and coasting with the current carried them to the vast Delta of the Athabasca River. There, before entering the lake, Pond built the first fort in the whole Mackenzie watershed and the first white man's house in Alberta. The exact site of his establishment is uncertain. It was most likely on a ridge of sand near the point where the Athabasca splits to send the Embarras River on its separate way to the lake (Embarras Portage). There, according to his successor Alexander Mackenzie, he

saw a vast concourse of the Knisteneaux and Chepewyan tribes, who used to carry their furs annually to Churchill the latter by the barren grounds, where they suffered innumerable hardships and were sometimes even starved to death. . . . Mr. Pond's reception and success was accordingly beyond his expectation, and he procured twice as many furs as his canoes would carry.

At one stroke Pond had established a trading post in the Mackenzie watershed, built the first white man's house in what is now Alberta and carried his goods to the heart of the Chipewyans' homeland, thereby ensuring that never again would they have to make the long, hard trip to deliver their furs to his Hudson's Bay Company rivals. Thenceforth, for many years Pond and his associates were to have the rich trade of the North all to themselves.

In the fall of 1779 Peter Pond returned to his new post and passed another busy year. When he came out in the spring he went east to the Grand Portage and the Detroit area and did not return to northwestern Canada for eighteen months. He spent the winter of 1781-82 at Lac La Ronge, where in a disagreement with one of his associates Etienne Waden was killed. This tragedy was one of the reasons that the loose partnership of independent traders broke up and once more they began competing with each other. Pond, a member of the larger faction, spent the winter of 1782-83 at Ile-à-la-Crosse.

Meanwhile, others of his former associates, we are not sure who, had continued to trade on the Athabasca River. The 1782-83 season, however, was most unsuccessful as according to Alexander Mackenzie the traders ". . . found, in every direction, the ravages of the small-pox, so that from the great diminution of the natives, they returned in the spring with no more than seven packages of beaver."

The great smallpox epidemic, which had started far away in American territory, swept northward through the Sioux to the tribes on the Canadian plains and then through the Crees to the Mackenzie watershed. In the fall of 1783, nothing daunted, Peter Pond returned to his house near Lake Athabasca, where, as well as trading, he continued to dream great dreams. That season he met some of the Chipewyans who had travelled with Samuel Hearne eleven years earlier and they explained the lay of the land in the vicinity of Great Slave Lake.

When Pond went down to Grand Portage in the spring of 1784 he found that the North West Company had been formed by an agreement that was to last for five years and in which he had been given only one share. Although naturally disappointed, he was not the only man whose feelings were hurt. Because of the upheaval and resultant jealousies, others had taken an uncooperative stance and a new firm, Gregory and McLeod, entered the picture and a new man, Alexander Mackenzie, came upon the scene. Once more northwestern Canada was to see bitter competition between strong independent traders fighting among themselves and with the Hudson's Bay Company. In 1785, after spending a year in Montreal and travelling to Washington, Peter Pond returned to the edge of the open marshes of Lake Athabasca. This time, however, he was to meet with opposition from the Gregory and McLeod firm. On their behalf, John Ross and his clerk, Laurent Leroux, built a post close to Pond's establishment. That year too Alexander Mackenzie set up shop for Gregory and McLeod at Ile-à-la-Crosse, which remained his headquarters for two years during the last of which he had his cousin Roderick Mackenzie as assistant.

Travelling as much as he could through the Slave River area, Peter Pond not only maintained his post until the spring of 1788 but set up a number of subsidiary posts. One, built in 1785 on Great Slave Lake near the mouth of the Slave River by Pond's man Cuthbert Grant, was opposed by another built for the Gregory and McLeod partnership by Laurent Leroux. Up the Peace River as early as 1786 another of Pond's posts, which Alexander Mackenzie called the Old Establishment, was probably built by a man named Boyer, near the mouth of the present-day Boyer River. As well as these, three other outposts came into existence on the Athabasca River itself. All we know of them comes from the journals of Philip Turnor and

Peter Fidler when in 1791 they descended that river to survey it and to locate Lake Athabasca on the map.

What appears to have been the oldest one is what Turnor noted as "an Old Canadian House on the East side [of the Athabasca River] which was left when they built one at the mouth of the Pillicon [Clearwater] River." This old one which had been abandoned was on the bank of the Athabasca directly east of the southern end of Mildred Lake. Peter Fidler commented that it had been built by a man named St. Germain or Buffalo Head. The next outpost in order of age, the one at the mouth of the Clearwater and the one Peter Fidler called "Mr. McLeod's house, [had] been built about 3 or 4 years back [*circa* 1787] but now nobody living at it." It was on the right bank of the Clearwater near present-day Fort McMurray, and, while unoccupied when Turnor's crew passed, nevertheless had a thriving garden planted with potatoes.

Still another and later house was farther downstream near the mouth of the Calumet River and not too far from the relatively recent oil sands works at Bitumount. Fidler noted its existence with the comment that the "French house is here" as a successor to "Mr. McLeod's house" and that in the Birch Hills to the west the traders procured bark for their canoes.

These, then, together with Pond's house, were the only traces of white men along the long, timber-fringed Athabasca River. Farther south at the Methy Portage at least three shacks had been thrown up. One of these, abandoned at the time Turnor's party passed, was on the Clearwater River at the north end of the portage and others were located on the shores of Methy Lake. In the whole vast wilderness extending north and west for hundreds of miles from Ile-à-la-Crosse to Great Slave Lake, these tiny clearings in the spruce and pine forests and an occasional canoe in summer or dog team in winter, provided the tenuous line of communication supporting the recent intrusion of European commerce into the far North. Though it was only a beginning, all that had been accomplished was due to a handful of hardy North West Company fur traders, of whom Peter Pond had been the spearhead.

The astute Pond and his associates had not only pushed a few hundred miles farther north than the Hudson's Bay Company but in doing so had also discovered and put into operation a transportation system capable of getting the furs out to the Montreal market some three thousand miles away. Transporting European goods of any sort—guns and hatchets, traps and textiles from England, beads and trinkets from Italy, brandy from France, rum from the West Indies, and tobacco from Brazil—and in return shipping out the furs to pay for them was done in several stages and required enormous effort. The toil inherent in crossing the twelve-mile Methy Portage alone was most arduous. With such distances and delays involved, it is not difficult to understand why the trip from Montreal to the Athabasca country took up most of the summer. Mackenzie noted that the fastest trip from Grand Portage to Fort Chipewyan was fifty-two days; two months were usually allowed.

While Pond and his associates were groping their way towards a system of transport, one of their first moves was to build the house which Fidler saw at the north end of the portage. He said it was "built for the purpose of keeping provisions in to meet the canoes at the Methy Carrying Place on their return from the Grand Portage. . . . The provisions were brought down Peace river in July or the beginning of August & then sent directly to this place, for the above purpose, where they remained till the arrival of the canoes."

In other words, the voyageurs going south from Pond's house took their furs and pemmican as far as the Methy Portage where they met their colleagues coming north. Then, having exchanged their loads, the northern men returned down the Clearwater and Athabasca while the southern crews doubled back towards Cumberland House and eventually to Grand Portage. For them the critical areas where ice might be found in either spring or fall were south of the Methy Portage at Peter Pond Lake and at Methy Lake. The voyageurs, despite the time-saving expedient of swapping loads halfway, were always under the pressure of the imminent onset of winter. Any delay from sickness, incapacity, broken canoes, or a head wind, involved the danger of starvation. It was this preoccupation with winter that made it impossible for the voyageurs to hunt or fish en route. All rations had to be carried and, when exhausted, replenished from fixed depots.

That was where the Indians' pemmican came to play its vital role in the fur business. Pemmican for the long trip up and down the Saskatchewan River between Lake Winnipeg and the western posts came from our prairies. So too did that needed as the traders worked up the Churchill River and to Ile-à-la-Crosse and by Peter Pond on his first trip to Lake Athabasca. It was only then that he and his associates discovered that the Peace River country could be an equally rich source of pemmican, and the problem of furnishing food for the northern posts and for the long trips was made much easier. Moreover, the Chipewyans, who hunted the migrating caribou mainly north and east of Lake Athabasca, could furnish at least part of the required supply of this rich and nutritious product.

When in 1791 Turnor and Fidler made their way down the Athabasca River the abundance of game animals came as a surprise to the Hudson's Bay surveyors and elicited many comments from them. When they could see the Birch Mountains off to the west, Turnor noted that the area was "a fine Country for Buffalo and Moose," and in his remarks about the Peace River country he said: "it's there they get all their dried provisions for their journeys. . . ." Farther down the Slave River his journal referred once more to this matter saying:

The land within seems level mostly good woods near the River and am informed that there are fine Grassy Plains with ledges of woods about which there are plenty of Buffalo and Moose, great quantities of Geese breed about this river and in the Plains the Cranes blue brown and white are Plenty beyond belief.

This, then, was the productive area into which Pond had carried the independent traders' commerce. Unfortunately he had also taken along his intractable temper which had led him to kill an opponent in the United States, had resulted in Waden's death in 1782, and in the spring of 1786 indirectly led to the sudden demise of his neighbour and competitor, John Ross. According to the great explorer David Thompson, Peter Pond "persuaded his men to rob Mr. Ross of a load of furs in open day. In the course of the altercation Mr. Ross was shot, really by accident, from a gun in the hand of a voyageur named Péché."

As a result, Alexander Mackenzie was sent in to supervise Pond and to manage matters at Pond's post. There in a flourishing condition he found the first patch of vegetables ever to be cleared out of Alberta's bush— ". . . as fine a kitchen garden as I ever saw in Canada." As a gardener Pond had done well but in other respects he had messed his nest and his days in the northwest were nearing their end. Nevertheless, during the winter of 1787-88 he and Mackenzie seem to have lived amicably. What is more important, Pond had ample time to communicate to the Scot his great dream of much further exploration and to fan the younger man's ambition to the heat necessary to carry it out.

Pond's great dream was nothing less than to find a relatively easy water route from Lake Athabasca to the Pacific coast. Now that Hearne's trip to the Coppermine River had killed the legendary Northwest Passage, Pond determined to find a fresh-water route to the Pacific. The hope that such a way existed was shared by some of his associates. As the North West Company's fur trade activities rolled ever farther west, transportation costs mounted; as a result, it was highly desirable to find a way west to tidewater. Although, on the one hand, it would divert the furs from Montreal, on the other, it would cut freight costs. Moreover, since there was a potentially rich fur market in the Orient, the North West Company would profit in at least two ways.

In 1785 Pond, who had gained a surprisingly good knowledge of the geography of North America and had travelled as far north as Great Slave Lake, made a trip to Montreal. With him he took the notes and ideas which enabled him to draw his very creditable map of 1785 which he presented to the United States Congress. While in Montreal Pond had a chance to read Cook's recently published *Voyages*. It did not take him long to arrive at the conclusion that the river which Cook had mentioned as flowing into the Pacific just might be the same as the great river which according to Indian report flowed west out of Great Slave Lake. Further enquiries and travels after he returned to his post in the Athabasca delta in 1785 supported this idea and encouraged him to go and find out for himself. Unfortunately for his theory and his hopes, the hand he had in Ross's murder the next year thwarted him.

In the spring of 1788 Pond, the toughened, adventurous, far-sighted man, left his post in Mackenzie's hands and his dream in Mackenzie's mind, and turning his back on the marshes of the Athabasca delta for the last time returned to Montreal. There he seems to have remained for about a year until he sold his interest in the North West Company for £800. Then he returned to his native Milford, Connecticut, where in 1807 he died in poverty.

There has been a tendency to overrate Pond's achievement. He was, however, much more than a mere crass trader. He had indeed lived in a violent manner, on a rugged frontier and in a rough era. Nevertheless, he had been the first white man to cross the Methy Portage and to discover not only the wealth of furs in the Athabasca basin but also the unsuspected plentitude of game animals in the bountiful Peace River country. The conception of the move into the Athabasca watershed was possibly not his but he was the man who realized it. After he had organized the trade along the Athabasca and set up a system of transport that made these riches available, he had looked farther afield. Impressed with the wealth to be won by penetrating to the Pacific coast and trading with the Orient, he had bent his more than usual gifts towards reaching these rich goals. Unfortunately, though he did not achieve his desire of finding a way to the Pacific Ocean and though he died in poverty, his had been an adventurous and a full life. He led the way in developing the northwest, laying the basis of our long-time water route to the Arctic and paving the way for further exploration in the far North. The conception of the plan for that exploration was Pond's—its execution fell to his disciple, Alexander Mackenzie, a luckier man.

At the great cross-roads of the northern waterways, Mackenzie took the torch which Peter Pond held out and soon set about finding just how important that cross-roads and that torch were. Not satisfied with the location of Pond's post, Mackenzie waited until his predecessor left and then sent his cousin, Roderick Mackenzie, to build its more convenient successor, Fort Chipewyan, on Old Fort Point on the south shore of Lake Athabasca. All the while, with the acquiescence of his partners in the North West Company, he made plans to carry out the exploration of which Pond had dreamed.

Starting from Fort Chipewyan on July 3, 1789, he crossed the wide expanse of water which he called the Lake of the Hills in company with Laurent Leroux who was taking his own canoe and supplies as far as his post on Great Slave Lake. Mackenzie's ". . . crew consisted of four [French] Canadians, two of whom were attended by their wives, and a German: we were accompanied also by an Indian, who had acquired the title of English Chief, and his two wives, in a small canoe, with two young Indians; his followers in another small canoe." The English Chief "was one of the followers of the chief who conducted Mr. Hearne to the copper-mine river. . . ." The French Canadians were François Barrieu, Charles Ducette, Joseph Landry and Pierre De Lorme.

At last Mackenzie was off on his great venture to test Pond's theories and to find a way to Cook's Inlet on the Pacific coast. The next day the party passed the mouth of the Peace River and entered the Slave. As far as Leroux' post on Great Slave Lake the route was familiar, but finally when, well west of there on June 25 they parted from Leroux, the prow of Mackenzie's canoe was heading into unexplored waters. Making rapid progress down the mighty river flowing west out of Great Slave Lake, the explorer reached tidewater at its mouth on July 14. But the ocean there turned out to be the frigid Arctic and not the balmy Pacific. Pond's 1785 map had been right after all, but reading Cook's *Voyages* had led him astray and now it led to a disgruntling end to Mackenzie's brave attempt to reach the Pacific. Well might he have called the river he had explored "the River of Disappointment." Other men, recognizing his great achievement, named it the Mackenzie. At last a white man had travelled its full length and in a fashion was able to show it on a map. Having now followed the watercourse all the way from the future site of Fort McMurray to the frozen sea, Mackenzie was able to confirm what Hearne had said some years previously. There was no Northwest Passage through the continent.

Even though he had followed the course of the Mackenzie River and thus proved that at least in that respect Pond's 1785 map was essentially correct, there were other features of the map which needed verification. How accurately had Pond located Lake Athabasca? He had shown its west end as some 35° west of Fort Churchill. If indeed this were true, then it would be some eleven hundred miles west of Hudson Bay and less than three hundred miles from the Pacific Ocean (at modern Juneau, Alaska). If Pond's map was correct, then it ought to be possible to find a short route to the coast. British geographers, however, expressed some doubt about its correctness and proposed that a qualified surveyor be sent to locate Lake Athabasca accurately. In due course, in a co-operative venture on the part of the British government and the Hudson's Bay Company, Philip Turnor, a surveyor of note, set out for the lake.

Taking Peter Fidler and others with him, Turnor picked out a new route by way of Garson and Watchusk lakes and the Christina River and made his way to Fort McMurray. On the way down the Christina, Fidler recorded seeing the famous Athabasca oil sands, saying: "Found great quantities of Bitumen a kind of Liquid Tar oozing out of the Banks on both sides of the river, in many Places, which has a very sulphurous smell & quite black like real Tar & in my opinion would be a very good substitute for that useful Mineral."

These were the same beds as those which Alexander Mackenzie reported somewhat lower down the Athabasca when during 1801 he sent the manuscript of his *Voyages* to the printer. Of them he said:

> At about twenty-four miles from the Fork, are some bitumenous fountains, into which a pole of twenty feet long may be inserted without the least resistance. The bitumen is in a fluid state, and when mixed with gum, or the resinous substance collected from the spruce fir, serves to gum the canoes. In its heated state it emits a smell like that of sea-coal. The banks of the river, which are there very elevated, discover veins of the same bitumenous quality.

Four days' paddling below that point took the party to Peter Pond's unoccupied house at the edge of the Delta. Eventually they reached Roderick Mackenzie's Fort Chipewyan on what we call Old Fort Point. Turnor was surprised at how well stocked the post was, saying: "I think this the compleatest Inland House I have seen in the Country, this is the Grand Magazine of the Athapiscow Country and I am informed they have a sufficient quantity of Trading Goods in this Country for at least two years to come. . . . "

Upon his arrival, Turnor determined the correct location of Fort Chipewyan, which turned out to be about 110° 30' west longitude at a latitude of 58° 37'. At last he knew and undoubtedly told Roderick Mackenzie how badly Peter Pond's dead reckoning had erred. Instead of being some eleven hundred miles west of Fort Churchill, it was less than half that, and instead of being less than three hundred miles from the Pacific coast, it was at least eight hundred.

At Fort Chipewyan he allowed his crew to relax and then on the evening of the fourth day headed north to carry his survey to Great Slave Lake by paddling as far as Goose Island. Next morning, in spite of a strong wind, they headed across the lake to land on the present site of the Fort Chipewyan settlement. Turnor described that shore as

an intire rock and many rocky Islands laying to South from which this part of the Lake is called the Lake of the Paps from their appearing hĕigh and round at a distance and no land seen beyond them, in the southern [Cree] Indian Tongue *Too-Toos Sack-a-ha-gan*, in the Chepawyan tongue *Thew Too-ah* or the Paps Lake. . . .Athapescow in the Southern Indian tongue signifies open country such as lakes with Willows and grass growing about them or swampy land without woods. *Kyte-hel-le-ca* in the Chepawyan tongue implies the same meaning but that name does not properly belong or is applied to any part but the South end. . . .

After describing the Delta as he saw it when working his way into the Rivière des Rochers, the party camped about 4 miles upstream of the mouth of the Peace River. Only then did Turnor find that "we had left the Sextant at the Canadian House though I had particularly enquired and was assured that it was in the Canoe." Since the only object of his trip was to survey, he had to go back for it. So next morning at 9:30 he headed back against the current, reached Old Fort Point after some ten hours' paddling, picked up the instrument, set out north again and did not camp until 6:30 the second evening. In a continuous remarkable trip his crew had taken him 45 miles back to Roderick Mackenzie's house, turned around and paddled another 75 miles until they stopped on the Slave River a few miles above Demicharge Rapids. In two full days and one night they had carried him 120 miles.

A few days later the party worked its way down the sixteen miles of rapids above our Fort Smith. In his journal Turnor noted the fact that "a Canadian and an Indian drowned here," while a little lower down "the Canadians Totally lost two Canoes and had five men drowned." In the latter case, which happened at the Rapids of the Drowned in 1786, the men and canoes were part of Cuthbert Grant's expedition on its way to start a post on Great Slave Lake. Travelling down the Slave River and commenting frequently on the abundance of buffalo, Turnor reached a "Canadian House" on Great Slave Lake on July 22.

Having gone that far, Turnor returned to Fort Chipewyan and then made a side trip which took him to the vicinity of Fond du Lac. There he was glad to hear ". . . the Indians say thĕir is a near way to Churchill water by proceeding up this river [Fond du Lac] and through a chain of small

Lakes to the Deer [Reindeer] Lake. . . ." On their return to Mackenzie's house they found Malcom Ross "building a House about 600 yards SSE of the Canadian Settlement." There Turnor remained for the winter of 1791-92 while he sent Peter Fidler out to winter with some Chipewyans along the Slave River.

At Fort Chipewyan earlier in the year he had learned of the continual forays the natives waged against each other and that the "Southern Indians [Crees] are going to War upon the Indians to the Westward of the Slave Lake." Now at the mouth of the Peace River he met three canoes of these Southern Indians containing seven men and three women on their way back rejoicing in the two scalps they carried and in the fact that they had also murdered one lone woman whom they had come upon. Their presence involved Fidler in a delicate situation. Neither these Crees nor the Chipewyans could speak each other's language, and he had to serve as interpreter. After the customary greetings of strangers, the Chipewyans, realizing that they were superior in numbers, discontinued their usual chit-chat and began discussing amongst themselves the pleasant prospect of killing the Crees. The latter, not understanding a word of this discussion, stood innocently by waiting for Fidler to interpret. It was some time before he could pay any attention to the Crees, but during that interval he talked the Chipewyans into a more peaceful frame of mind. Then after a while, never realizing how close the hand of death had been, the Crees went their way.

In the spring of 1792, after Fidler had returned to Fort Chipewyan, Turnor's party left the Athabasca country, this time by way of the Methy Portage, and went on to Cumberland House and York Factory. They had spent two years making the trip into the far northwest but the time had been well spent. At last someone had charted the route of the great waterway as far as Great Slave Lake and determined the location and the outline of Lake Athabasca. Its eastern end had turned out to be a mere four hundred miles from Hudson Bay, much closer than anyone had realized, and, moreover, Turnor had heard of a water route from it to the Bay which upon further investigation might eliminate the long roundabout way by Methy Portage. During the next few years the Hudson's Bay Company was to follow up this rumour and to send another surveyor to seek this hoped for short cut from Churchill to Lake Athabasca, but the route proved to be impractical.

The North West Company was not so vitally concerned about a route east out of Lake Athabasca as it was with a way to the Pacific, and Alexander Mackenzie, dreaming of an outlet to the ocean, kept that goal—Pond's old goal—before their eyes. This search had led him down the Mackenzie River and to disappointment. Then, after meeting Turnor and Fidler on their way north to Lake Athabasca, he set off for England where he studied surveying and astronomy in order to fit himself for another attempt to find a western outlet. On his way back in August 1792 near the Grand Rapids of the Saskatchewan, he again met Peter Fidler, who noted that Mackenzie "is now fitted out with the necessary instruments to make the ensuing summer a journey across the Rocky Mountains up Peace River to the Western Ocean. . . ."

Early in October 1792, equipped with new knowledge and new equipment, Mackenzie set out on his next venture, saying: "Having made every necessary preparation, I left Fort Chipewyan, to proceed up the Peace River." These preparations involved taking along some gold guineas "to traffic with the Russians" at the west coast. They also included sending an advance party some hundreds of miles up the Peace River to near the mouth of the Smoky River to build Fort Fork where he planned to winter and from which he was to set off upstream in the spring.

This time he not only had a much better idea of where he was going but for the first time he knew where he was starting from. This time, while he had no idea where his voyage up the Peace would take him or how when he reached the Rocky Mountains he would ever find a way across them and down to the Pacific, he nevertheless knew that the distance to tidewater was about eight hundred miles and probably double that by the winding route the rivers would force him to take. At last the framework of northwestern Canada was being sketched. Now that the distance to the Pacific Ocean was known, this stubborn and courageous explorer had a better idea of the magnitude of the task that still lay before him in getting to the coast.

To carry out his task, Mackenzie needed all the toughness and hardihood of which only the better fur traders were capable. He also needed the support of the nine valiant crewmen who backed him up. These were Alexander MacKay, a fellow Scot, who was second in command of the expedition, "Joseph Landry, Charles Ducette, François Beaulieux, Baptiste Bisson, François Courtois, and Jacques Beauchamp with two Indians, as hunters and interpreters." With them on May 9, 1793, he set forth west from Fort Fork. After toil and tribulation that would have daunted other men, he arrived at tidewater. There in the Dean Channel he wrote on a large rock: "Alexander Mackenzie, from Canada, by land, the twenty-second of July, one thousand seven hundred and ninety-three." He had achieved his goal.

The trip back to Fort Fork took the party a little over a month and from there Mackenzie returned to Fort Chipewyan where he spent the following winter. Now his horizon and his company's and indeed Lake Athabasca's had been greatly expanded. As he stood looking out over the calm, beautiful lake or across its storm-tossed whitecaps to the north shore, or looked west to Potato Island in the narrowing channel leading its waters north, he saw an enlarged world. That channel sweeping by Potato Island had assumed a new meaning. It was now more than ever the junction point of the northwestern part of the continent. From it the waters of the Slave and Mackenzie rivers led north fourteen hundred miles to the Arctic Ocean. To it but moving west through the lake itself came the waters gathered from all over northern Saskatchewan. Year after year, the flood of the great Athabasca River brought tidings from the edge of the prairies and from the connecting water links leading to Lake Winnipeg, the Great Lakes and Montreal. Lastly came the waters of the great Peace River, providing a water route to the summit of the faraway Rocky Mountains. In his mind's eye Mackenzie could see this junction leading to an ever expanding trading kingdom limited only by the Arctic and Pacific oceans to the north and west, by the Spanish settlements in Mexico, and by the tiny

Russian outposts in Alaska. And beyond that kingdom lay the riches of trading with the Orient. Here indeed was a stage upon which he and his partners, amply provided with courage and capital, could act out a commercial drama rarely equalled in brilliance.

For Mackenzie the great dreamer was an equally great doer. During the next few years, carrying out his dreams, he and his associates pushed posts ever farther westward up the Peace and finally to the mouth of the Columbia River. A vast area soon came under their control, the area which the North West Company's highlanders called New Caledonia and from which their men traded with Mexicans far to the south and with Russians capturing sea otters amongst the ice floes of Alaska. Much of this expansion was planned and controlled from the great Emporium of the North, Fort Chipewyan. Looking out upon the blue expanse of Lake Athabasca, great men had dreamed great dreams and from the fort at the cross-roads of the North, hardy men had carried them out.

CHAPTER THREE

Bitter Battles at Fort Chipewyan

In 1789, the same summer that Alexander Mackenzie set out on his way to the Arctic Ocean, Angus Shaw, another venturesome Northwester, ascended the Beaver River from Ile-à-la-Crosse and on Moose Lake built the first white man's house to be erected in what is now the cultivated part of Alberta. Six years later, in 1795, the Northwesters' drive up the North Saskatchewan River, also spearheaded by Shaw, saw their Fort Augustus established. Nearby were the Hudson's Bay Company's Edmonton House and a post owned by Richardson and Ogilvie, who were later to become shareholders in the X Y Company. These moves by the three companies were their first attempts to enter the vast area between the lower reaches of Alberta's North Saskatchewan River and the Peace River. Bisecting that northeastern quarter of the future province of Alberta, of course, lay the middle portion of the Athabasca River—the stretch from modern Athabasca town to Fort McMurray.

After building posts near modern Edmonton it was but a step for the fur traders and especially the North West Company men to investigate this large area. From Edmonton House the distance to the Athabasca River was about a hundred miles; from the North West Company's Fort George and the adjacent Hudson's Bay Company's Buckingham House near modern Elk Point the distance to our Fort McMurray was nearly twice that. Throughout all this region was the forest broken only by a number of large solitary lakes, Lac La Biche, Lakes Wolf, Christina and several others, the havens for uncounted waterfowl from sandpipers to swans and from pintails to pelicans.

The first record of a south-bound trip through this forest is in the journal Peter Fidler kept at Buckingham House next door to Fort George in which, on March 2, 1797, he noted the arrival of the North West Company's express from the Athabasca district. These men on snowshoes, mushing along behind their dog teams, were breaking what was soon to become an important trail. Undoubtedly they had skirted the Athabasca and its rapids between our Fort McMurray and the mouth of House River and then ascended its spruce-locked valley and passing Lac La Biche had cut across to Fort George. Undoubtedly too in choosing this route they had been guided by a native intimately familiar with all the lakes they crossed and the valleys they followed.

Before long Peter Fidler was caught up in the Hudson's Bay Company's drive towards the middle Athabasca River when he was sent out to counteract the new North West Company posts set up in its watershed. In the fall of 1798 David Thompson, his one-time fellow surveyor who was now working for the opposition company, established the first of these on Lac La Biche. Then the following spring, riding around by Fort Augustus and heading north to strike the Pembina River, this same explorer descended that stream until he found himself on the Athabasca. Dropping down it he paused at the mouth of Lesser Slave Lake River and then ascended it to Lesser Slave Lake. Having put that large body of water on his map, he returned to the Athabasca and descended it to modern Fort McMurray, whence he went east over the Methy Portage. On his trip he mapped the Athabasca River all the way downstream from the mouth of Lesser Slave Lake River.

While David Thompson was leaving the Athabasca country by the Methy Portage, Peter Fidler, who was to be accompanied by William Flett and others, was getting ready for his trip up the winding Beaver River to Lac La Biche. There in the fall of 1799 he built the Hudson's Bay Company's Greenwich House. From it the next February he made his way down the winding Lac La Biche River and ascended the Athabasca until he came to the second post the North West Company had in the general area. It was at the mouth of Lesser Slave Lake River and had been built in 1799 after David Thompson's trip.

By this time the X Y Company had become a serious factor in the trade. When in the autumn of 1799 Sir Alexander Mackenzie fell out with the North West Company, he gathered together a few smaller fur trading concerns and in 1800 amalgamated them into the New North West Company, which because it marked its bales with the letters X Y became known as the X Y Company. In October of that year, according to Fidler, this company sent some men down the Athabasca River to Lake Athabasca "& had the misfortune to loose several pieces of Goods . . . & 2 men nearly drowned — 5 canoes — they carried goods over land from Edmonton House to the Summer berry [Pembina] river a Distance of 20 or 30 miles. . . ." Their misadventure was probably the first of a long line of accidents caused by the Grand Rapids.

While all this activity was taking place along the Athabasca above its junction with the Clearwater, the North West Company posts farther north were settling down to a routine way of life. By this time the company had posts on Great Slave Lake and even farther north, and its men had a thorough knowledge of the broad Peace River's lower five hundred miles. In that vast region from Fort McMurray north where their trade was most lucrative their monopoly was unchallenged.

This monopoly, however, which their courage and hardihood had procured for them did little to endear them to their Chipewyan customers. It had, in fact, not only embittered and intimidated the natives but also had hardened the traders until they became oppressive and unbearably brutal towards them. A few years previously the Chipewyans had made gruelling trips each year to purchase some of their wants from the white men at Hudson Bay and as soon as the Northwesters had carried goods into the heart of their area, the basin of Lake Athabasca, they had welcomed them with open arms. Then, rightly or wrongly but with some reason, the traders began to consider their customers as the most backward Indians with whom they had ever dealt. Moreover, the Chipewyans, no longer willing to carry their goods all the way to the Bay and thus maintain some measure of independence, came to rely absolutely upon the Northwesters. Such a development led to a mutual loss of respect: to overbearing oppression on the one hand and nearly abject submission on the other, to scorn on the part of the whites and hatred on that of the natives.

One cause of this hatred involved the traders' treatment of women. In their journals Philip Turnor and Malcom Ross both mentioned the friction caused by the Northwesters' brutality. Turnor, for instance, stated that:

> . . . the method by which they get most of the Che-pá-wy-an Women is by the Masters seizing them for their Husbands or Fathers debts and then selling them to their men from five hundred to two thousand Livres and if the Father or Husband or any of them resist the only satisfaction they get is a beating and they are frequently not satisfied with taking the Woman but their Gun and Tent likewise.

Chipewyan women's lives were hard. Within their own communities they had become accustomed to being wrested from their husbands by a more powerful tribesman, and the rest of the band, particularly the men, gave the matter little thought. Now, however, when the white men acquired these women in much the same fashion, the native men naturally got up in arms.

While such an observation as Turnor's must have been somewhat coloured by inter-company rivalry, it is probable that it was fairly accurate. We do not have to depend entirely on Hudson's Bay Company men's reports of such incidents, however, because a look at the journal kept at Fort Chipewyan in 1799 by James McKenzie, the North West Company's factor there, corroborates what their rivals said. Among many other references, he records his own treatment of the daughter of Saurarda, one of the natives. This man

> brought his daughter, who deserted in the course of the winter from Morin, at Slave Lake, in order to be returned to her husband [Morin]. Mr. Porter wrote me, by Morin's orders, to sell her to the highest bidder and debit Morin for the amount.
>
> Two advantages may be reached from this affair; the first is that it will assist to discharge the debts of a man unable to do it by any other means, for he is neither good middleman, foreman, steersman, interpreter nor carpenter; the second is that it may be the means of thickling some

lecherous miser to part with some of his hoard. I therefore kept the woman to be disposed of in the season when the Peace River bucks look out for women, in the month of May. . . .

I offered Morin's wife (to take care of her till the arrival of Mr. Finlay) first to Etier, then to Dusablon and then to old Marcil, but she refused all three *tour à tour*, and, to convince them how heartily she hated them all three, she set up her pipes at the bare mention of their names. . . . She had a young *Ojijauke* on board her frigate on its way to this world, but how far advanced in the voyage, I have not enquired.

On May 22, 1800, once the ice was out of the Athabasca River, McKenzie's journal reports the arrival of the North West Company's first competitors in the persons of two men, Perrons and Bellegarde, who came representing the recently incorporated X Y Company. That day these men, who had brought three canoes of goods, were at Bustard Island and had come with the intention of building near the older company's post. The next day they camped at Little Island across the narrow neck of water from McKenzie's establishment. "In order to keep them from building a Fort on *Pointe du Sable*, the prettiest spot for that purpose on this side of the lake, Mr. Finlay marked it out for the North West Company. . . ."

These entries do not state positively that the X Y Company did build on the little island in question. Neither do they identify the island for us, but it was probably English Island, which in comparison with Potato Island might well be referred to as little. This brings up the question of the exact

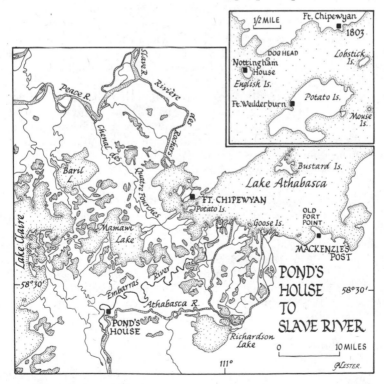

location of the Northwesters' Fort Chipewyan of James McKenzie's time. Peter Fidler, who built the Hudson's Bay Company's Nottingham House on English Island in 1802, states that the Fort Chipewyan of the time was three-quarters of a mile away across a neck of water. Presumably then, the Fort Chipewyan of that time was either on the shore of the small bay later occupied by Colin Fraser's establishment or immediately west of it on the low point now occupied by a number of shacks.

James McKenzie's journal indicates that the fort in which he lived in 1800 was in a bad state of repair and that the palisades were beginning to rot away. No one knows when Roderick Mackenzie's post on Old Fort Point was abandoned, but from the above evidence its successor on the north shore must have been seven or eight years old when James McKenzie complained of its condition. His journal also throws a little light on another of his company's posts presided over by James Porter which seems to have been on the west side of Lake Claire and to have been in operation as early as 1799.

In any event, now that Alexander Mackenzie had broken with the North West Company and swung his massive support behind the new X Y Company, that outfit was ready to battle the Northwesters for a share of the trade of the Athabasca district. As it turned out, the X Y Company never succeeded in matching the might of its older rival. For now, after a dozen years in the North, the North West Company was strongly entrenched. The very number of its posts scattered along the Peace River, at Great Slave Lake, and at other strategic points, was an indication of its strength. All of these were under the command of the headquarters on Lake Athabasca, Fort Chipewyan, the great Emporium of the North.

The new company girded its loins in an endeavour to unseat its rival and in the course of the next two or three years it poured many men and much money into its Athabasca venture. By the end of that time it had not only set up the post in opposition to Fort Chipewyan but had established four posts on the Peace River (including one near the mouth of the Smoky River), as well as others built on Great Slave Lake, at Fort Liard and even on Great Bear Lake. The opposition between the two Montreal based companies was made more bitter by the fact that many of the officers of the new company were former employees of the older North West. In the fierce competition between these traders, principles of fair play and honesty played little part. In the resultant cat-and-dog fray, no action was too brutal, no deed too despicable to work on the enemy.

During these companies' fierce competition the quantities of liquor poured out to the natives in all the region west of the Great Lakes reached new heights. In 1800 when they were beginning their battle, 10,098 gallons of spirits were used; by 1803, near the close of the competition, over 21,000 gallons were taken in. In three years the quantity had doubled. This expenditure was ruinous, and with it came reduced returns. Well might the Hudson's Bay Company, watching these rivals, feel that bankruptcy faced them both.

Into this fray in 1802 the Hudson's Bay Company sent poor Peter Fidler to sandwich himself between the two rivals on Lake Athabasca and to wave the company's flag. Though he was a good trader and a courageous man, a feeble wave was all that could be expected when in the Athabasca area his 17-man party was to oppose the X Y Company with nearly 100 men and the North West Company with some 175. Nevertheless, as his journal for August 7, 1802, states, he started for Lake Athabasca with Thomas Swain and five canoes "to build two Trading Houses, one at the Athapescow Lake and the other up Peace River—as this last place is the only one to make dry provisions at, to supply the Canoes out in the Spring."

Finally on September 18 Fidler and his party crossed to the north side of Lake Athabasca. Almost immediately he despatched Mr. Swain with three canoes and nine men to select a suitable site for a post well up the Peace River. Swain built his Mansfield House at or near modern Fort Vermilion, nearly two hundred miles straight west of Chipewyan as the crow flies. Then, with his eight remaining men, Fidler searched for a site for his own Nottingham House. In the end, he built it on a small bay on the east side of what, because his post was there, has ever since been known as English Island. Across the narrow gap between it and the north shore stood the North West Company's Fort Chipewyan. Now all three companies had houses in sight of each other, all more or less guarding both main routes leading out of Lake Athabasca: the Rivière des Rochers and the Quatre Fourches channel.

Within a few days of Fidler's arrival, some of his Chipewyan friends came in and explained that while they would like to trade with him, they were fearful of his company's stability in the area. To combat both Fidler and the X Y Company, the Northwesters spread the word that they would soon drive both of their rivals away and threatened the Chipewyans with dire punishment if they traded with these recent interlopers. For the next four years as white men wrangled, the little pinpoint of European intrusion into the vast pine-clad wilderness exuded bitterness. In the summer when most of the traders were away in their canoes taking their furs to eastern Canada, all was as peaceful as if white men had never existed. In the fall when the rival traders's canoes made their way past the outlying islands and headed for the three groups of little bark-thatched huts, hatred and jealousies paddled in with them. And all through the bitter winter, the Beavers, Chipewyans and Crees, hunting far back at Namur or Margaret lakes or along the Salt River, smiled as they told of the antics of the trading rivals or muttered as they recalled some recent indignities heaped on their own heads.

The Indians were particularly bitter against the North West Company men who, exercising the tyranny made possible by their dominating position, made life miserable for any Indian who dared to sympathize or trade with either of the other companies. To secure meat and pemmican the X Y Company had some posts dotted here and there for hundreds of miles along the Peace River, but the Northwesters, by an outpouring of liquor and cajolery combined with brutality, soon made it too risky for the Beaver Indians to trade with them and supply them with meat. Similarly, at the Hudson's Bay Company's Mansfield House (near our Fort Vermilion) Thomas Swain got very few furs, and more crippling still, no pemmican. On January 23, 1803, he and his men returned to Nottingham House, reporting that it was no use trying to do any business up the Peace River.

This put Fidler and all his men in a precarious position. It was essential to get pemmican from the plains of the Peace River country both to augment the food supply at Nottingham House and to provide provisions for their trip out in the spring. The Northwesters, seeing the Hudson's Bay Company's weak point, had struck at it and thereby threatened Fidler's whole enterprise. After thinking this over, Fidler set his men to redouble their efforts to get fish, so as to have enough to dry for their requirements in the spring.

All the while the Northwesters continued their aggressive tactics. On one occasion during the winter of 1802-03 Fidler wrote: "An Indian came over here & told us that the Old Co. had pillaged him of 23 MBr, which he had in credit last fall at our house, he owed them not a single skin—he was bringing them here." In May when the Indians began bringing in their furs the Northwesters stepped up their reign of violence, and on May 5 two of their employees burned up one of Fidler's canoes. A few days later, "the Old Coy sent people to make a tent and remain near us to watch and to keep away Indians from our house." The trading season was rapidly drawing to a close, but in the last days many Chipewyans and Beavers came in, only to be confronted by the malevolent Northwesters in their tent nearby.

When at last the ice went out and Fidler carried away the meagre returns of his frustrating winter, he put James Kirkness in charge of Nottingham House and left George Cromarty and Robert Flett to help him. On September 12, 1803, when he returned to Nottingham House, he not only discovered that the North West Company was in the process of moving east along the lake shore to the site which Fort Chipewyan was to occupy for well over a hundred years, but he was also greeted with discouraging news. Once more Swain had been defeated in his struggle to maintain Mansfield House up the Peace River. On the other hand, Kirkness reported that "36 hunters have died this season in the environs of this lake, which loss in killing skins will be considerably felt in the winter—besides casting a melancholy gloom on nearly all the rest." Another of the epidemics to which the natives were particularly vulnerable had swept the land.

For about three weeks affairs at Nottingham House remained peaceable, but on October 20 "Old Company men came over here and began to build a smaller house close to ours, to watch any Indians which may come to us, also to observe that we do not go to any Indians privately—this is the first instance of their ever building a watch house over us."

What the Northwesters may have been doing to the X Y Company men we do not know, but they probably made it just as difficult for them. Since the X Y Company and the Hudson's Bay Company were the underdogs in the area, the relations between their two staffs were relatively cordial and each helped the other to repel the war-like activity directed against them. On one occasion Fidler stepped in and undoubtedly averted a tragedy. His journal tells ". . . the New Coy Master and the Old Co's met upon the Lake & quarreled much about the Indians altho they then had nothing—and it likely proving serious as they had got the Ground marked out, Pistols there and even arrangement made for an attack upon each other, I went to them and put an end to the dispute in an amicable manner."

During this time the journal reports the death of St. Germain, "called

Buffalo Head." He was sixty-six years old and had been in charge of one or other of the North West Company's posts in the Peace River country. Here undoubtedly was the progenitor of all the St. Germains who for generations were to play such a large part in that area. Moreover, this must have been the man after whom the Buffalo Head Hills and Buffalo Head Prairie, south of Fort Vermilion, were named.

About the middle of May when Fidler was getting ready to take his furs out, David Thompson descended the Peace River from his winter quarters near the mouth of the Smoky River. In 1802 Thompson, who two or three years earlier had surveyed the Athabasca River, carried his instruments by way of the North West Company house on the west end of Lesser Slave Lake to Alexander Mackenzie's old Fort Fork. There he spent about a year before setting off with a team of dogs in March 1804 to ascend the Peace River to his company's most westerly post near modern Fort St. John. From there, still by dog team, he retraced his route to Fort Fork and continued along the river's ice to Horseshoe House, which was some fifteen miles northeast of the present town of Manning. As soon as the ice went out he dropped downstream in a canoe, noting various fur trading posts, until on May 12 he arrived at the "Athabaska House." At that time it was on the site where it remained for well over a century as the Fort Chipewyan we know. Then after relaxing for three days, he made his way up the Athabasca to the company's trading post at the mouth of the Clearwater and thence across the Methy Portage.

When David Thompson descended the Peace River from Fort St. John to Fort Chipewyan he made its first accurate survey. Then when he ascended the Athabasca to the mouth of the Clearwater, the spot he had visited five years earlier, he completed his voyage around an area of about 40,000 square miles. And from this vast, heavily forested region bounded on the south by Lesser Slave Lake, on the west and north by the Peace River, and on the east by the Athabasca, from this area which had North West Company posts all around it, came most of the richest furs ever sent to European markets. In it one or two hundred Indian families, Beavers, Crees and Chipewyans and a few interloping Iroquois, made a passable but sometimes hungry and never an easy living. It contained many streams and minor rivers—one of them over three hundred miles long—abounding in beaver, otters, mink and martens. In the numerous lakes of which Claire with its 640 square miles and Utikuma with its 130 were the largest, pike, pickerel, trout and the ever reliable whitefish, teemed. Breeding by the thousands, geese, swans and other wildfowl shared the grassy borders of these lakes and the 1.5 million acres of the reedy Peace-Athabasca Delta. Pasturing on the area's sedge meadows, hundreds of buffalo trampled the winter snows while in summer moose, wading belly-deep, gorged on succulent aquatic vegetation or in winter rattled their antlers amongst frozen willows. In the fall evenings, echoing from birch or pine ridges, the moans of the bull elk haunted the hilltops, coughing, grunting, roaring and whistling in the pleading urgency of the mating season. In short, this huge area between the Peace and the Athabasca rivers provided the Indians with sufficient game for their own needs together with a surplus to sell to the traders.

Into this area the Northwesters first brought horses from the vicinity of Edmonton by way of Lesser Slave Lake, Dunvegan and Fort Vermilion to Fort Chipewyan. These horses were to enable them to haul meat from Indian camps and fish from the Lake Athabasca fisheries to the fort. Using horses which could move much more than dogs, the company could effect significant economies by cutting down the number of dogs which had to be fed meat or fish and also the number of men who had to drive them and to catch fish for their sustenance. Of these first horses to reach Fort Chipewyan, Fidler wrote on May 20, 1804: "A Batteaux belonging to the Old Co. arrived here from their upper settlements in the Peace River with 3 horses—these are the first animals of the kind that was ever at this lake."

By that time he was on the point of taking his meagre returns to Cumberland House from which he came back to Nottingham House early in September 1804. On the way north he met two Crees and an Iroquois, who told him that during the summer the Chipewyans, timid though they had always been, had not been able to endure the bullying of the North-westers and at Fond du Lac on the east end of Lake Athabasca had killed the two Northwesters in charge there and destroyed their post. Moreover, near Fort Chipewyan they had killed four more of that company's men. Fidler, when he heard the news, doubted its truth, but he commented, "should it be true it is what the Canadians had richly deserved—they are very severe with them." Near the mouth of the Athabasca he ran into some Chipewyans who were hiding. When they found out who he was, they came out, confirmed the news of the killings and said they now lived in fear of revenge.

During the ensuing season the trading pattern was much as it had been for the previous years with some slight co-operation between the Hudson's Bay Company's men and those of the X Y Company. The Chipewyans, of course, dared not come to any of the posts. On April 28, 1805, Fidler recorded that Robert Flett was drowned in the lake. On May 6, he recorded his reaction to another misfortune.

> . . . at 8 am 2 Canadians from Peace River came here in a canoe each in one belonging to each company with Circular Letters to all the Pro-prietors of Both Companies that a junction of the two Companies had taken place last October in Montreal. . . . Now that both Companies have joined we shall stand a much worse chance than before to get any Skins—as they have threatened that should such an event take place, as has now happened, they would soon force us all out of this Quarter—& as we are so very few we have little chance.

After the amalgamation the Northwesters outdid themselves to harrass Fidler. Two days after the news of the union of the two companies, "The French set fire to all our wood that we had collected with great labor and carried down to the water's edge ready for rafting to build a new house with." Nevertheless, Fidler and a few faithful adherents returned to Lake Athabasca in the fall of 1805 to find that his opponents had built a small house two hundred yards away. As soon as he arrived, they came and pitched a tent within four yards of his house. Fidler's food supply for the winter was dangerously low and he immediately sent his men out to kill the ducks which were gathering for their fall migration. Samuel Black of the North West Company sent men to follow Fidler's men to "shout & hallow" and scare the birds away. The same day Black's men pulled up his garden and attempted to set fire to his house.

The bullying and obstruction were such that Fidler and his people were forced to capitulate to their oppressors during the winter of 1805-06 and the following spring they left the area. The Hudson's Bay Company's first attempt to trade in the vital Athabasca country had failed. A year later Fidler went on to conduct the company's final survey of the eastern approaches to Lake Athabasca, his work putting the finishing touches to whatever hopes still lingered of making use of those waterways for trade purposes. In the course of his survey he travelled north through Saskatchewan's Reindeer Lake to the larger body of water which he named Wollaston Lake and then continued towards Lake Athabasca until near the North West Company's Fond du Lac outpost he connected his survey with the one he and Turnor had made in 1791.

For the next nine years the North West Company remained in sole and undisturbed possession of the fur trade from Lake Athabasca down the whole of the Mackenzie watershed and up the total length of the Peace River to its headwaters in the Rocky Mountains. During those years it expanded its trade, sending Simon Fraser to build Fort George in 1807 and to descend the Fraser River to tidewater a year later. Supplying those posts and supporting this activity fell upon Fort Chipewyan. At the same time, by sending David Thompson up the North Saskatchewan River and across the mountains during the four years after 1807 and then for a couple of years after that having him go up the extreme headwaters of the Athabasca in the Jasper area and over to the Columbia, the company was able to do business all the way to the mouth of that river. This drive towards the Pacific coast gave them control of such places as Spokane Fort in 1810 and Fort Kamloops in 1812. As they had done when they first entered the Athabasca basin, the resourceful, determined men of the North West Company pressed on west until by argument, bargaining or sheer masterfulness, they had won the Indians over to their will. Thereby they laid claim to perhaps one-quarter of the continent. And at least half of that amazing advance westward had been channelled through Fort Chipewyan.

To cope with this great expansion, Fort Chipewyan on its new site had to be up-graded and rebuilt until it became the most impressive stronghold in northwestern Canada. It was, moreover, on a most strategic site, just at the entrance to the main channel out of Lake Athabasca, at the logical spot to control the fur trade which in increasing amounts was being carried on down the Slave and Mackenzie rivers and up the Peace River far into New Caledonia. To it the Northwesters' autumn brigades brought their goods from Fort William for redistribution to all the posts beyond. In return, the furs from these other widely scattered posts not only found their way during the summer but remained there for months, ready to be taken south and east the following spring. The distances involved and the nature of the climate were such that had it not been for the presence of this major depot on Lake Athabasca it would have been impossible to develop the trade at these far-flung posts, for furs from them reached Montreal in two stages after having spent the best part of a year at Fort Chipewyan.

CHAPTER FOUR

The Six-Year Battle on Lake Athabasca

Change and competition were ultimately to upset the measured routine of the relatively new Fort Chipewyan. It came from an aroused and re-vitalized Hudson's Bay Company which in 1815 once more challenged the North West Company in the Athabasca basin. That year the English company hired Colin Robertson, a dominating man, to master-mind it, and once more for nearly six long years Fort Chipewyan buzzed with con-spiracies and conflicts of armed and angry men.

On account of other commitments during 1815 Robertson, a former North West Company employee, directed the attack but left the actual assault to John Clarke, who was also a former Northwester. In the fall of 1815 Clarke, with his sixteen canoes and his ninety-eight-man brigade, amply laden with trading goods but woefully lacking in provisions, set out from Cumberland House to beard the North West lion in his Fort Chipewyan den. In due course in the first week of October, the leading canoes, filled with men already tightening their L'Assomption sashes from hunger, pushed their way through the reedy delta to emerge upon the clear, chilly waters of Lake Athabasca. With paddles dripping in the sunlight, they swung around Goose Island and headed for Potato Island. The Northwesters at Fort Chipewyan, already warned of their approach by their colleagues at Ile-à-la-Crosse who had prevented the Indians from selling food to them, assembled outside their palisades to watch as canoe after canoe was beached on the north shore of the island a mere mile across the channel. Although they outnumbered the English invaders, the Northwesters may well have watched with some trepidation as this new force landed on the rocky outcrop then called Coal Island but today known as Potato. For, whereas in 1802 Peter Fidler had settled on English Island with some seventeen men, this expeditionary force had more than a hundred.

Clambering ashore on Potato Island, Clarke quickly sorted out his lieutenants and their platoons, and because they were near starvation, hustled most of them off to regions where with luck they could kill game. He set Duncan Campbell and another Roderick of the ubiquitous Mackenzies to supervise fourteen men as they chopped trees to build their new post, Fort Wedderburn, on the northwest side of the island. Aulay McAulay and Vital Bourassa and thirteen men he sent to Great Slave Lake. Thomas Thomas, Jr., and twelve men he turned back up the Athabasca to build at some point what was to be called Berens House, in the midst of a land said to abound in meat and pemmican located perhaps as far upstream as the mouth of the Clearwater. François Decoigne had led his forces over to Lesser Slave Lake. Clarke himself hurriedly prepared to take six officers and forty-eight men up the Peace River to start other posts but above all else to secure pemmican with which to eke out his dwindling supplies.

This then was the force which, carrying out Robertson's instructions, Clarke had assembled to assault the Northwesters' stronghold, the Athabasca district. But though they presented a formidable threat to John McGillivray and his Fort Chipewyan associates, he had already devised a scheme to humble them.

As in five half-loaded canoes Clarke's Peace River force paddled around the point of the Dog Head, the North West Company's tactics began to reveal themselves. Open bloodshed ill suited that company's policy; starvation was a better weapon. The machinery needed to bring this about was all prepared. All that was required was a signal to touch it off and John McGillivray of the North West Company gave that signal. A few days earlier he had sent out instructions bidding the Indians to keep ahead of the Hudson's Bay Company's men, to drive all game back from the river and on no account to have anything to do with them or to feed them. The English party was forced by starvation to stop at Loon River. Meanwhile, Clarke had gone ahead as far as Fort Vermilion. Sixteen men turned back from Loon River towards Lake Athabasca, but the river froze and they had to abandon their canoes and make their way on foot. One by one, individuals fell out on the way. Three only reached Fort Wedderburn. The rest perished from starvation. In due course the Northwesters captured Clarke and some of the other men who had ascended the river.

The men at Fort Wedderburn under Duncan Campbell, however, depending on fish, could not be starved into submission. Neither could those under Thomas Thomas at Berens House because they obtained much of their sustenance from the fishery near the Old Fort and the rest of it from the big game animals of their area. Nevertheless, the Hudson's Bay Company's great assault had fizzled out.

Paradoxically the second round during the season of 1816-17 was much more eventful and much more violent but did not result in any loss of life. When on September 18 Clarke's brigade arrived at Fort Wedderburn he was welcomed by the fact that the Northwesters had come across the narrow channel from Fort Chipewyan and built a blockhouse right at the corner of the English company's house. With it McLeod's numerous men dominated the entrance to Fort Wedderburn and prevented Indians from trading there. Well might Clarke suspect that high-jinks were in store for him.

Within a few days weapons began to rattle in the hands of various hot-tempered Scots. Hector McNeil, taking care not to jab his claymore through the bark of his canoe, stepped ashore from a North West Company craft. Hamish McVicar came running out of Fort Wedderburn swinging his sword, and as the silent spruces of Potato Island echoed to the clash of blade on blade, McNeil was wounded and McVicar disarmed. The motionless Indians watched silently but every highland heart beat with fierce pride. When he heard of McNeil's wounds, McLeod sent over a strong force of Mackenzies and McGillivrays along with Thomas McMurray and seized a number of Hudson's Bay Company Scots. The clans had gathered and clashed.

Eventually, by a trick, the Northwesters captured Clarke and held him for the rest of the winter. That year's round in the war went to the Northwesters. So did the 1817-18 season, making three rounds, all of them won by the North West Company. Then in the fall of 1818 an aroused Hudson's Bay Company stood ready to back the angry Colin Robertson. He in turn took to the field to command all that company's affairs in the Athabasca basin. On September 21 he and his brigade of twenty-two canoes and over one hundred men entered Lake Athabasca and headed across the chilly blue water for Potato Island.

For the time being Robertson appeared to be in the driver's seat and likely to remain there unless some event should cast up. But when events needed casting up the Northwesters did not usually sit idly hoping. They soon contrived an event which took much of the starch out of Robertson's rosy prospects. One dawn in his ramshackle Fort Wedderburn, one of his men wakened him to report that at the fishery Etienne Carriveau had been shot accidentally and that his associates had brought his body to the fort to be buried. In naturally low spirits Colin got up thinking of the funeral service he had to conduct and ordered breakfast. As he sat down to eat he heard a commotion outside. As Robertson told of it in a letter he wrote while a prisoner in his opponent's fort:

> I got up, went to my bedroom as was my custom, put a pistol as I thought into my pocket, and went towards the place where the man was standing, where I saw Mr. Simon McGillivray. I was relating to him what had happened, and if they had any private quarrels to adjust this was not a proper occasion; at this time Black with eight or ten men made a rush from behind, and in a moment I was surrounded. In the struggle my pistol dropped down and got entangled in my clothes and in the attempt to find it, went off. At the report of the pistol they rushed and closed on me, and dragged me to the beach, where I happened to disengage myself and made some resistance by laying about with the empty pistol. . . . When placed in the canoe, I made an attempt to upset it in the hopes of making my escape by swimming, when Black drew his pistol upon me. This had little or no effect, and as I did not succeed it was owing to my strength being exhausted. On my arrival at this place I rushed into the Indian Hall.

Though Robertson did not escape from captivity until the following June at Île-à-la-Crosse, the Hudson's Bay Company's cause in the Mackenzie watershed made more progress than it had ever done. He had established the Athabasca district for his company on a scale never approached previously. His outlying posts along the Peace River and at Lesser Slave Lake did well and when the 1818-19 season closed impartial observers might well have concluded that round four had been a draw.

The Hudson's Bay Company's 1819-20 Athabasca venture was a continuation of its dogged determination to gain a foothold in that vast fur-rich area. Once more Colin Robertson took charge of the assault but this time he guided it from the new St. Mary's post far up the Peace River. His prediction that during that winter the weakening North West Company would provoke less friction turned out to be correct. The Hudson's Bay Company had come in with plenty of goods and plenty of men, and taking a leaf from the Northwesters' book, had added a legal officer to its armament. It had brought in a constable—not a policeman in the sense that we know them, but a representative of Canadian courts—bearing a warrant for the arrest of Samuel Black, the Northwesters' gadfly who had seized Colin Robertson the previous year.

As soon as Robertson reached Lake Athabasca he immediately spread his many men far and wide over the Mackenzie watershed; John Yale at Colvile House, Robert McVicar and Pierre St. Germain at Great Slave Lake, Aulay McAulay at Berens House and Peter Andries who went to Fond du Lac and established Harrison's House. Berens House needs further mention. In 1815 Thomas Thomas, Jr., had built a Berens House which according to William Brown's 1820 *Report of the Athabasca District* was at the "chutes of Rivière Labiche [Athabasca River]." During the summer of 1819, according to the same source, Joseph Greill built a new Berens House at the mouth of Pierre au Calumet River and Aulay McAulay went upstream to manage it.

Alexander McDonald and Dr. William Todd, the first physician ever to practise in what is now Alberta, helped to hold Fort Wedderburn, while the redoubtable John Clarke was kept out of the actual Mackenzie watershed but left in an auxiliary role back at Île-à-la-Crosse. The previous year Colin Robertson had found Fort Wedderburn in a deplorable condition, the "chimneys, doors and joists having been removed in preparation for a rebuilding which was interrupted for lack of provisions. It was proposed to remove the building during the summer of 1819 to a point where they would not be so dominated by the N.W.C. Fort Chipewyan." For by that time the Northwesters had built bastions beside it so that Alexander McDonald wrote: "their buildings now flank us on both sides, and with the desperadoes they have, our lives are in the greatest danger." During the summer of 1819 Aulay McAulay, to get away from the Northwesters' bastions, had thrown up a hastily built new Fort Wedderburn on a nearby site. Into this hurriedly and poorly built post Alexander McDonald and Dr. Todd moved in the fall of 1819, only to see the Northwesters build another "Watch House" very close to it. To us this building of watch houses and these petty—although sometimes deadly—enmities smack of childishness, but yet in the bitterly hostile and distorted context of the lives of these courageous men such actions seemed natural.

When on his way to eastern Canada, Colin Robertson, who had spent the winter near modern Peace River, reached Fort Wedderburn on May 23, 1820, he found that McDonald and Dr. Todd had spent a watchful but interesting winter. As Robertson wrote, Dr. Todd's "profession has given him an astonishing influence over the natives, from the circumstance of hooping cough having got amongst their children. Even the Indians and children of the N.W. Co. have come over for advice and assistance. You who have some knowledge of the Indian Character, may form some idea of the effects of his application—what a change! . . . two or three successful operations gave the Indians such confidence in the power of his medicines, that they not only love, but are dreadfully afraid of him."

If, however, the Northwesters had been little more than a nuisance at Fort Wedderburn, they had caused the collapse of Aulay McAulay's venture at Berens House where he had hoped to do a good trade in pemmican and dried meat. At Berens House he was in direct competition with his rivals' Pierre au Calumet House which at intervals since Fidler's 1791 trip down the river they had occupied as a provision post, and he had to close his post and go to Fort Wedderburn. Captain John Franklin, the Arctic explorer who became the guest of John Stewart in March 1820 at Pierre au Calumet, recorded that it "[was] built on the summit of a steep bank, rising almost perpendicular to the height of one hundred and eighty feet, commands an extensive prospect along the fine river, and over the plains which stretch out several miles back of it. . . . This house receives its name from the place where the stone is procured of which many of the pipes of the Canadians and Indians is made."

The company's disappointment at Berens House was more than offset by good news and good returns from most of Colin Robertson's other outposts. When in June 1820 he left Fort Wedderburn for the last time at the close of the rough and tumble battle for predominance, he may well have been proud of the part he had played and looked forward to starting a new round in the war the following fall.

It was during this fifth round that the first overland Arctic Exploring Expedition mounted by the British government reached Lake Athabasca—the first white men not connected with the fur trade ever to do so. Captain John Franklin, who was on his second visit to the Arctic shoreline, led it by way of the fur traders' route down the Mackenzie watershed and found its efforts unintentionally hampered by the fur trade fray. Franklin and a young midshipman, George Back, who was later to become famous as an Arctic explorer, arrived at Fort Chipewyan near the end of March 1820. The following July they were joined there by their colleagues, midshipman Hood and Dr. John Richardson, the second physician to visit Alberta and a man who made a major contribution to the natural history of northwestern Canada. During his prolonged stay at Fort Chipewyan Franklin picked up considerable information. One of the many interesting men he met was a Chipewyan named Rabbit's Head, who proved to be a step-son of the famous leader Matonabbee. As an adolescent he had actually been to the mouth of the Coppermine River with Hearne.

The guidance of the sixth and final round in the inter-company bout, which started the fall after Franklin's departure, fell to the lot of the most remarkable man in all the long history of the Canadian fur trade, George Simpson, a little wispy—but waspy—book-keeping type of man. Nevertheless, Simpson, the little Scot of about thirty-three years of age when he left England and rather suddenly found himself sent down the Athabasca River and catapulted into the midst of the fray on Potato Island, was a brave fighter whose intelligence, adroitness and subtlety helped him win most of his battles. Fortunately his very detailed journal for the winter of 1821-22 reveals much of the man himself and of the conditions on Lake Athabasca.

On September 9, Simpson, who for the next several months was to command more than 130 officers and men, "exclusive of guides, interpreters and Iroquois" but including Amable Grignon, who though unable to read or write, was a constable for the District of Montreal and an important part of Simpson's party, left Ile-à-la-Crosse. They passed the site of our Fort McMurray eight days later and reached the fork of the Embarras River on September 19. Though Simpson must have been appalled by the run-down condition of Fort Wedderburn, he was probably not surprised to learn that all summer long from their watch house adjacent to the fort the Northwesters had "frequently paraded in front of our Gates exhibiting their swords & pistols." He soon learned that of the chief men over at Fort Chipewyan two were also Scots, George Keith and James Leith, while the third, Edward Smith, was of unspecified ethnic origin. Even though Simpson was momentarily under scrutiny from unfriendly eyes in the watch house, he quickly turned his hand to despatch his winter crews to the outposts up the Peace River and down the Slave. Nearer to Fort Wedderburn he sent Aulay McAulay back to what he called the Forks of the Pembina (mouth of the Christina River) to "establish a post there in opposition to the N.W." As it turned out, McAulay failed to build there. Joseph Greill, a German, was sent to Berens House where McAulay had been starved out the previous winter.

Having attended to these details, Simpson had time to write up his journal in which he regretted that disease had caused "great mortality amongst the Beaver Indians this year." A couple of weeks later in a most adroit way he solved another problem. A Chipewyan wife who had deserted her husband and eloped with his friend, did not get very far before her lawful spouse caught up with her and brought her back. ". . . her paramour had absconded and thereby in all probability saved his scalp." At that point the problem was dropped on Simpson's plate.

> The Indian whose woman committed the "Faux pas" a few days ago, entreated I would inform him if she would remain faithful to him during the Winter. After the necessary ceremony I set his mind to rest on that subject, and gave a private lecture to the Lady threatening to transform her into a dog if she repeated the sin, she appeared very penitent and promised to conduct herself in a more becoming manner in future.

This problem, however, only added a bit of humour to Simpson's sojourn. Far more serious was that presented by the Northwesters at the watch house of which Simon McGillivray took charge. It was "twelve yards distance from our Bastion and projects about five yards beyond the front of our Fort towards the Lake. . . . In order to remove this eye sore I requested Mr. Oxley to superintend the erection of a few Stockades to run in a line from the corner of our Bastion towards the face of the bank."

Out stamped McGillivray and several of his supporters and ordered Oxley to stop. Whereupon Simpson and his crew facing up to McGillivray and his men "each armed with a dirk and a brace of large pistols . . . held openly to view in their hands" told Oxley to go on building. During the ensuing verbal argument over the boundary line between the two establishments Simpson made his point. Just then

> my Terrier Dog Boxer (a very playful fellow) was amusing himself with a stick close to Soucisses feet, and while the Bully was regarding him with an ill natured look, as if about to give him a kick, I with a smile addressed the dog, "come here Boxer, you do not seem to be aware that you are committing a trespass." McGillivray with a good deal of asperity observed: "We have no intention to molest your dog Sir." to which I replied: "nor shall you his Master with impunity."

Two hours later Simpson's stockade was finished.

Other similar incidents were almost daily occurrences until on October 23 the Northwesters rafted timber over to the site and began erecting a bastion "at a distance of two feet from our Bastion," thereby encroaching about three feet on the Hudson's Bay Company's property. Simpson sent Brown to tell them to stop, whereupon McGillivray and his associates in the richest of their several Scottish brogues ordered Brown to commit a number of unedifying acts against his own person, the mildest of which was "to drop dead." So Simpson and his men prepared to sally forth to "resist the encroachment by force if necessary."

Just then, by one of those curious coincidences which throughout Simpson's life always demonstrated that upon every occasion a handful of subtlety beat two fistfuls of sword hilts, Amable Grignon, the constable, "who had been absent since the 18th Inst. unexpectedly arrived." A sheer coincidence, but a brilliant one. But in Simpson's life coincidences frequently came in pairs and Grignon "on learning the circumstances of the case he informed me that he had a Warrant in his possession against the said Simon McGillivray and would by virtue of that instrument apprehend him."

That took the affair out of Simpson's hands and placed it in those of the law to which he had to bow, saying that

> I could not interfere or give any sanction or instructions to him in his Official capacity as a Constable, that whatever was done in that way must be on his own responsibility, but that it was my province to protect the Company's rights and that I was now about to act in conformity: he rejoined, that he intended to do his duty, and that he would call upon

those around him to assist in the Kings-name if necessary; I then said, that if Legally called upon for protection or assistance, we had no alternative.

Quite unmindful of Grignon the constable, of course, and solely to protect his employer's property, Simpson called for arms and ammunition for his men, "shewed the example by loading my double barrel'd gun and pistols with Ball" and sallied forth. The Northwesters faced up to them, led by McGillivray "with his hand on the hilt of his Dagger." Then

> when close to each other I said, "Mr. McGillivray I shall be glad to have some further conversation with you on the subject of this boundary line," he was about to reply when Mr. Grignon collered him and said "I arrest you in the Kings name." he made some resistance and the Officer called out "I demand your assistance in the Kings name" on which two of our people rushed upon the prisoner disarmed and conveyed him into Fort Wedderburn.

Without Simpson laying a hand on him and purely because of the fortuitous presence of Amable Grignon, poor McGillivray found himself a prisoner "venting his spleen in a torrent of abuse."

Finally the long winter wore away and as the hours of daylight lengthened and everyone looked forward to spring, Simpson began thinking of the time when he would take his brigade to Norway House and planning what his crews would do at Lake Athabasca during the summer. One thing was certain. Fort Wedderburn would have to be rebuilt, and as early as April he set his men to cutting logs for a new fort. Then too, before the season advanced too far some of his staff cut and hauled ice to preserve food in the ice house during the summer. Others were kept busy "attending the charcoal fire" so that the blacksmith might have fuel for his forge. It is probable that Potato Island had been used for some years as a site for burning charcoal and so at times came to be referred to as Coal Island.

Simpson also worked out plans for a rearrangement of his staff for the year to come. He sent Robert Clouston to take over Berens House, with instructions that if the Indians wanted him to abandon its existing site and move it to the mouth of the Christina River, he was to do so. When about a month later Simpson's canoe ascended the long, straight stretch of the Athabasca he found Berens House abandoned and a new one under construction at the mouth of our Mackay River. Since Simpson did not expect to be back the following year, he appointed William Brown to take charge of Fort Wedderburn.

On May 23, Simpson and many of his officers left Fort Wedderburn with the furs. As he travelled south and east, visions of the Grand Rapids of the Saskatchewan were rarely far from his mind. For along that stretch of some three miles the vast volume of water tumbling down to the level of Lake Winnipeg foamed and roared in a series of boiling cascades. But it was not the rapids that Simpson dreaded. To by-pass them most travellers took to a narrow portage path, and during the bitterness of the last few years this path had been the scene of many an ambush. Along it on June 21, 1819, when he thought Colin Robertson to be a prisoner of the marching Northwesters, Governor Williams had attacked that company's brigade and captured many of its leading men. At the same spot on June 20, 1820, the Northwesters had again arrested Colin Robertson. And now it was June 18, 1821, and Simpson, recalling the oft repeated threats of the previous winter—threats that if they did not get him before that they would certainly do so at Grand Rapids—approached the portage with trepidation and with extra precautions. "I fully calculated on meeting the N.W. at the Foot of the Rapid this morning, and therefore made the necessary defensive preparations; . . ." If he were to run the rapids, he had to unload some of his men and lighten the canoe "as it was considered dangerous to run the Rapid with the full complement, and in six minutes got to the Basin of the Upper Portage, a distance of about two miles: this is considered the finest run in North America, and altho' the swell is heavy it is by no means a dangerous rapid; . . ."

To his surprise and relief, as the canoe pitched over the lowest breaker, sped through the last of the whirling bubbles and finally glided out into the quiet water, Simpson realized that he had weathered the rapids and warded off capture. Surely the Northwesters had softened up more than he had dared to hope. But that was not his only surprise. A short distance ahead John, one of the numerous McLeods, hailed him by name and holding out the hand of friendship delivered the amazing announcement that the two companies had amalgamated.

The Northwesters had been knocked out in the sixth round. The war was over. Its battles had been fought at trading posts all over the West. But of all the war's battles none were fought with more bitterness than those on Lake Athabasca's northern shore, when clashing swords faced flashing dirks and when pistol shots echoed off the pre-Cambrian rocks and died away in the dark, non-committal forests.

CHAPTER FIVE

Governor George Simpson

From Simpson's *Journal* and his 1821-22 *Report of the Athabasca District*, supplemented by William Brown's report for the same year, we can gain a good insight into the conditions of the Lake Athabasca area, its natives and the logistics of the fur trade as its activities revolved about Fort Wedderburn and Fort Chipewyan.

Brown, standing on Potato Island and letting his eyes and his mind wander over the vast wilderness extending in every direction, declared that "This District may be considered as the most plentiful in the North, both in regard of Furs and Provisions." To the west, looking out over the marshy Delta so wide that only on the clearest days were the faint blue outlines of the hills beyond it visible, ranged a heavy concentration of buffalo. Off to the southwest and the northwest, moose were plentiful and to the east, all the way along and beyond the 150-mile northern shoreline, caribou wandered in great herds. Within the vast lake's clear, cold waters thousands of trout, pike and whitefish migrated from place to place and were to be taken with relative ease. In short, plenty of food was available, sometimes a mere eighteen miles away at a fishery and sometimes a hundred miles away in the forest. The main problem, however, was to get it when it was needed and frequently it arrived not a moment too soon.

Then, of course, there were the fur-bearing animals, and normally the area abounded in beaver, muskrat, mink and marten. Occasionally, for one reason or another, all of these animals had a bad year. As William Brown said: "In the year Seventeen hundred and Ninety-five and Eighteen hundred and twelve an epidemic distemper took place amongst the Beaver which carried off great numbers of them." Similarly, the muskrats occasionally suffered. ". . . when the water is high for a few years they become very numerous, but when low they entirely disappear."

The third resource of the area, the links between the white traders and the fur and game animals, were the native peoples—Crees, Beavers and

41

Chipewyans—who brought both furs and food to the posts. The Crees were more concentrated towards the south and, perhaps because they were well known to the traders, occasioned little comment. In Simpson's journal the Beaver Indians came in for an occasional favourable reference. While he regarded them as "naturally indolent," he had a good word for them, saying that they were:

of a bold Manly character, quick in resenting injuries, but possessing none of that detestable treachery, which characterises the Chipewyans, nor have they any of their selfish, covetous and avaricious dispositions . . . they seldom or never intermarry with neighbouring Tribes and it is against their Religious tenets to have connexion with the Civilized, so that there are no Beaver Indian half breeds. . . .

As for the Chipewyans, however, he regretted to say:

I cannot point out a solitary good trait . . . all their dealings are tainted with a degree of low Cunning which one would think it difficult for an uncultivated savage to acquire; they are covetous to an extreme, false and cowardly; . . . the whole Tribe does not possess one particle of honor and to the feelings of gratitude they are total Strangers; . . . such Wretches are only fit to inhabit the inhospitable clime they live in and no one who has had an opportunity of knowing them will commiserate their situation.

Hard words indeed—but words written in the midst of the unnatural heat of his campaign with the Northwesters. It is interesting to wonder what the Chipewyans might have written about the extremely dishonourable conduct of white men if only these natives had been literate.

On two occasions Simpson noted what to him seemed callous indifference to suffering. Of the first he said:

Three families of our Indians have taken their departure for their hunting grounds, and made ample promises. They mean to leave an old man, the head of one of the Families on the Bustard Island to Perish, as he is too infirm to travel. This barbarous practice is I understand peculiar to the Chipewyans.

Of the second, he wrote:

The "Bustards" Wife died this morning, or more properly speaking a termination was put to her sufferings as she was actually buried before the vital spark was extinguished; the relations demonstrated their grief by clamorous lamentations and the destruction of their clothes.

While Simpson's comments were generally quite sound, his opinion, like any other man's, cannot be regarded as wholly objective. Furthermore, of course, these and similar observations quoted give only the traders' assessment of the Indians. Unfortunately their opinions, the only written ones we have, undoubtedly painted a darker picture than the facts seen from the natives' point of view would warrant. The red men and the white possessed cultures which varied so greatly from each other that neither race could effectively see through the curtain that kept their ideas apart. Though the Indians' customs, beliefs and practices seen through the white man's eyes may have looked strange, nevertheless, the Chipewyans had developed them in their response to gaining their livelihood from a harsh and unforgiving land. To the Chipewyans' credit, however, is William Brown's opinion that while they were not as good hunters as the Crees, they were much more provident and therefore did not suffer as much. Furthermore, for many years, the Chipewyans were reluctant to partake of the dubious delights of the white man's liquor. In the end, unfortunately, they became as blind devotees of firewater as any other Indians.

Having dealt ever so lightly with the natives and the fauna of the area, perhaps we should look more closely at the white man's activities there. As Simpson wrote, probably with a wry smile over a well-turned phrase, "Philanthropy is not the exclusive object of our visits to these Northern Regions, but that to it are coupled interested motives, and Beaver is the grand bone of contention." The men were there and the posts had been built solely to obtain furs for export. To enable them to serve this function the staffs had to be fed—with meat when it was available, and more often with fish. Although the system and the provisions improved after Simpson left Fort Wedderburn and assumed control of all the Hudson's Bay Company's Canadian operation, that improvement came partly as a result of his hungry winter of 1820-21.

The main sources of food, of course, were the three fisheries; near Roderick Mackenzie's old fort, at Goose Island and at Big Island (our Bustard Island). Just as the Indians had been responsible for teaching the white man so many of the other secrets necessary for survival in the northern lands, so it appears that they were responsible for teaching the whites how to set nets beneath the ice. Once the ice froze solidly enough to bear their weight, the fishermen had a long winter's work before them, work which needed stamina and experience. For them the in-between seasons of freeze-up and spring break-up were the hazardous and least rewarding times. All too often during these seasons men lost their lives or had serious misadventures such as the one Simpson recorded on November 11, 1820.

The four men who were sent to the Big Island on the 3rd had nearly perished; their Canoe was set fast in the Lake, and being unable either to proceed or return, they providentially got to a small Island where they remained six days without any sustenance until the Ice was sufficiently strong to bear.

During such seasons hunger usually prevailed at the fort. On October

19, 1820, Simpson's journal records: "Received a supply of fish from the Big Island this Evening: for the last three days we have lived entirely on flour." Again about a week later he complained that: "Our stock of Provisions is now reduced to four bags of Flour, and if the lake does not soon set fast, I fear we shall be exposed to serious privations."

The importance of fish in Fort Wedderburn's economy is indicated by the figures which William Brown compiled showing the fort's provisions for the twelve months ending June 1, 1821.

Fish - No. 28,264	Tongues - 28 lbs.
Fat - 351 lbs.	Swans - No. 3
Fresh meat - 7,587 lbs.	Geese - No. 427
Dry meat - 1,960 lbs.	Ducks - No. 12
Beat meat - 593 lbs.	

All the meat reaching the fort came from the Indians who sometimes brought it in but more frequently sent word that they had killed a beast or two and let the traders come out to get it. Usually, of course, the carcass lay several miles away, as was the case on December 20 when Simpson remarked: "The six trains that started for meat on the 6th Instant returned with about 1,000 lbs Wt., it is dearly bought as our people have been away 16 days and the consumption of Fish on such Voyages is very great."

Because as much meat as possible had to be saved to feed the outgoing brigades in the spring, it was used only when fish failed. When both fish and meat failed the occupants had to resort to flour. This expensive commodity was brought in not for daily use but to be held in reserve if all other food ran out. While in future years the staff at Fort Chipewyan occasionally went hungry, the food situation during the days of competition in Simpson's time was at its very worst. Moreover, as Simpson said in March 1820:

The consumption of provisions at this place is incredible, the Officer's Mess including three House Servants expends about 90 lbs Buffalo Meat p̌ Diem, this may seem a paradox, as we have seldom more than nine sitters at Table, but when it is known that some of these men eat from 8 to 10 lbs p̌ day it is explained, and some of these Gluttons have the assurance to complain that they are half starved.

The staff at Fort Wedderburn, of course, varied from perhaps fifty for short periods down to the officers and six men who were there on March 1 after Simpson had sent as many as possible to the shacks at the fisheries to catch their own food. In times of scarcity other men were frequently sent out to live with the Indians. The personnel of the fort included women as well as a number of half-breed children. The women, however, were not merely useless hangers-on but were indispensable for such tasks as making fur clothing and leather moccasins. In February one of them, the wife of Lamallice, the best interpreter, was in some danger of being sent away temporarily with her husband, but to Simpson's surprise she said that: "if she was permitted to remain at the Fort, her Family would not require any allowance for 20 Days; it appears that in anticipation of a scarcity of provisions this thrifty amazon has out of the Rations served to her family (even when the Officers' mess was on short allowance) laid up a stock of about 200 fish; I have therefore permitted her to remain." Her unusual thrift undoubtedly raised her further in his estimation.

Simpson, of course, also had his "woman," a half-breed who became pregnant during the winter and the next fall presented the world with the first of his many "bits of brown" as he called those children he had by native women. While having a native wife was almost a necessity for a fur trader, it also fitted well into Simpson's virile temperament and with his official stance which was that:

> Connubial alliances are the best security we can have of the goodwill of the Natives, I have therefore recommended the Gentlemen to form connections with the principal Families immediately on their arrival, which is no difficult matter as the offer of their Wives & Daughters is the first token of their Friendship & hospitality.

The Indian women were proud of the prestige of having a white husband and, of course, found the shelter of the fort preferable to nomadic life in the snow-filled forest. Their presence within the palisades ensured that their relatives would bring in furs and meat to trade.

While every effort had been made during the winter of 1820-21 to hoard fish and meat for the use of the outgoing spring brigade, Simpson's endeavours came to nothing, for on May 23 on the eve of its departure he had to record:

> This is another Fast day with us and I fear our Canoe men will be in a wretched state before we get to Isle ala Crosse having only 1 Bag Pemican, a little dried meat & a few Geese to maintain 20 men and four passengers for about nine days.

Some months previously he had written to Francis Heron at Edmonton House and to John Lewes at Lesser Slave Lake, exhorting them to send pemmican to meet the brigade at Ile-à-la-Crosse. All that winter the problem of supplying food for his transport system was always near the top of Simpson's priorities. In the future, he applied himself to honing the transport system to a fine edge of efficiency, but during that winter it gave him considerable concern.

The link from Fort Wedderburn to Norway House was only one in a most extensive system which the Hudson's Bay Company had copied from the pioneering North West Company. Actually the company's inland transport system began at York Factory, the terminus for vessels from England. From there all the goods were shipped to Norway House near Lake Winnipeg and then those for the Athabasca district went on to the third depot in the chain, Fort Wedderburn, and later to Fort Chipewyan. Goods arriving at Norway House one year were forwarded about the middle of June the following year by the Methy Portage brigade. That brigade arrived at the portage in time to meet the south-bound brigade from Fort

Wedderburn and exchanged trade goods for furs. James Keith, a former Northwester who after the amalgamation of the companies took charge of the Hudson's Bay Company's newly acquired Fort Chipewyan, recorded the stages of one such journey from York Factory very succinctly:

> Their progress inwards as follows—15 days from Y Factory to Split Lake thence to Burnt Wood Carrying Place on Height of Lands that divides the York & Churchill Waters 13 days thence to Frog Portage the Point of junction between the Haye River Norway H. & Nelson River Routes 10 days—thence to Isle a la Crosse 10 days, thence to Portage Loche [Methy Portage] (including & in that River) 10 In the Portage 5 & thence hither in 7 days. 73 days in all. . . .

There were about forty portages where boats and canoes had to be transported, "& about as many dicharges or Partial carrying places where only part or the whole of the Canoes require to be transported equal to 80. . . ."

Even before the amalgamation the Hudson's Bay Company's Governor William Williams had been studying the system and, realising that the Methy Portage was a bottleneck on the way to Lake Athabasca, gave orders "To leave four men and a Superintendent to improve the Portage at Lac Laloche in such a way that Horses and Carts may be employed to convey Goods across." Unfortunately, Mr. Heron at Edmonton House who was to provide the horses was unable to deliver them at the portage that year. What Williams had in mind was to start replacing the glamourous canoe with the more prosaic, but more efficient, York type of boat; at the time he planned to have them hauled across the portage and continue on their way. As more careful plans were worked out the boats would be beached at the ends of the portage and their loads taken across by carts. Trying to follow Williams's suggestion, Simpson at Fort Wedderburn had intended to build a couple of boats but was unable to do so during that frantic winter of 1820-21.

But as well as thinking about transport across the continent, Simpson gave ample attention to the local Fort Wedderburn scene. There, of course, dogs were prominent and on November 5 he commented that since the snow had come both the natives and his men had begun to prepare their animals for the winter's work.

> These useful animals have certainly no sinecure of it in this Country; from the beginning of November until the latter end of May they are daily in Harness, hard wrought and sparingly fed; if in tolerable condition at the end of the season, many of them are eaten by their Masters, and those who have the good fortune of being so lean as to escape the Kettle are allowed to starve the rest of the year. They are a great article of trafic among the Canadians who value a dog according to his points as we estimate a Horse in the civilized world. Three active dogs have been known to run ten miles within the hour drawing a cariole and passenger with the driver standing behind and fifty pounds of luggage; a Thousand to fifteen hundred livres is no unusual price for a good train, say 3 dogs. By proper attention to the breeding of dogs the Company may make a

very profitable trade of them and in spring I intend to issue an Order that none shall keep bitches except the Compy., by this arrangement we shall always have a good stock of dogs, and can supply the people at fair prices.

His active mind suggested other possible beasts of burden, for he wrote to Peter Andries at Harrison's House, requesting him to "Ask your Indians to secure in Spring half a dozen Carriboo or Rein Deer Fawns; if properly broke in I think they will be very useful on the Rivers & Lakes instead of Dogs." However, nothing seems to have come of this idea even though about the same time he was writing,

We are this season greatly in want of dogs, and if the Horse had not been got from Peace River we must have foregone the comfort of Fires: half a dozen Horses may be kept here at little expense, and they would be found of most essential benefit in hauling fish, and other necessary work about the Fort, which occupies more than one half of our people, whereas three men with six horses and a sufficient number of dogs could do all the draught work throughout the Winter.

While the Northwesters had been using horses at Fort Chipewyan since 1804, this appears to have been the first Hudson's Bay Company horse to reach Lake Athabasca.

Epidemics amongst the natives were a recurring theme in most of the traders' journals. In May of 1820 William Brown had written: "The trade appears to have suffered severely in this district from the privations of the measles and whooping cough which carried off a considerable number of the Indians." The previous year Dr. Todd pointed out one of the deplorable features of whooping cough which was: "a disease particularly distressing amongst the Indians as well for its long continuance as its depriving them of the Means of subsistence the whole of their caution in approaching an animal being rendered abortive by a single cough."

Simpson, however, had many other problems to occupy his attention including being expected to supply some staff and food stuffs to send to Franklin's party, which by that time was north of Great Slave Lake. On October 1, 1820, when sending two canoes north, he noted that they bore the two Eskimos destined for Franklin's party. These two, certainly the first Eskimos to mingle with their hereditary enemies the Chipewyans at Fort Chipewyan, had been hired at Fort Churchill. Now by way of the fur traders' route they were on their way to serve as interpreters when Franklin should finally make contact with their compatriots along the Arctic shoreline. These two, whose names were Tattannoeuck and Hoeootoerock (the Belly and the Ear), turned out to be hardy, resourceful men whom the explorer nicknamed Augustus and Junius.

These two were not the only members of unusual race to make their appearance at Fort Chipewyan, for while Simon McGillivray was held prisoner in Fort Wedderburn he had occasion to complain of Glasgow the cook's cruelty to his half-breed children. Simpson investigated the charge, which he found groundless, but could not refrain from a bit of sarcasm. " . . .

the man happens to be a Negro and the children have taken umbrage at his complexion, it being a shade darker than their own."

So with Glasgow the Negro, Eskimos, the Beaver Indian Pouce Coupée, who traded there, and Tête Jaune the Iroquois, who from time to time signed on with the Hudson's Bay Company, Simpson had a busy winter. At the same time he acquired a thorough knowledge of the fur trade and by combining that with his great intelligence, business acumen and drive, he soon won promotion. Upon his return from Fort Chipewyan that spring of 1821, he was made Governor of the company's Northern Territory and by 1839 was elevated to Governor-in-Chief of all the Hudson's Bay Company's Canadian territories and affairs. For, over a period of well-nigh forty years, with his far-seeing and masterful mind he was to guide more than half of our present day Canada along a benign and peaceful road.

When George Simpson's canoe glided away from Fort Wedderburn he did not know that the bitter conflict of the last few years had ended with the amalgamation of the two companies. A new era of peaceful monopoly, which, in the Athabasca district at least, was destined to endure for over sixty years, had commenced. Henceforth, the staffs of the two companies were to work together, the good men from each to be reconciled and retained and the poor ones weeded out and moved away. One of each pair of competing posts, usually the better built North West Company one, was refurbished and continued in operation while the other was abandoned. On Lake Athabasca, the headquarters of the vast northern region, Fort Wedderburn was left to disintegrate, while Fort Chipewyan started on a new career which for all of the next century was to see it dominate the North.

Both the natives and the Hudson's Bay Company gained by the return of peace. The main problem the company had to face was the demoralization of the Indians which had been brought on by the competitive outlay of goods and the lavish outpouring of liquor. Once it had no rivals, the Hudson's Bay Company quickly set about decreasing the amount of liquor given to the Indians and by 1828 ceased handing it out altogether. That year, when Simpson passed through Fort Chipewyan on his way to British Columbia and the Oregon country, he was able to write:

> Liquor, they never talk of now, and it is singular enough that those Indians, who but a few years ago were nearly unmanageable, from the bad habits contracted in the hottest opposition ever known in the Indian country; should be the first to fall in with our wishes, in simplifying the Trade by reducing it to a regular system of buying & Selling in barter.

After the amalgamation of the companies, new and more efficient procedures made themselves felt at Fort Chipewyan. William Brown took charge of the establishment which so recently had been the North West Company's post. The following year James Keith, a former Northwester, became the fort's Chief Factor and continued in that capacity until 1826. Berens House at Pierre au Calumet was closed out so that along the Athabasca, as far up as present-day Fort McMurray and even beyond that up the Clearwater River to the Methy Portage, no posts were left in operation. Harrison's House at Fond du Lac probably remained in business as an outpost devoting its attention mainly to supplying caribou pemmican to Fort Chipewyan.

Now that the former competition was over, the problems of the food supply became less acute, but even then hunger occasionally stalked the fort. And hunger was not confined to the men and their dogs but at least once reached out to the few scrawny horses used to haul fish. During the winter of 1822 the supply of hay ran out and these gaunt beasts were kept barely alive by being fed fish.

Once spring returned to the magnificent lake and ducks and geese abounded, other changes came into effect. On September 29, 1823, Samuel Black, who so recently had been one of Simpson's inveterate foes but who by this time was a company employee, arrived at Fort Chipewyan with four loaded boats, "the first boats ever fitted out for Athabasca." As James Keith reported, he had been seventy-three days bringing them from York Factory, but their greater capacity than canoes had effected a significant saving in costs. As a matter of interest, they had left York Factory two weeks after the company's Northern Council meeting there had decreed that:

> The Boat Builder at Fort Chipewyan be employed during the winter in boat building, and that two Boats additional to the four now stationed at Portage La Loche, be brought thither next spring.

These boats were much safer on the large lakes of the northwest and carried about three times as much lading as the former North West Company's freight canoes. For a long time canoes continued in use at Fort Chipewyan but they were kept mainly for express trips.

More than ever now that the era of boats had arrived, Fort Chipewyan began to flourish as the headquarters of the northwest and the cross-roads of the long transport routes. From the west came company stalwarts, mainly former Northwesters, who but a few weeks previously had been serving in Oregon or the Okanagan valley. From the north came rugged men accustomed to dealing with Yellowknives, Dogribs or Eskimos. Finally, from the south came instructions for further explorations or ventures up the Liard or the Finlay rivers. All of them came by water along the Athabasca, the broad, safe channel flowing north through the interminable greenery of the summer forests or leading the Orkney boatmen along mile after mile of its nearly incredible autumn blaze of yellow and gold. But when winter came and the lake boomed with the cold, Fort Chipewyan kept in touch with the outer world by at least one express in which the dog team made its way across the pressure ridges and over the rough snow-covered ice on the Athabasca and Peace rivers and night after night camped up the bank in the shelter of the silent spruces. For such an express ran regularly each winter from Fort Carlton on the Saskatchewan River to Edmonton House and thence by way of Lesser Slave Lake, Dunvegan and Forts Vermilion and Chipewyan and back via Ile-à-la-Crosse to Carlton. Of all the northern posts, only Edmonton House did not come under Fort Chipewyan's control and was its only rival.

George Simpson had seen possibilities in the upstart Edmonton House. With a team of dogs during the winter of 1822-23 he visited the scene of his recent Lake Athabasca tribulations and travelled to Fort Chipewyan. Following the route of the express in reverse, he went on to Dunvegan and crossed over the 350 miles to the North Saskatchewan River. Then in the fall of 1824 he ordered a pack trail cut through the forest from Edmonton House to the recently established Fort Assiniboine on the middle section of the Athabasca River. He decreed that thenceforth personnel and goods going across the Rocky Mountains should ascend the North Saskatchewan River to Edmonton House, cross the seventy-mile portage to Fort Assiniboine by pack horses, work their way up the Athabasca River to its headwaters near Jasper and after crossing the summit of the mountains proceed down the Columbia River to the coast. From then on Fort Chipewyan was out of bounds to Oregon-based personnel.

Nevertheless, the fort on the vast lake continued consolidating its position as the connecting link to the northern part of the territory which we call British Columbia but which the Gaelic fur traders called New Caledonia, and also to all the tremendous area drained by the Mackenzie River. To it reported men who were ever pushing the frontier of the company's knowledge farther back—up the Finlay River and up the Liard and Nahannie rivers. For a thousand miles west into the maze of British Columbia's mountains and for a thousand miles north down to the Arctic ice floes, Fort Chipewyan directed further exploration. And from these areas for many thousand square miles it drew increasing harvests of furs.

From 1822 to 1826, the fort's director, James Keith, appears to have had an easy time. According to his 1824 Journal, the winter establishment included four officers, forty-nine employees, seventeen women and adult children, twenty-three children of both sexes, seven widows, boarders, pensioners, and five of their children, for a very large total of over 105 souls.

The demand for fresh meat to feed such a number was high, the standard daily ration per man, when the yield of the forests allowed, was eight pounds of fresh meat or two pounds of pemmican. Securing anything approaching that quantity demanded the skills of people who were intimately familiar with both the country around the lake and the ways of the animals which lived in it. No amount of white application to mastering the requisite skills could pre-empt those of one who was born there, and as a result half a dozen Indian hunters were employed. In explaining how they were paid Keith said that they were

. . . allowed for every Lar[ge] animal (Female, Buffaloe or Moose deer) 5 M Beavr & for every male of the same specie 4 M.B.—for every full grown rein Deer half the foregoing prices & for younger animals in Proportion, but are only paid for what they furnish to the Fort & not for their own consumption; are supplied with a reasonable quantity of ammunition & Tobacco gratuitously for every ten animals furnished are allowed 3/4 Quart spirits equal to 1 Gall Indian rum.

Perhaps it would be a good idea at this point to try to lay to rest a long standing canard that an Indian who wanted to buy a gun had to pile beaver skins one upon the other until the stack equalled the height of the gun. The old flintlocks were about five feet long and a pile of beaver pelts that high would be the equivalent of an ordinary hunter's catch of beaver during a two-year period. Actually, in most of Canada the price of a gun was about ten beaver skins. Far down the Mackenzie River, where the costs of shipping goods in and carrying the furs out to Hudson Bay were extremely high, a gun never cost more than twenty beaver skins, and in those days on the New York fur market such a skin sold for about $1.90.

To obtain their guns and other necessities, relatively few Crees traded at Fort Chipewyan. In 1823 Keith considered that a population of 593 Chipewyan dealt there as compared to some 60 Crees. For many reasons, including inter-tribal enmity, the numbers fluctuated. Keith recorded the details of one row related in August 1824 by a band of victorious Chipewyans.

At Vermilion Chutes a hunting party of seven young Beaver Indians met a band of ten Chipewyan families led by Old Fool. For about a week the two groups camped peaceably together and gambled until the more successful Chipewyans won all the stakes. At that point the Beavers, who were accustomed to browbeat their usually inoffensive neighbours, started a disturbance and threatened not only to pillage the Chipewyans and take their younger women by force, but to kill any men who resisted. Old Fool and the older men of the Chipewyan band tried to smooth the affair over and succeeded so far as to retreat with their families to an island some fifteen miles down the Peace River.

The next morning, however, four vigorous young Beaver men followed them and demanded the surrender of some women and property. But the Chipewyans, at the end of their patience, captured and disarmed the young men who as Keith said became "as humble and suppliant as they were lately fierce and unaccommodating—though too late—the train was laid, the match applied and the explosion must take place." They killed the Beavers, mangled the corpses and left the island littered with bits of their bodies. They then made their way back through the Delta and a couple of days later told Keith of the incident.

As a rule, relations between the traders and the Chipewyans were on a good footing and the white men found them amenable to reason. Shortly after 1821 the company began to worry about the continued supply of the furred animals whose presence in the area was the main reason for the establishment of Fort Chipewyan. In this respect more than a century and a half ago the Hudson's Bay Company was the first corporation to think of or practise conservation in Canada. In 1825 the Northern Council directed against killing beaver during the summer months. Executing the order involved no small amount of explaining to the trappers, but the natives finally adopted this practice. Most of them soon came to realize the importance to their continued supply of the white man's goods of maintaining a steady number of fur-bearing animals in the region. It appears that only the Indians alien to the area, the Iroquois, trapped without regard to the future.

When in 1828 George Simpson paid the Chipewyans and the Beavers of Fort Chipewyan another visit, he was able to say of them:

> Their country is in good condition and improving every successive year: they are without exception the best Beaver hunters we know, rarely kill except when the animal is in Season, use the Ice Chissel principally, never destroy all the inmates of a Lodge and generally allow three, or four years elapse before revisiting their last Hunting grounds.

As well as beavers, muskrats were also a lucrative source of revenue to the natives. Occasionally, however, disease or climatic conditions killed them off. In 1825, for instance, James Keith declared that the spring hunt for them was almost an entire failure and this he attributed to a combination of the peculiar state of the ice and water and "the annoyance from the Foxes & wolverines—last year this place turned out about 8,000 Muskrats & this year little above 3,000." Similarly, in 1827, his successor, Alexander Stewart, commented:

> Our Hunters accompanied with several other Chipewyans, paid us a visit saying they are much disappointed in the Rat Hunt. the water in all the small Lakes having withdrawn in consequence of the cold, thereby leaving the Rat Houses on dry land, when the inhabitants must of course have froze, and ultimately destroy some thousands of those little animals.

It was Stewart who was on hand in the middle of August 1828 to welcome Governor Simpson, who was on his way to inspect the posts in New Caledonia and Oregon. By that time Simpson had acquired his reputation as a swift traveller, which he demonstrated by reaching the post on Lake Athabasca in an express canoe manned by picked voyageurs six hours short of a month after he had left York Factory. His arrival caught the local staff by surprise, but when looking across the water towards Bustard Island they perceived two canoes displaying the Governor's flag, they gave him the "best reception in our power—and on coming ashore, the Cos Standard being hoisted he was saluted by some discharges from our old Iron Cohorn . . . and here the Govrs. Piper amused & astonished the natives, in fact, they pretended to think him the greatest Chief of the Whole, tho' they knew the Govr. was Master."

This piper was never stationed at Fort Chipewyan but later on he had a son who was to have a profound influence on its future. This man, the first Colin Fraser, had been recently recruited from the Scottish highlands for the purpose of adding a touch of colour and ceremony to Simpson's processions back and forth across the land. Archibald McDonald, another Highlander who accompanied Simpson on this trip, confessed, however, that Fraser's music made "but a poor accordance with the pole and the paddle."

During his brief visit, Simpson was glad to renew acquaintances with some of the Chipewyans he had known a few years earlier. Perhaps not having them under foot all the time had softened his earlier harsh criticism for on this visit he praised them for the way they had fallen in line with the company's conservation policies, saying ". . . they are without exception the best Beaver hunters we know." On this trip he learned that Pouce Coupée, "a good old man and a regular good fur hunter," had died a few months previously. On the whole he was pleased with the "great regularity and Oeconomy" with which the local business was being conducted. Archibald McDonald, however, who after writing that "all the buildings about this place are in a state of decay" also said: "Our departure from Fort Chipewyan—the great emporium of the North in days of yore—was as imposing as the firing of guns, heavy cheers from master and men on rocks, and the waving of flags, and songs in abundance on our part could make it."

CHAPTER SIX

Fort Chipewyan—Headquarters of the North

As the memories of the governor's visit faded, the reliant folk at Fort Chipewyan, isolated by hundreds of miles from any other post, quickly resumed the routine of their compact centre of civilization. Already, less than ten years after the bitter fights of the days of competition, the Hudson's Bay Company's monopoly rule had brought relative peace and contentment to all this vast region. Never grabbing for every last penny, the company's attitude was strict and formal but beneficent. A sense of the responsibilities it bore is perhaps best set out in a memorandum written at the time, saying: "and as the posts must to a certain extent be maintained to preserve the Indians who could not now exist without amunition and other necessaries the expences cannot be curtailed in proportion to the returns."

While this attitude was undoubtedly the wise one for a company which had a long-time monopoly interest in the natives and the harvest of their trap lines, it was prompted by the directors in England who partook of the humanitarian outlook sweeping that country at the time. The Indians, although regarded as backward, were nevertheless thought of as human beings who merited and responded to considerate treatment. As a result of this outlook, assisted by the fact that most of the traders had taken native wives, relations between the company and the Indians settled into a pattern where each trusted, respected and helped the other—a pattern which was to come down the decades until recent times.

The immediate outcome of these policies and practices was that although the tally of employees of Fort Chipewyan itself may have remained relatively constant, the number of Métis families who considered its immediate environs as their home began gradually to increase. Moreover, after 1821 the Indians all over the North started the practice of leaving their aged or infirm to camp near the companies' forts, where in dire emergencies the white men could ensure them against starvation. To have taken these invalids back with them and thereby to have exposed them to all the rigours of winter travelling in the inhospitable forest would not only have resulted in their death but would have formed a serious impediment to the progress of the fit. At times this led to a dearth of food at Fort Chipewyan but it also cemented the friendship and respect existing between white men and red. By the time of Simpson's 1828 trip Fort Chipewyan had entered upon a routine which was to continue till some sixty years later the puff of civilization's steam engines shattered its long-time calm. Even then for a generation or two along the remote waterways of the North the word of the Hudson's Bay traders was to remain the real law of the land.

Simpson and the Northern Council, which he dominated, soon began to place more emphasis on the practice of each post developing whatever agriculture its climate justified. Evidently their wishes began to be taken seriously along the Peace River and by May 1833 we find William MacKintosh of Dunvegan writing to John Charles, the Chief Factor at Fort Chipewyan, saying:

> . . . I can say little about farming in Peace River all I know is that Barley and potatoes thrive tolerably well but I doubt if wheat will . . . it certainly is an object worth trial to raise Flour for Athabasca, but I have no hope that any thing of the kind will be effective with Canadians alone. there is no country better adapted for Cattle there is plenty of luxuriant grass and Hay can be got in abundance if there were Scythes to mow it.

A month later, the Minutes of the Northern Council decreed that:

> In order to save expense of transporting flour from the Depot to Athabasca and McKenzie's River District; it is resolved That the Gentlemen in charge of posts in Peace River where the climate and soil are favourable to cultivation be directed to devote their attention to that important object forthwith, and it is intended that these districts shall depend on Peace River alone for their flour after the close of Outfit 1834.

But the agricultural policy evidently contemplated more than flour for MacKintosh, writing to Charles again, said: "In the Month of June a Party of my Beaver Indians, brought 2 Cows, 1 Heifer & a Young Bull, the Cows have no Milk & doubtful if they are in Calf."

Evidently in 1834 the first cows ever to graze along the flats of the Peace River had reached Dunvegan after their mosquito- and horsefly-infested trip from John Rowand's Edmonton pasture. Probably due to Charles's reluctance, no cattle seem to have reached Fort Chipewyan until 1835 when Captain George Back, who was on his way to explore the Barren Lands river which now bears his name, reported their arrival there.

> On the 23d of May, some boats laden with furs, &c. arrived from the post on Peace River, whence they also brought a cow and calf, and thereby supplied us with luxuries till then untasted at Chipewyan.

Others seem to have come shortly thereafter, because in June 1836 Edward Smith, the new factor at Fort Chipewyan, wrote McPherson at Fort Simpson, saying:

> The cattle here now and a horse is for your district, and you will endeavour to take them with you say a cow a bull and a calf, the other bull and cow is for Slave Lake. [Presumably Great Slave Lake.]

The milk and butter obtained from these forlorn Fort Chipewyan cows would be highly regarded as luxuries. So too would be the produce of the traders' often sadly ineffective gardens. Occasionally turnips were fit to harvest. As the years rolled along the Fort Chipewyan staff seem to have been more adept at caring for their patches of potatoes planted either on Potato Island or around the little bay near the fort and their production increased. When, however, the potato crop was favourable, the tubers added variety to the otherwise near perpetual diet of fish.

From year to year the catch of fish on which they relied for the bulk of their food supply varied. Up to February 1832 the yield had been 30,179 fish, but even by March 8, 1835, the season's catch had been only 22,444 averaging four pounds each. At a different season, such as during July 1836, there might be "Bad news from the fishery. Laprize is taking no Fish Saturday with 10 nets he only took 5 white Fish & this morning's visit with 11 nets only gave 3 Fish." The periods of freeze-up and break-up were usually hungry times at the fort and hazardous times at the fisheries. On October 26, 1837, the journal reports: "two nets have been lost and the people there are in a starving state, the ice is still too Weak to admit of setting nets, but the first cold Weather will remove all danger for the safety of the nets. . . ." Despite that prediction, until the end of November "The fishery is not productive, owing to the extreme low state of the water." On one such occasion the journalist explained that "We could get Fowl from the Indians but then our stock of ammunition will not afford us to employ hunters to kill Game."

But scarcity could strike in other ways besides a shortage of fish. Muskrats were a delectable and important item on the menu of both trappers and traders. In their pushups in the wide-spread marshes these animals, however, suffered their own diseases and problems. On September 29, 1834, for instance, the Indians said ". . . the Musquash that has been so plentiful for this two last seasons have disappeared the low water destroy's them. . . ." Evidently the water was exceptionally low that fall for on November 10 ". . . Measured on the rocks at Little Portage the depth from high water mark to its present level 13 1/2 feet Walked on the sand over the place where Nets were usually set at this season of the year. . . ."

During the next year Edward Smith, the factor, had another and a more serious worry—disease. "The Influenze that so severely afflicted us incoming broke out here in the middle of October, to this date there has been fifteen deaths amongst the Indians." The epidemic spread and was later reported to have swept the country between the Peace River and Great Slave Lake and to have extended west beyond Fort Dunvegan, carrying away many more of the native inhabitants. From time to time, measles, smallpox, whooping cough and influenza are frequently mentioned as affecting the people in the fort and living about the lake. Serious outbreaks of diseases are recorded so often that in that regard it is almost impossible to tell the difference between what was normal and what was exceptional.

The year 1835 was doubly hard on the occupants of Fort Chipewyan. Not only did they suffer from the depressing news coming in from the various Indian bands, but their liquor had been cut off. That year the Northern Council, following its first step of 1826 when it had forbidden giving liquor to Indians, now prohibited the serving of liquor to all classes of its employees. It could well be that a disgruntled entry in the journal of January 1836 was in part egged on by the recent prohibition. It said: "We are freezing in our Barn of a House. Near the fire one side burns and the other freezes . . . the man is unfortunate who is condemned to pass the winter in such a rotten Fabric in this climate."

But better times were ahead for even at that time some steps had been taken to rebuild Fort Chipewyan and they seem to have gone on to a successful conclusion within a year or so. In the course of such rebuilding, the blacksmith's services would be called upon to make hinges and other hardware and probably with that in mind an entry in the journal pointed out that twenty-seven cords of birch wood had been cut for charcoal. Other entries indicate that preparing charcoal presumably over on "Coal" Island was given a high priority.

With a staff kept comfortably busy with the manifold duties and chores of the important, if not luxurious, fort, this key post at the cross-roads of the northern trade routes had settled down to the orderly pursuit of business which was to be its role for many decades. Nevertheless, while it had been busily ironing out its changing role on Lake Athabasca, outsiders not interested in the fur trade had become curious about the vast territory extending some six hundred miles north across the Barren Lands and about the exact delineation of the Arctic shoreline. Various marine expeditions had fought their way into the ice floes north of the mainland. Then in 1825, to supplement their activities, Captain John Franklin once more took the fur traders' route past Fort Chipewyan. Accompanied by Dr. John Richardson and Lieutenant George Back, who had been with him three years earlier, and some new men, Franklin stopped at the old post. In July that year his party crossed the Methy Portage, which had to be negotiated by the sweat of his crew men because even then no draught animals had been sent there. While the map accompanying his report of this expedition showed a set of buildings at our Fort McMurray, he passed them without comment, presumably because they were not occupied at the time. Neither was Berens House nor the post across the Athabasca River from it at Pierre au Calumet.

Once more the traders at Fort Chipewyan pitched in to help him along, and in 1827, after having accomplished some more survey work with the assistance of the Hudson's Bay Company's Peter Warren Dease, the exploring party returned south through that post. It paused long enough at the fort on the rock to observe how faithfully the factor there—and indeed at each of the other posts—had carried out the company's instructions that the Sabbath day should be duly observed and that a service be read. While there, also, Franklin had two vehicles constructed which he took upstream to the Methy Portage to enable the crews to roll the expedition's boats across it.

Six years were to elapse before another non-fur-trade explorer set forth down the Slave River and again it was the indefatigable George Back. This time he was leading a search party trying to find Captain John Ross, who in 1829 had sailed for the polar regions and now four years later was presumed to have met with some misadventure. Once more the Hudson's Bay Company gave Back what help it could and in the fall of 1833, with the assistance of one of its traders, he went on to build a huddle of shacks at the east end of Great Slave Lake, which he called Fort Reliance. There he spent the winter, planning to start his search for Ross in the spring by crossing the height of land until he could reach and descend the stream then known as Great Fish River but now named in his honour.

On March 26, 1834, a messenger from Fort Resolution arrived at Fort Reliance bearing the second of a duplicate set of packets sent from York Factory and stating that the first set had been forwarded from Fort Resolution—a mere two hundred miles away—a month previously and most surely had gone astray. He then told Back what he knew about the bearers of the first set. To begin with, he said that Back's faithful friend, Augustus (Tattannoeuck), the Eskimo interpreter who had gone with him on the previous Franklin expedition and had since been living along the shores of Hudson Bay, had heard of the present trip. He was so determined to take part in it that during the winter he had walked over fifteen hundred miles until he had reached Fort Resolution. From there Augustus, a French Canadian and an Iroquois, none of whom could speak the others' language, had started out with the first message. After an absence of eighteen days the Canadian and the Iroquois returned to Fort Resolution with the first packet and stated that they had all gotten lost and that Augustus, without gun, bow or arrows and with only ten pounds of pemmican, had left them and pressed on to find his way to Back's Fort Reliance.

On March 29, three days after Back had received that second packet, another messenger arrived bearing the first as well as a letter from McDonell at Fort Resolution, saying that the same day the Canadian and the Iroquois had come in still carrying the first message, McDonell had sent it out again with two other Iroquois who were also to look for Augustus. But once more, after a lapse of another eighteen days, they too came in reporting failure and the fact that they also had gotten lost. At that point McDonell had sent off this the first of the pair of duplicate packets which the Iroquois had returned to him. There could be no doubt now that the faithful Augustus had perished.

But on April 25 at Fort Reliance where messengers from other white men were usually as scarce as food had been all winter, another burst into Back's room and handed him a third packet. This one, having no relation to the previous two, was obviously of English origin and its bearer exclaimed: "He is returned sir." Back, still sorrowing over the fate of his faithful Eskimo, cried out: "What! Augustus—Thank God." Only to hear the reply: "Captain Ross, sir—Captain Ross is returned."

The amazing speed with which that last message had crossed Canada illustrates the surpassing efficiency of the Hudson's Bay Company's organization. Two separate packets had been mailed from London, England, to the company's factor at Sault Ste. Marie, one by way of Montreal and the other along an American route. Both of them reached Back, one on April 25 and the second on May 7. The last one he received took about ninety days to come from the Sault, some 2,500 miles through the bitterness of the Canadian winter.

Delighted that according to these messages the navy captain, the object of his search, had reached England, Back wondered what to do now that he no longer needed to proceed. Since spring had come and he was within striking distance of the Great Fish River, he wisely concluded that he had better explore it. So he set out and mapped it to its mouth at the Arctic Ocean and returned to spend a second hungry winter making scientific observations at his Fort Reliance. Anyone seeking to understand typical hardships, the hunger and starvation which the Chipewyans endured during these two winters or their apparent harshness and callousness towards their less fortunate kin can gain some further impression and compassion for these natives from Back's comments about this period. He said it "had been pregnant with more than ordinary evils to the different tribes inhabiting the country about Slave Lake and the McKenzie River," and noted that:

forty of the choicest hunters among the Chipewyans had been destroyed by actual famine; many others had not yet been heard of; and the scattered survivors, from the rigours of the climate, and the difficulty of procuring a single animal, had experienced the severest hardships which even their hardy natures were capable of sustaining. . . .

For the neglect or abandonment by the more active hunters of the sick and feeble of their tribe, some allowance may be made, on account of the peculiarity of their circumstances. To follow and keep up with the migratory animals which constitute their food, is essential to the preservation, not only of the hunters themselves, but of the whole encampment. An infirm or diseased savage is not merely useless; he is a positive clog and encumbrance on the motions of the rest. No wonder then, if occasionally, in the impatience or necessity of the chase, he is left behind to the mercy of chance.

While allowing for the fact that Back, although also starving at times, could not even then have seen through Indian eyes, his comments provide one of the truest insights into the way of life in the northern forests even after the fur traders' goods had helped to soften its harshness.

Decade after decade, much of Fort Chipewyan's fascination has lain in the continued flow of adventurous men like Back who lived there for a time and enjoyed its hospitality. To it as the cross-roads of the North during all of the nineteenth and part of the twentieth centuries came a succession of strong men marching determinedly onward to continue the West's ever expanding and ever continuing exploration. Such a typical traveller was John McLean, who was to remain one of the lesser lights in the fur trade hierarchy. He had spent some time in Ontario, three years in the mountainous interior of British Columbia, and five years in Labrador, before being stationed at Great Slave Lake.

Like all of his associates, he knew most of the company's other adventurous men and like many of them he met George Back on his comings and goings. He also met many of the lesser luminaries of the fur trade—the Orkney boatmen and the sturdy race of voyageurs, compounded of the mixed blood of French, Scottish, Iroquois and other Indian races. Their faithful toil with pole, paddle or dogs alternated with weeks of indolent loafing. Largely anonymous except indirectly by their monuments—the hundreds of lakes, rivers and rapids named after them all over Canada —they too opened up the Canada we know. A worthy representative of this breed was the voyageur John McLean met in a brigade of canoes in 1833 as he ascended the Peace River from Fort Chipewyan. As he wrote:

an old man with a white head and wrinkled face, sitting in the centre of one of them, I made up to him, and after saluting him à la Française, presented him with a piece of tobacco—the Indian letter of introduction. I enquired of him how long it was since he had left home.

"Sixty-two years, Monsieur," was the reply; and as the canoes assembled around us, he pointed out to me his sons, and his son's sons, to the third and fourth generation.

After Captain Back left Fort Chipewyan in 1836 the Hudson's Bay Company decided to play a greater part in the British attempt to map out the Arctic coastline. In what proved to be a successful adventure in which Fort Chipewyan became slightly involved, the company employed two of its outstanding men, Thomas Simpson, a young relation of its famous governor, and Peter Warren Dease, a travel-hardened practical trader. Starting in 1837 these two spent three years in the far North and cleared up much of the mystery of the ice-girt shoreline. Some evidence of these men's ability may be seen in Thomas Simpson's remarkable feat of walking from the vicinity of today's Winnipeg to Fort Chipewyan to join the expedition. He covered this distance on foot in the heart of winter and arrived on February 1, 1837—1400 miles in sixty-three days, an average of 22 miles each short wintry day.

At the same time other Hudson's Bay Company men were busily exploring in other directions and from time to time news drifted into Fort Chipewyan of their discoveries or of new posts they established whose personnel and supplies would have to be handled through the post on the rock. In 1834 John McLeod pushed west to Dease Lake and found the headwaters of the Stikine River, which reached the ocean near today's town of Wrangell, Alaska. Two years later, Robert Campbell set out from Fort Simpson and by May 1840 was ascending the headwaters of the Liard River, naming Frances Lake after George Simpson's recent white bride and Pelly River after the English governor of the company. In 1843 he descended the Pelly to its junction with the Lewes River, which he named after John L. Lewes, one-time postmaster at Lesser Slave Lake and later chief factor of the Mackenzie River District, and of whom we shall hear further. In 1848 Campbell built Fort Selkirk on the Yukon River and finally pushed downstream till he came to Fort Yukon, where he found his old friend, W. L. Hardisty, who had arrived at that point by descending the Mackenzie River, crossing the mountains and paddling down the Porcupine River. That far west the two company men rather anxiously feared a collision with the Russian traders who resented the Hudson's Bay Company's intrusion.

All of this exploration greatly expanded Fort Chipewyan's horizon as men en route to or from the new places paused to sit and swap yarns by its blazing fireplaces. During much of the early part of Campbell's time in the Yukon Fort Chipewyan had remained free of non-company explorers, but on September 23, 1843, an investigator of another type arrived—J. H. Lefroy, a scientist concerned with magnetic and other phenomena.· On his way west from Toronto he had fallen in with John McLean who was heading for Great Slave Lake and the two crossed the Methy Portage about the same time. Of it McLean wrote that while at last horses were stationed at the portage, they were not taken there by the company but rather by

a number of half-breeds, with their horses, from the Saskatchewan, awaiting our arrival, in the expectation of being employed to transport goods. Nor were they disappointed; sooner than undergo the harrassing toil of carrying the outfit across a portage of twelve miles, the men hired the half-breeds, parting with their most valuable articles in payment.

The interesting letters Lefroy sent home help us to visualize Fort Chipewyan.

It is a square area, fenced by high palisades, and containing low one-storied buildings on three sides. Nearly all of them display nothing but parchment windows . . . flour is the scarcest article; bread is unknown. . . . Our fireplaces are like small sentry boxes, and filled with logs upright which is the way they arrange them, give an immense heat. . . . These are "the holidays," a season of fête, kept by all the Canadians, and one in which the solitary gentlemen in charge of outposts assemble if they can at the nearest Fort. We are now expecting one from Slave Lake. So you see winter travelling cannot be very disagreeable when a man prefers a journey on snowshoes of seven or eight days to passing his Xmas quite alone . . . we drank "absent friends" in a bottle of Madeira, "very particular" Madeira indeed, for it was the only bottle in Athabasca. I brought it in my canteen.

After he got settled down for the winter, the charm of Fort Chipewyan soaked into his system.

It stands on rather an exposed knoll of naked granite rocks, facing an arm of the lake with an island of black pines opposite, looking so rigid unmoved and lifeless over its frozen surface, that one wonders that summer can ever thaw them. The prettiest point in the neighbourhood is called the Pointe des Morts from the burial ground which is placed there. When I first arrived the birch and poplar trees around it had not lost their foliage and the dark monumental pines which form a perfect thicket within it, made up a very pretty scene, the lake gave the background. I used to notice a number of boughs, some fresh some faded, hung here and there upon the fence. This was done by the women of the Fort. Those who had lost a child pluck a bough and set it over its grave every time they pass; it is an act of recollection whose simplicity makes it even, I think, beautiful. . . .The Indians sometimes suffer terribly. Last year there was a complete famine on the Mackenzies R. and two unhappy Scotchmen who were travelling with an express were knocked on the head in their encampment one night, and devoured by some starving women, who had previously murdered their husbands and children in the same way.

These two men, John Spence and Murdo Morrison, who were taking messages to Fort McPherson on the Peel River during the winter of 1842-43, were indeed killed and eaten. This example of the lengths to which hunger drove the Indians is but one of many such cannibalistic incidents. Few indeed, of course, involved white men. When John L. Lewes in charge of the Mackenzie District wrote to Sir George Simpson, Governor of the Hudson's Bay Company, asking how the murderers of Spence and Morrison should be punished, Simpson replied that they should not be punished because, abhorrent as the idea of cannibalism was to white men, even they sometimes had to resort to it and that these two poor women were mere victims of their intense sufferings. At times both George Simpson and his company's policies could be very harsh, but this episode shows as perhaps few others do the man's humanity and compassion.

On March 5 Lefroy left Fort Chipewyan to take some magnetic readings at Fort Simpson and there once more he met his former companion John McLean, who had come in to replace John L. Lewes "who had the misfortune to blow his right hand off last September." In Lefroy's *Autobiography* he dealt with this incident more fully, saying:

It was a terrible accident to happen far from surgical aid, but he had as an assistant a young fellow of nerve and decision, named, I think, Pears [Peers], who tried to dress the stump. To stop the bleeding he tied up every vein and artery he could get at; he then bathed the wound with a decoction of epinette, which is much used in the country for external applications; and although much reduced by loss of blood, Lewes's strength of constitution enabled him to gradually recover.

A year after Lefroy left Fort Chipewyan, Sir John Franklin, then fifty-nine years old, set off on another of his sea voyages to the Arctic Ocean. When by 1848 no news of the expedition had reached England, the British government set on foot a series of searches that was to last several years and was rather incidentally to involve Fort Chipewyan. One of the men chosen to lead one of the many search parties was Dr. John Richardson who had been with Franklin on his earlier trips through Lake Athabasca. Since Richardson was also getting along in years, Sir George Simpson saw to it that an outstanding employee, Dr. John Rae, was chosen as his second in command. Simpson had always felt, and probably correctly, that in contrast to his company's explorers, the naval men who led overland parties had detracted from their effectiveness by encumbering themselves with too much equipment. Rae, on the other hand, had demonstrated remarkable ability to support his travelling by hunting and fishing as he went along. As it turned out, Rae was to justify Simpson's faith in him and, although not the originator of the idea of an explorer living off the land, he was to become the foremost exponent of that idea.

In any event, in June 1848 Richardson and Rae passed through Fort Chipewyan on their way to the mouth of the Mackenzie River and the Coppermine River. During the spring of 1849 Richardson returned to England, whereas Rae continued the search for Franklin for another year. That fall, with his headquarters at Fort Simpson, he reverted to his role of fur trader as the Chief Factor of the Mackenzie District, which included the posts in the Yukon. Then once more during the winter of 1850-51 John Rae searched the northern edge of the Barren Lands for any news of the fate of Franklin and his party. Finally on his way out of the far North Rae passed through Fort Chipewyan, as he said in one of his letters:

During the winter of 1851-52 I proceeded to England, having travelled on snow shoes from Athabasca [Fort Chipewyan] to St. Paul's, a distance of 1,730 statute miles, being aided by dogs for the last four hundred and fifty miles, which four hundred and fifty were accomplished in ten days.

As one who frequently crossed the Methy Portage, Rae added his voice to that of others who advocated stationing company horses there—advice which for some reason Sir George Simpson was reluctant to take. In December 1850, undoubtedly countering one of Rae's arguments, Simpson remarked:

Oxen & Carts, I think, would answer much better than horses, & prove less expensive, keeping them during the winter at Isle à la Crosse, driving them to the portage on the last ice & back to the Wintering grounds on the first ice in the fall.

He evidently took steps to send oxen to that point, but when Rae passed it going south in 1851 they had failed to arrive, for he wrote Simpson, saying:

The oxen that were sent from Fort Pitt for the Portage La Loche transport business, ran away in the woods before reaching Green Lake, and will not be available for this summer.

Rae was one of the great explorers of the Arctic coastline and the Barren Lands. In awarding the Founders Gold Medal of the Royal Geographical Society, the chairman complimented him for "boldness never surpassed" and singled out Rae's 1850-51 expedition. On it he said that Rae had set out accompanied by two men only, and, trusting solely for shelter to snow-houses, which he taught his men to build, accomplished a distance of 1,060 miles in 39 days, or 27 miles per day including stoppages— a feat which has never been equalled in Arctic travelling.

The great traveller was not present to receive the medal but it was most fitting that a man of like calibre, Sir George Back, who had also been a frequent visitor at Fort Chipewyan, accepted it on his behalf.

George Simpson, Governor-in-Chief of the Hudson's Bay Company Territories
(*dson's Bay Company*)

Colin Fraser sorting a shipment of furs worth $35,000 (*Provincial Archives of Alberta*)

Traders Lessard and Picard examining furs on a northern buying trip *(Provincial Archives of Alberta)*

Fort Chipewyan, 1891, showing the fort to the right of the Anglican church
(Geological Survey of Canada)

Nativity Mission at Fort Chipewyan, 1922 *(Research Council of Alberta)*

"Shot" Fousseneuve, famous voyageur *(Bob Duncan)*

Steamer *Grahame* at Smith Landing, 1892 *(Hudson's Bay Company)*

Colin Fraser's scows leaving Athabasca Landing *(Provincial Archives of Alberta)*

ATHABASCA.

COPYRIGHT
ERNEST BROWN,

H B CO'S STEAMER ATHABASCA LANDING - 49 - 1896.

PHOTO BY

Tracking on the Athabasca River *(Provincial Archives of Alberta)*

(above) The *Athabasca River* built 1912 which in 1915 replaced the *Peace River (Hudson's Bay Company)*

(left) Steamer *Athabasca* at Athabasca Landing, 1896, with three scows in foreground *(Provincial Archives of Alberta)*

Grand Rapids of the Athabasca, showing Hudson's Bay Company fur scows on way up river *(Provincial Archives of Alberta)*

Steamer *Fort McMurray* sunk near Vermilion Chutes *(Hudson's Bay Company)*

Sydney C. Ells (*Public Archives of Canada*)

Lt.-Col. Jim Cornwall (*Provincial Archives of Alberta*)

Sgt. H. "Nitchie" Thorne *(Provincial Archives of Alberta)*

Mickey Ryan *(Provincial Archives of Alberta)*

Great Canadian Oil Sands plant *(Photographic Services, Gov't. of Alberta)*

Dr. Karl A. Clark (*Provincial Archives of Alberta*)

GCOS bucket-wheel excavator – 150 feet from trucks to top – eating into face of oil sands (*GCOS*)

Another view of excavator showing the 30-foot diameter
bucket-wheel *(Photographic Services, Gov't. of Alberta)*

(above) Another view of excavator *(Photographic Services,
Gov't. of Alberta)*

(right) One of the nine 75-ton trucks *(GCOS)*

A 30-foot diameter bucket-wheel, showing the second excavator in the background
(*Photographic Services, Gov't. of Alberta*)

CHAPTER SEVEN

Missionaries Focus on Fort Chipewyan

A few years before the furore over the Franklin parties kept Fort Chipewyan on its toes, a new element in the community's make-up slipped in quietly from the west. Two days before Christmas 1841, James Evans, the Western Superintendent of Wesleyan Missions, rejoiced as his sleigh dogs, finally detecting Fort Chipewyan ahead, pricked up their ears and spurted up to the palisade. There, Colin Campbell, the factor, welcomed him and there he remained about a month before he set off across the ice heading for faraway Norway House. With a similar welcome the factors at Fort Dunvegan and Fort Vermilion had received him when, after visiting the recently arrived R. T. Rundle, the first resident missionary at Fort Edmonton, he had set out during the winter to become the first itinerant missionary to reach the Peace River country and Lake Athabasca. In view of the fact that by that time he had already invented his famous Cree syllabic, which was to enable the Indians to communicate in writing, it is perhaps unfortunate that his church was not able to follow up his visit by establishing a mission at Fort Chipewyan.

It was, moreover, disappointing to the Indians, who had long hoped to learn more than mere hearsay about the white man's religion. For they, in common with their kin all over the West, were eager to learn the new magic and had become curious about the white man's God. Part of this curiosity had been excited by the voyageurs and by the Roman Catholic Iroquois who had come from Caughnawaga; it had also come from observing and at times participating in church services which the Hudson's Bay Company management insisted be held at their posts. For instance, as a reiteration of the acknowledged customs of years, the Minutes of the Council of the Northern Department for 1823 had resolved:

That for the more effectual civilization and moral improvement of the families attached to the different establishments and the Indians—Every

65

Sunday when circumstances permit, divine Service be publickly read with becoming solemnity, either once or twice a day, to be regulated by the number of people and other circumstances, at which every man woman and child resident must attend, together with such of the Indians who may be at hand, as it may be found proper to admit.

Over the years the post journals make frequent reference to such religious practices. One written in June 1842, a few months after James Evans's visit, showing the Indians' desire to try to fall in line with the new magic, said: " . . . the few with whom I have conversed upon the subject of Religion seemed very desirous of being instructed and of embracing Christianity."

The fruit was ready to be picked by the first missionary who would reside at Fort Chipewyan and help to assuage the Indians' spiritual hunger. To their regret, the Wesleyans had to leave these pickings to their rivals the Roman Catholics, who, while they did indeed gather the fruit, did so at a terrific cost in devotion and hardship—a cost borne willingly and even jubilantly by the Oblates of Mary Immaculate.

As might be expected, the priests entered the Lake Athabasca region by way of Ile-à-la-Crosse and the Methy Portage. Father Thibault, the first resident Roman Catholic missionary at Fort Edmonton, pointed the way. When visiting Cold Lake in 1844 he let it be known that he hoped to go on to Ile-à-la-Crosse the next year, and news of his intention spread to Lake Athabasca and even to Great Slave Lake. There it was picked up by the pagan patriarch, Beaulieu, a leader amongst the Chipewyans and a man who in his time was said to have killed an enemy or two. He was the son of a Chipewyan mother by the earliest of the Beaulieus to enter the far West. Like his father, François, the mighty venturer who had been the first man with some white blood in his veins to settle along the Slave River and who had accompanied Alexander Mackenzie on his trip to the Pacific Ocean, he too was a man of action. As such, in 1845, loading his canoe with as many of his wives, children and grandchildren as he could take along, this younger Beaulieu set out for Ile-à-la-Crosse. There, for several days in a large brush structure built by the Chipewyans he listened to Father Thibault and became one of his first converts.

Following up Thibault's success, Father Alexander Taché reached Fort Chipewyan on September 2, 1847. It was at the time when to all appearances all the waterfowl of the far North, swans, geese and ducks by the thousands, congregate on the Delta marshes. Consequently some two hundred Chipewyan and fifteen Cree hunters had also assembled in camps near the fort. But according to the church records "they laid their guns aside, and left themselves entirely in the hands of the man of prayer." On September 5, Father Taché celebrated the first mass ever to be said in the region, and before his departure three weeks later he baptised "194 persons, mostly Chipewyans, and mostly children, their parents to be left for consideration on a later visit."

The cross had come to Fort Chipewyan—a cross which, through hunger, frost and hardship, devoted hands, male or female, ever held aloft. Other priestly visits followed, but it was left to Father Faraud to build the first mission about a mile west of the fort on high, rocky ground overlooking the lake. This he dedicated on September 8, 1851, as the Nativity Mission. Despite his many travels to other stations, he made Lake Athabasca his headquarters for the ten-year period 1848-59. His accomplishments there were impressive. As he wrote:

The first year, I built a house and a chapel. The second year, I turned the swamps into fields and gardens. The third year, I built a new church, a new house, a kitchen, a stable, and a house for the men in our employment. Later on I began, and in four years I completed, a large church, which would not look too bad even in a town.

Seeking additional contact with the Chipewyans, the Oblates established a subsidiary mission at Fond du Lac in 1853 when Father Grollier accompanied the Hudson's Bay Company personnel as they went to reopen their Harrison's House which had been virtually abandoned about thirty years earlier. There during 1855 Father Grollier built his combined chapel and residence—a little log hut twenty-seven feet by seventeen.

About the same time, other Roman Catholic missionaries had been visiting various isolated posts throughout northern Alberta. In these activities many of the famous northern priests played their strenuous parts—men such as Fathers Bourassa, Clut, Faraud, Lacombe, Remas, Vegreville and others. In addition to their other missions, they established Lac La Biche (1852), St. Albert (1861) and Dunvegan (1867).

Of these, the mission at Lac La Biche was to become a key point in the chain of communication with those of the Mackenzie watershed. There in 1856, following up the visits of various priests, Bishop Taché laid the foundations for a more elaborate set of mission buildings at a new location on what we know today as Mission Bay. Then in a bold stroke which was really to be one of the earliest moves in testing the navigability of the middle portion of the Athabasca River, he set out for Fort Chipewyan. Paddling his canoe across the placid lake, his crew followed the zig-zag windings of the Lac La Biche River until it entered the Athabasca and then set forth to try the white water of that mighty stream. With plenty of excitement but no significant mishap, they sped along and seven days later reached Fort Chipewyan. Bishop Taché's trip was to be a milestone in the history of transportation in the North, a milestone which, though not to be noticed again for over a decade, was the first peal in the knell of the Methy Portage.

During that decade (in 1862) another of the heroic northern priests arrived at Fort Chipewyan. While it may be invidious to highlight one priest more than another, one stands out as the symbol of all Roman Catholic missionary effort in the far North. For sixty-nine years in total, through frost, ice and blizzard, hunger and hardship, mosquitoes and muskeg, Father Grouard, probably the most famous of the throng of devoted priests, ministered to his flock. After Bishop Taché's trip down the Athabasca, he took steps to build the Lac La Biche mission into a place of considerable importance, and to establish a group of Grey Nuns there. His next move, taken in 1867, was to send out more heroic nuns, this time to

Fort Providence on the west end of Great Slave Lake. Instead of taking the more orthodox route through Ile-à-la-Crosse, these came overland from St. Boniface and, in their squealing, jolting Red River carts, spent fifty-three days before peering through the bush ahead they could see the sod-roofed buildings of the Lac La Biche mission and the waters of the beautiful lake.

Their trip from St. Boniface, alternately plagued by dust, mosquitoes and mud, had been more wearying than thrilling. Their thrills lay ahead of them for Bishop Faraud had decided to take them north by the route Bishop Taché had picked out some ten years earlier—down the Lac La Biche River and thence through the Grand Rapids of the Athabasca. On it, in addition to the mosquitoes, they were plagued by horseflies, and faced the possibility of a watery death in the white cascades. Their voyage across the peaceful lake where the sun shone and with great white swans and pelicans gliding gracefully out of their way, and down past beds of water lilies fringing the somnolent Lac La Biche River, did little to prepare them for its lower rough water. It took them three days to reach the Athabasca, but during the last two the nuns, swatting horseflies, marched along the muddy bank in order to lighten the barge which the men had difficulty working through the shallow rocky rapids.

Once on the mighty Athabasca their barge, the first scow ever to take up the challenge of the furious cascades of the middle section of the roaring river, glided effortlessly downstream. The nuns were entranced by the beauty of the August foliage but all too soon bored by the sameness of the headlands, mud banks and endless forest. Before long, however, their boredom changed to electrifying fear as they approached the roar of the Grand Rapids, landed at their head and stared in silence at the awful cascades through which the voyageurs would have to manoeuvre their craft.

If, however, the foreman of the crew felt fear, he did not allow it to show for he had promised to run a scow down in safety. He was twenty-six-year-old Louis Fousseneuve, standing six feet three and never had he feared any reasonable risk. From his buffalo hunting days he had been known as Shot—a shortening of "Sure Shot"—a mighty hunter and a mighty man. Under his direction the men began carrying the goods over the half-mile portage. That done, bishop, priests, voyageurs and nuns, turned to the task of easing the barge down the furious, treacherous rapids. Along with the men the five valiant women buckled on the harnesses of the towing lines and, clambering and slipping, bruising themselves on rocks and falling full length in mud, they fought to keep control of their craft. Eventually, without loss of goods or lives, they got down the Grand Rapids and the next eighty-seven miles of cascades which brought them to the mouth of the Clearwater and once more to calm waters. Shot had succeeded; the first freight scow had run the rapids—the first nail had been driven into the coffin of the old Methy Portage.

Finally, long overdue, on August 13, 1867, the barge bearing Bishop Faraud's nuns drew up to the rocks below the Nativity Mission. By then the sisters, destined for the hardships of Fort Providence, had some conception of the world of the waterways. They had withstood their baptism of boiling, white water. The priests and brothers at the mission had been expecting them but to the few Indians about, five white women all in one batch was a seven-days' wonder, to be inspected, touched and regarded with awe. True enough, for a period of four years starting in 1859 Mrs. Robert Campbell, the chief factor's wife, a woman fresh from Scotland, had resided at Fort Chipewyan, but these nuns were in a different category. Even the white men at the fort had been impressed, and the writer of the post journal, noting the return of Bishop Faraud, added the incredulous comment: "There appeared to be a good many females on board."

But a pleasant surprise awaited these females, for they were to participate in Father Clut's consecration as a bishop. Indeed, the ceremony had been postponed for weeks awaiting Bishop Faraud's arrival with them. That delay, however, was insignificant when compared to the total time that had elapsed since his appointment had been confirmed in August 1864. News of his promotion did not reach him at Fort Providence until January 1866, when he was told that, when convenient, he would be raised to that high office at Lac La Biche. Bishop Faraud had hoped to have the participation of Bishops Taché and Grandin at the ceremony, but as the time approached and these two had to go to Europe, he decided to perform it himself. Consequently, when leaving the Nativity Mission in 1867 to meet the nuns at Lac La Biche, he exclaimed to Father Clut:

We will wait no longer. You have already been a bishop for three years! Prepare for consecration. Call together a concourse of Indians; I expect to be back here with the nuns by the middle of July at the latest.

But the middle of July passed and then the end of July, and the first week of August went by with no sign of Bishop Faraud and his nuns. Provisions of all sorts ran short and for a while the Indians fasted but finally had to disperse to hunt. And not till August 13 did the priests, straining their eyes looking out over the lake, see the bishop's barge.

Although most of the Indians had left, the spectators were augmented by the priests' neighbours, the officers of Fort Chipewyan, mostly Protestant, as well as by all the largely Catholic staff who came to pay their respects to their fellow northerner. As the fort journal reported: "The men returned from the hay making this afternoon in order to be present at the Ceremony of Consecrating the New Bishop." In such a manner, Bishop Clut entered the field of his episcopal duties. In such a manner, too, in the quiet little speck of white civilization that was Fort Chipewyan, its most important event of 1867 passed into history. Three thousand miles away and 330 décharges or portages away, a still more important event held the limelight. For on July 1, 1867, some six weeks before Fort Chipewyan's celebration, Confederation that was to be the start of Canada's nationhood, had been carried off with proper pomp and more imposing ceremonies. To the total half-breed and white population of some two thousand and to five or six thousand Indians in the area we know as the Province of Alberta, Confederation meant nothing. Because the area was owned by the Hudson's Bay Company and not by Canada, Confederation had neither factual nor legal significance. At the time, Edmonton House and its older colleague, Fort Chipewyan, and less than a dozen outlying fur trade posts all tributary to these two, together with a few isolated mission stations, were all that white men had to show for a century of occupation of Alberta. Since, however, each of these communities occupied such a little space compared to the vast silent forest that encompassed all of them, they had made no appreciable mark on the area. Outside these minute cleared spots, it was exactly the same beautiful wilderness that it had been when the first Indians had discovered it. To the old-time residents of the Fort Chipewyan settlement looking back over the three previous decades, little indeed had changed. Of course, Roman Catholic missionaries had come to settle there and Anglican missionaries had passed through, and now even nuns on their way to the mission at Fort Providence had come to try to soften some of the harshness of the North, but the daily round at the settlement was essentially what it always had been.

During those decades the vast territory lying north of the Liard River and west of the Mackenzie River—the Yukon—had become known through the exertions of men like John Bell, W. L. Hardisty and Robert Campbell, and from time to time they had dropped in to Fort Chipewyan to tell of their adventures. In due course two of them became chief factors at Fort Chipewyan; John Bell, who left there in 1855, and Robert Campbell, who succeeded him in that office on the rugged rock looking out across Lake Athabasca. Prior to that, however, Campbell had decided to visit Scotland and leaving Fort Simpson on November 30, 1852, and changing dogs and sometimes travelling companions, he stamped into Fort Chipewyan on Christmas Day. Relaxing there until January 4, he slipped into his snowshoes, headed south over the Methy Portage and reached Fort Garry on February 23, only to pause for a day or so before continuing to Crow Wing on the Mississippi River. From there on March 13 by stage, railway and steamship, he made his way to England, where he landed on April 13. For distance travelled on snowshoes, his march of three thousand miles from Fort Simpson to Crow Wing established a record which remained unbeaten until in 1877 J. S. Camsell broke it by walking from Fort Liard to the same destination.

While visiting his old home in Scotland, Campbell became engaged to be married. Then after spending a year in Britain he returned to Fort Simpson, and a year later in 1855 became chief factor of the Athabasca District with headquarters at Fort Chipewyan. In that capacity he was critical of the inadequate transport facilities on the Methy Portage. When he crossed the portage in 1854 he found that the brigades had to depend on one ox and a cart which was stationed there and upon the services of a few dozen pack horses which when needed could never be found. He wrote urging that a proper road be cut across it and that a reasonable number of oxen and carts be kept there in charge of a couple of men. Since Campbell remained at Fort Chipewyan until 1863, he was probably the man who was energetic enough to see such a method of transport started there.

But Robert Campbell also had more personal concerns on his mind. For in the spring of 1859 his bride-to-be, accompanied by her sister, set out on the six-thousand-mile trip to Fort Chipewyan and in due course these two became the first white women to appear there. Campbell went to meet his future bride at Norway House, where the Rev. Mr. Brooking married them. Then on May 14, 1860, the Campbells were blessed with a son, James, the first white boy ever to be born in the Mackenzie watershed and the second in all Alberta. In due course Campbell's sister-in-law returned to Scotland.

During the winter of 1861, the winter packet brought Campbell word that his old friend Sir George Simpson had died the previous September. Forty years had elapsed since this inexperienced young Scot had cut his fur-trade teeth at Fort Chipewyan during that winter of bitter warfare. For all of those years Simpson had led the Canadian operations of the Hudson's Bay Company and brought them to an amazing peak of efficiency. Many men loved him and many others hated him violently, but all respected the outstanding ability of this man, one of the greatest Canadians of his era.

During Robert Campbell's sojourn at Fort Chipewyan the discipline and forethought exercised at the post tended more and more to ward off starvation, but occasionally its spectre stalked the settlement. Success or failure in fishing or hunting was perhaps the thought always uppermost in the residents' minds as weeks of hunger alternated with periods of plenty. Some years water levels in the Delta were extremely high and during others they dropped drastically. During years of low water the muskrats froze; under certain conditions of both high water and low, the fishermen had problems. Problems, however, were not confined to wild creatures as occasionally the dogs, which were essential in winter travelling and in hauling fish across the miles of ice to the post, caught diseases. In October 1858 "Dogs still going mad: out of 40 dogs in use last winter there are now only about 12 old, almost useless ones—A great misfortune this. . . ." By November more dogs had died. The year before bad luck had hit the small cattle herd. On November 2 "the Bull died this morning." The next day "The cow has fallen sick & wont eat anything. . . ." Within a week it too was dead.

The cattle were kept for their milk and butter. With the shortage of pasture they could have contributed little to the meat supply. Caribou, on the other hand, did and in December 1850 the journalist rejoiced when he wrote that caribou were reported "not far off from the Fort." About a year later word of hard times came in from Fort Vermilion where they were having to eat their horses. Near that post, which relied mainly on moose, a crust had formed on the snow and the hunters could not approach these animals because of the noise they made in breaking through it. Furthermore, one of their Indians employed as a paid hunter had died recently and the other two had fallen sick. "The Indians dying of starvation."

At both Fort Vermilion and Fort Chipewyan potatoes came to figure heavily in the menus. Over the years the art of cultivating them had improved and the crops became much larger; the yield grew fitfully to 290 kegs in 1853 and 400 kegs in 1860. Meanwhile, of course, the garden patch so arduously drained by Father Faraud made life easier for the priests who undoubtedly cultivated it more assiduously than the fur trade employees worked their plots.

Generally the priests and the fur traders, white men facing all the rigours of travelling in the North, respected each other's ability and enjoyed each other's company. The men who kept the fort journal in 1858, however, grudgingly accepted the need to observe the Romish feasts, and on June 29 wrote:

> St. Peter's day. kept holy & of course no work done. It is my humble opinion that St. Peter doesn't care a d——n for the honor done to his memory this day: he certainly wont be so [melted?] by such soft -sawder as to open Heaven's Gates to the fools who have this day neglected their duty to do him such mighty soap sud honor.

All this while the Church of England, although it did not figure immediately in the history of Fort Chipewyan, had not been inactive. The first of its missionaries to visit the far North was Archdeacon James Hunter, who in 1858 spent a full year among the Indians at Fort Simpson. The Reverend William Kirkby succeeded him and was in turn followed by Rev. Robert MacDonald in 1862. When word reached England in 1865 that MacDonald was in failing health "and was obliged to leave his work, and that Romish priests were in readiness to succeed to it," an appeal for an immediate replacement was made.

William Carpenter Bompas responded and reached Fort Chipewyan on October 23, 1865. Fortunately the news of MacDonald's decline was premature, so that he continued his work at Fort Simpson while Bompas accepted a "roving commission" to proselytize in the Athabasca district, on the Peace River, and on Great Bear and Great Slave lakes. Such frequent travel was necessary because the English missions were very understaffed. Bompas wrote the following in regard to the Athabasca District, but could have applied it to any of his other charges: "If I leave this district a second time unoccupied, the Indians will lose all confidence in the permanence and reliability of our instruction, and will be thrown more completely than ever into the arms of Rome." Up to the time of Canada's Confederation, however, the Anglicans still had no mission building at Fort Chipewyan.

In 1867 events were afoot which were to lead Fort Chipewyan into a new era. The nuns, for instance, who had remained for Bishop Clut's ordination and had then gone on to Fort Providence, were a sign of changing times. With their missions growing and the added needs of the Sisters' establishment, the Catholic fathers found it necessary to bring increasing quantities of goods into the north country. In the past the Hudson's Bay Company had been reasonably generous to them and had hauled in their supplies, but Bishop Taché could see a day coming when the priests would be well advised to handle their own freight. To start with, he had a trail cut through the woods from a point on the Fort Pitt-Fort Edmonton route, near our St. Paul des Métis, to the new Lac La Biche mission which he soon built up as a storage depot.

During the half century since David Thompson and Peter Fidler had abandoned their trading posts at Lac La Biche, various fur trade messengers urging their dog teams back and forth on their trips to the junction of the Clearwater and the Athabasca and on to Fort Chipewyan had cut across by that lake. As early as 1805 Antoine Desjarlais had found Lac La Biche a desirable place to live and he was soon joined by Joseph Cardinal and some of his relatives, and others. Moreover, until about 1825 the lake had been on the route used by the fur traders' brigades heading for the mountains and the Pacific coast. From its waters they had paddled down the Lac La Biche River to the Athabasca and then had ascended that stream to Jasper. In the course of decades Lac La Biche had come to be a significant half-breed community, and now Bishop Taché's move was to make it even more significant. That, however, was incidental for the good bishop's plan was much more far reaching—nothing less than re-orienting the freight route to the far North and pioneering a way down the Athabasca. To him goes the credit for bringing into being what later became the commercial waterway down the middle section of the Athabasca, a route which for half a century was destined to carry all the commerce of the far North.

While the credit for the idea goes to him, its headaches fell most heavily on Bishop Faraud and Bishop Clut. The day after Christmas 1869, after seeing his first nuns well established at Fort Providence, Bishop Faraud strapped on his snowshoes and set out for Lac La Biche. When he reached there in February 1870 he turned his hand to building the first freight barge which, when autumn came, was to be loaded with goods and sent off to the northern missions. Thenceforth for some twenty years he made his headquarters at Lac La Biche, where he supervised the northern transport and kept making improvements in it.

The delivery of his first load of northern supplies, however, was fraught with more than usual difficulties and tragedies. When in the spring of 1870 they were being hauled overland in Red River carts from Fort Carlton to Lac La Biche they did so under harrowing circumstances. That spring the terrible epidemic of smallpox sweeping north across western Canada laid its hand on the Métis drivers. Of the fourteen who had left Lac La Biche to make the return trip, eight died of the disease en route or after they reached home. When, however, the barge loaded with supplies left the mission dock with Bishop Clut in command, he rejoiced that at last the great venture was under way—the first freight shipment to try conclusions with the new route. His crew of Lac La Biche voyageurs seemed capable of facing up to the cascades of the Athabasca and of taking care of his clutch of northern novices—two priests recently arrived from France, two prospective lay brothers, Marie Marguerite, a postulant for the Grey Nuns at Fort Providence, and a little orphan girl.

During the month it took the bishop to shepherd his charges as far as the mouth of the Clearwater River, he plumbed the depths of discouragement. On September 7, as the voyageurs listening to the roar of the Grand Rapids tied their barge to the bank and peered through the obscurity of rapidly falling snow at the seething water ahead, their courage forsook them. They rebelled, deserted Bishop Clut and walked back to Lac La Biche. The bishop's problems were compounded by a severe illness which prostrated Sister Marie Marguerite. Somehow he and his small following levered the barge ashore, pitched a tent for the young nun and left her and the orphan girl in charge of Father Roure, a lay brother and a loyal Métis. Then for four or five days, slipping in the mud and the slush from a fresh fall of snow, Bishop Clut, Father Lecorre and two brothers made their way to the recently built Fort McMurray. Because the trader was away, some three weeks elapsed before the bishop was able to obtain a barge and a crew to return to the foot of the Grand Rapids on October 1. The ailing sister's condition had worsened, and while the new crew got the mission's barge and goods to the calmer waters below, the practically unconscious girl was carried across. Five days later the scow had successfully negotiated the remaining rough water and reached Fort McMurray. On October 9 the first load of mission goods reached Fort Chipewyan, where Sister Marie Marguerite was carried ashore and put to bed. A few days later she died. Bishop Clut's whole venture had been a gruelling experience. Nevertheless the first load of freight had descended the Grand Rapids.

Year by year other barge loads followed, but the dangers of descending the Grand Rapids led Bishop Faraud to try to find a way of avoiding them by cutting a 140-mile road to Fort McMurray. In spite of some serious disagreements with his colleagues, he put men to work on that task in 1870 but before the end of the following year when some 70 miles had been hacked out, he had to abandon the idea. His trail, however, was to be the forerunner of other roads that ultimately worked their way over the sand hills, muskegs and deadfall between these two points. A third, which at this time Henry John Moberly picked out from Fort McMurray to Cold Lake and recommended that the Hudson's Bay Company cut out, never got started. Gradually, however, a trail—or rather a path trodden mainly by occasional missionaries—did come into existence between Lac La Biche and Fort McMurray.

Along this path in 1875 Bishop Clut sent Brother Alexis. Tracking his boat upstream from the Nativity Mission the brother, who was also transferring a comely Cree orphan girl to Lac La Biche, had the assistance of an Iroquois named Louis Lafrance and two half-breeds. At Fort McMurray these two refused to track any farther up the rough high water, so Brother Alexis split his party. Expecting these men to follow when the water level lowered, he pushed on early in July accompanied by the orphan girl and Louis Lafrance.

After a considerable lay-over the two boatmen resumed their trip and worked their craft up the Athabasca until in due course they clambered ashore to cook a meal at the mouth of House River. Approaching the sodden remains of a previous fire they were startled to find human bones picked clean. Fearing that enemies might be in the vicinity, they hastened to report their discovery to Bishop Faraud at Lac La Biche. He was surprised to see them and to learn that Brother Alexis had been on his way and alarmed that he had not shown up. Immediately he sent a crew of men to the ashes of the fire at the mouth of House River.

Nearby they made several grizzly discoveries; the dismembered remains of Brother Alexis, a bloody hatchet, and evidence that not only had a part of the victim's flesh been eaten but that a piece had been carried away for future consumption. Of the fate of the convent-reared Cree girl the gnarled cottonwoods and the mutely swaying spruce trees revealed no trace. Another secret had been added to the dark mystery of the silent, ferny forest. Another tale had been added to be heard with bated breath and many a glance over their shoulders into the dark aisles of creaking trees, as the voyageurs, seeking reassurance, prodded their campfire into a brighter flame.

Though the forest never revealed its secret of the girl's fate, weeks later its very indifference to the Iroquois' existence finally forced him into the open. In the meantime, he had travelled north and west until hunger had driven him to prowl around and steal from a camp of Fort Vermilion Crees. From ambush one of them finally shot the prowler, who, wearing only a piece of white tent canvas, turned out to be Louis Lafrance.

A better route for the mission's freight was the constant preoccupation of the Lac La Biche priests. Since Bishop Faraud's trail had been too much for them, the energetic young Father Collignon decided to avoid having to navigate the Lac La Biche River by cutting a route more or less along it to the Athabasca River. Though he persisted for years, his trail was not finished until 1878, but for a dozen years after that it bore the priests' freight.

Valiant indeed were the northern priests who in winter or summer travelled the brittle forests or the mighty stream from the mouth of the Lac La Biche River to that of the Clearwater. With them as with the Hudson's Bay Company it was a rule that, if possible, no man travelled alone; if some accident befell, there was always at least one companion along to help. During the winter, of course, they travelled with a sled drawn by their faithful dogs. Starting before sunrise from Fort McMurray, for instance, they urged their team forward and ran to keep up with it. Up out of the valley of the Athabasca they sped, rising with the ridge between the Horse and the Hangingstone rivers to gain the level tableland and then swung to the west to cross Cameron Creek and to touch the rim of the Horse River gorge. Before long it was ten o'clock and time for rest and lunch, washed down with hot tea. Half an hour later saw them following the edge of the river valley again and at times crossing it to cut off a bend until in sight of the blue hills rising three hundred feet above the stream ten miles away, they swung more to the south. Up over the shoulder of the hills they went, only to drop once more to cross the little headwater creeks feeding the Horse River. Across them they pressed and across the first tributaries of the House River, and at its mouth finally regained the Athabasca some ten miles above the Grand Rapids.

Pushing along through the forest, skirting windfall, hurrying through the sparse black spruces with their hanging moss and their clustery, twiggy tops and fairly flying over open frozen muskeg, they crossed many a creek and passed many a familiar landmark. Here and there they noted a moose track or the erratic trail left by a hunting weasel and once in a while a squirrel undaunted by the cold, scolded shrilly, unaware of an owl silent and listening on the top of a nearby tree. Always there was something for alert eyes to note even if it was only the bright red rose hips or a few sparse crimson cranberries, frozen and dejectedly clinging to branches long since bereft of leaves. Sometimes indeed it was a small flock of pine grosbeaks who, with their rosy breasts and the scarlet stripes down their backs, scorned the winter's snows.

Eventually while there was still an hour of daylight left to enable them to see to make camp, they sought the shelter of some creek valley handy to dry wood. While one man got firewood and gathered a bit of birch bark to kindle a blaze, the other, using a snowshoe as a shovel, cleared a space perhaps a dozen feet square. While his companion laid the logs in a pile extending all the way across the clearing and set them ablaze, he cut spruce or preferably aromatic balsam boughs for the mattress of the bed which covered much of the other side of the space and spread blankets or buffalo robes over it.

Then it was time to break out the fish to thaw for the dogs, to boil water for tea and cook whatever supper they had. Once it was over, the logs were kept blazing brightly while a pipe or so incited tales of adventures of other camps. But they turned in early, lying with their feet to the fire, which, with luck, lasted all night, and watched the millions of stars sparkling so clearly out of the vast sky. Soon, regardless of a temperature of thirty to forty below, sleep induced by the crack of exploding pockets of resin in the logs came to relax tired limbs and make them ready for another tramp. Thus passed another night on the trail, a night endurable if not enjoyable.

Not all trips passed so uneventfully, and at times in blizzards travellers lost toes or fingers or indeed their lives. Neither were all summer trips exempt from hardships of the type experienced by Bishop Faraud in 1880. After a winter of grave illness at Fort Providence, he started for Lac La Biche. High water in the Athabasca held his party back so much that by the time they reached the mouth of the House River their provisions were exhausted. Knowing that it was only a four-day trip through the woods to Lac La Biche, the bishop sent a half-breed to hasten there on foot while the rest of the party continued to drag their craft upstream.

A day or so later they met a camp of Crees who could spare them only a mouthful of dried meat. It staved off the worst of the hunger pangs, and since they expected relief from Lac La Biche within a few days, they pressed slowly upstream. Exhaustion and hunger soon stopped them and the travellers lay down to wait for succor. Except for a few buds they picked off nearby branches, three long days passed without a morsel of food. As a last resort the little Indian boy with Bishop Faraud lit a fire to boil his moccasins to make them more easily edible. The wisp of smoke rising from the tiny blaze saved them, for, by the merest chance, as the relief party sent out to look for them was hurrying past down the river, they smelled the smoke. And what of the half-breed who was hurrying on to Lac La Biche? He shot a bear, fed upon it and went on his way rejoicing. But his feeding and rejoicing took so much time that instead of reaching Bishop Grouard at the lake in four days, it took him eleven days.

One more story had been added to the roster to be told over campfires along the mighty Athabasca—one of the recorded accounts in contrast to many an unrevealed tragedy forever locked away with the secrets of every mile and creek mouth on each of the river's shadowy, forested banks.

CHAPTER EIGHT

Moberly Builds Fort McMurray

For a couple of years after Bishop Faraud started his barges hurtling their way down the Grand Rapids, the Hudson's Bay Company observed their progress with interest. Then in a move aimed at developing this section of the Athabasca River, it started Fort McMurray. On May 9, 1870, the Fort Chipewyan journal said: "Got Mr. Moberly [Henry or Harry J.] ready and he started in the Evening with a boat manned by 8 men who were to assist him in beginning a new Post at the Forks of the Athabasca and Clearwater Rivers—The boat is to proceed on to Portage La Loche [Methy] with the rest of the Brigade and Mr. Moberly will remain and get the necessary buildings up during the Summer."

On a spot where he found traces of old buildings, possibly the remains of the abortive Berens House which Thomas Thomas had started in 1815, he built his new post which was named to honour William McMurray, the officer in charge of Fort Chipewyan. By the fall Moberly had put up a store, men's houses and a carpenter shop and the next year erected a good residence. From then on to the present the site was to be continuously occupied, although not always by the Hudson's Bay Company. Moreover, within a year it was to see one of the first of a long line of self-sufficient characters which later on were to swarm in there.

This was Dutch Henry, an independent trader who had already spent two years farther north and who arrived clutching a pack of furs he was taking to Lac La Biche. Moberly welcomed him and, stuffing his precious furs under the counter, the wanderer waited for the flood waters to subside. Unfortunately the building caught fire and in his efforts to save it, Dutch Henry climbed on to the bark roof, only to be blasted off by an explosion of gun powder stored in the attic. Hearing the outburst, Moberly came running from his somewhat distant garden and nearly collided with Henry rushing blindly to soak his face in the river. Moberly was able to save some items and when he thought the fire, which had practically destroyed the store, could do no further damage, rushed to the river to refresh himself. Only then did he find why the Dutch adventurer did not answer his calls to help fight the fire. Hearing a groan from nearby bushes, he looked in and discovered the victim. "He was a weird sight. His hair, eyebrows and whiskers were gone, his eyes tight closed, and his round pink face swollen out of all semblance to that of a human being. His nose though short was still visible—a small red ball just discernible in the middle of his bulging cheeks."

While nursing Dutch Henry back to health, Moberly faced another problem, this time in the field of human relations. One of his Indian hunters had two wives, one old and the other young. Bishop Clut on his way through Fort McMurray told him that he must dispense with one of them, and since he had two children by the older one, he kept her and officially married her. But the arrangement did not work out too well and two months later he asked Moberly to write the bishop and tell him that he had taken the wrong woman, but had corrected his error by replacing the older wife with the younger. The bishop, he thought, could not object as he still had only one wife. "I declined to interfere, telling the man he might explain the matter when next he met the bishop. The attempt to explain to his lordship must have been amusing if ineffectual, for he had promptly to take back the first wife."

If this problem of natives having more than one wife vexed the priests, it posed a vastly different dilemma for a confused Indian. No matter which way he looked he was in trouble: on the one hand by damnation in the remote future by an angry God and on the other, denunciation here and now by an aroused woman. In this respect the Church of England gave him more elbow room which undoubtedly saved a lot of in-fighting. It allowed an Indian to keep the wives he had at the time of his conversion, but forbad him to marry any more. This applied even if one of his wives died; he was not allowed to replace her until, as sometimes happened, death swept away his supply of spouses, when, of course, he could take another—but only one.

Such problems slid lightly off the shoulders of Henry John Moberly, who in his time and, of course, one at a time, had taken several Indian women into his household. Of far greater concern were the problems of transportation which the company had placed in his hands. Indeed, Fort McMurray had been built and Henry John placed in charge of it mainly because it was necessary to upgrade the transportation system and to be ready for the day when changes taking place in western Canada would make a better one possible. About 1873 as one move in that direction, Moberly carried out his orders to study the river from his post downstream to the rapids at Fitzgerald to see if it would be practical to operate steamboats on that stretch of water. He reported that it would be eminently practical. About that time too, he was given the responsibility of taking charge of getting goods over the Methy Portage.

At last, after the back-breaking Methy Portage had been in existence for ninety-two years, the Hudson's Bay Company decided to bring some order into the hitherto haphazard manner in which oxen had been used there by maintaining a herd of these draft animals at Fort McMurray and making that post responsible for the official operation of the portage. By the spring of 1874 Moberly had supervised cutting a proper cart road across it from the south end to the point where it started its steep descent to the Clearwater, and that summer succeeded in continuing the road down that difficult hill. As Chief Factor Donald Ross of Fort Vermilion wrote in July 1874: "No more carrying on the much dreaded Portage Hill which is now a thing of the past. Everybody is delighted and no wonder, for it has been the ruin of many an able man." By the spring of the next year Moberly had a herd of oxen pasturing on the rich grasses at the mouth of the Clearwater River.

The Athabasca River, however, pays no attention to human plans. The very next spring, early in April, it rose and threw up an ice jam, spreading devastation over the flats at Fort McMurray. As Moberly wrote, it "drove the ice two miles up the Clearwater in piles forty or fifty feet high. In less than an hour the water rose fifty-seven feet, flooding the whole flat and mowing down trees, some three feet in diameter, like grass." The flood swept away one of the fort buildings and for five days before it subsided enough for them to reoccupy the soggy fort, Moberly and his men had to camp on the hillside. The thirty-seven draft oxen were less fortunate. Before Moberly had time to think about them, the one lonesome survivor, wet and bedraggled, struggled up to the fort for company.

The loss of the oxen, which within a few weeks had been expected to move freight over the Methy Portage, was a severe blow. Only speedy action could avert costly delays. Moberly, however, as his biography asserts, was equal to the occasion and

> Taking four men, each with his blanket and gun on his back, I made a bee line for Lac La Biche, the nearest post in the Saskatchewan District. Here I found one of our old officers, Mr. W. E. Traill, in charge, and with his assistance bought every available horse or ox capable of hauling a cart and started for home with my purchases.
>
> We had a heart-breaking return trip, wading through snow and water to our knees and crossing creeks and rivers swollen to their banks. The journey to Lac La Biche took seven days, the return to McMurray thirteen. An additional three days found us at Methy Portage. Two days later the first brigade arrived and the situation was thus neatly saved.

In March 1878 Moberly was transferred to Fort Vermilion. His eight-year sojourn at Fort McMurray took place during a period of unrivalled importance to western Canada, as the East, beginning to see some virtue in it after all, reached out to take control of it. Those years were filled with new ventures: in 1871 Prime Minister John A. Macdonald promised to build a railway to the Pacific coast; in 1872 Sandford Fleming, in charge of finding a route for it, sent the first of many surveying parties into the field; by 1874 the Mounted Police had been organized and had reached the prairies and during the next year built one of their barracks at Fort Saskatchewan. As they were erecting them, the Hudson's Bay Company's *Northcote*, the first steamboat ever to work its way that far up the river, steamed past bound for Fort Edmonton where it found that the CPR surveyors had slashed their trial lines nearby. Hard on their heels came the single-wire telegraph line from the East, which reached Edmonton in 1877. An era of change had barged into the West, change which was to transform the land south of the Athabasca River but which for many a decade, except in bringing it new mechanical means of transportation, was to have little effect on the Mackenzie watershed.

While all this had been going on, Fort Chipewyan folk had been mending their fishing nets and tanning their moose skins as they had done for decades. When Moberly had left there in 1870 the population of the fort stood at seventy-eight. This included three or four officers, perhaps thirty-five other employees, with a score or so of their women and children, and a few widows, boarders or pensioners. According to the Reverend Father Emile Petitot, the native population in the area in 1862 was about nine hundred Chipewyans and three hundred Crees. After the smallpox swept over the area about 1870 those numbers would have suffered a drastic decline.

During most of the year the population of the Fort Chipewyan community was usually less than a hundred, but spring and autumn brought renewed life to the shores of its bay. For then the Indians came in, bringing their furs to trade in the spring and assembling again in the fall to receive credits of ammunition and supplies to enable them to trap throughout the coming winter. At both seasons practically all the Beavers, Crees or Chipewyans who traded at the post camped for a short spell along the lake shore and Fort Chipewyan resounded with the howling of dogs and the merry shouts of children.

Starting about 1872 Roderick MacFarlane, the chief factor of the district, had the badly run-down old fort entirely rebuilt into a new imposing stronghold. As for MacFarlane himself, the famous Captain W. F. Butler who travelled with him to Fort Chipewyan during the winter of 1872 stated:

> Few men have led, even in the hard regions of the north, a life of greater toil than Roderick MacFarlane. . . . For seventeen years [far down the Mackenzie River] he had remained cut off from the outer world; yet his mind had never permitted itself to sink amidst the oppressive solitudes by which he was surrounded. . . .

Entering the service of the Hudson's Bay Company when he was nineteen, this young Scot found himself posted to Fort Simpson in 1853. During nearly a score of years when he was stationed here and there along the Mackenzie, he became one of the most noted northern travellers and also one of Canada's early outstanding naturalists. In this field fortunately he received inspiration and encouragement from Robert Kennicott, a pioneer in northern ornithology. Kennicott, a young American undeterred by any possible hardships, set off alone to pursue his hobby in the Mackenzie watershed and in 1859 at the Methy Portage fell in with the chief factor of the Mackenzie District, Bernard Ross, a man of similar leanings, and a few weeks later met MacFarlane. Over the years the adventurous American, in conjunction with Bernard Ross and MacFarlane, revealed to the world much of the fascination of the natural history of Canada's northland, the breeding ground of vast flocks of the continent's migratory birds. In their own ways, Kennicott, the American, and Captain Butler, the British army man who came ten years later and wrote *The Wild North Land*, each contributed towards turning the eyes of the world to northwestern Canada. But of the three, MacFarlane, who year after year sent box after box of specimens to the Smithsonian Institute and to the Royal Scottish Museum and wrote two excellent works on the natural history of the North, was perhaps the foremost.

When Butler left Fort Chipewyan in March 1873, Roderick MacFarlane, loath to lose his company, accompanied him as far as the Quatre Fourches before turning back to his post. From the forks Butler's path lay over the ice of Lake Mamawi and Lake Claire and the adjacent windswept marsh lined by scant fringes of willows and destitute of larger timber. Violent storms were frequent, filling the air with stinging snow and piling it into dense drifts. There was also little shelter or wood along the way and few distinguishing landmarks. Across this dangerous and desolate stretch Butler and his dogs set out in the company of three half-breed voyageurs with whom he had little rapport. One of them indeed, whom he referred to as Harper, had an especially bad reputation. A few years previously he and an inexperienced young Hudson's Bay Company clerk by the name of MacRae had gone out in bitter weather with two dog teams to bring back the meat of three moose cached along the southwest shore of Lake Claire. They had loaded the meat and set out for the fort when a stinging snowstorm blew up and they lost their way. Harper, knowing of MacRae's inexperience and aware of the fact that he had only three matches left, decided to abandon him. Leaving him to drive both teams, Harper strode on ahead and disappeared into the blinding snow.

Finally, when MacRae let the dogs have their way, they led him into a thin screen of willows, where on trying to make a fire his three matches flashed and fizzled out. Though he had lots of food it was frozen brick hard. Deserted, virtually without food and unable to make a fire, he and the dogs camped the night and the next day made their way to an open sulphurous spring where, shelterless, they remained waiting for the storm to blow itself out.

Harper in the meantime returned to a camp at Quatre Fourches where he feigned surprise that MacRae, whom he said had preceded him, had not shown up. Going on to Fort Chipewyan, he told the same story, but there the factor sent him back with a search party. Acting on the theory that dead men tell no tales, Harper deliberately misled it along the lake's northern shore while another two days were lost before the party returned to the fort. There, suspicious of Harper, the factor sent out another party led by a keen-eyed French half-breed who headed for Lake Claire's southwestern shore, and finally came to a faint trace in the drifted snow which indicated the passage of a snowshoe. Following several barely perceptible marks, the party came to the first fireless campsite and noted the trail taken the next morning. Certain that at any moment they would come upon MacRae's frozen corpse, they made their way to the spring. There, frost-bitten, hungry but safe, sat the victim of Harper's desertion. Five days had passed but he and the dogs were still alive.

As quickly as possible he was loaded on a sleigh and taken to the fort where he recovered. As for Harper, he was assessed some formal punishment but the far heavier penalty lay in the horror and distaste that he was ever after accorded throughout the region.

While Butler was making his way west up the Peace River towards the mountains, affairs at Fort Chipewyan fell back into their routine ways until in 1874 Bishop Clut deemed it necessary to establish a school with teaching nuns there. As a result, he called upon the services of the Sisters of Charity at Fort Providence and they sent Sisters Lapointe, St. Michael and Domithilda to serve at Fort Chipewyan. Within a week of their arrival late in July, they had cleared out a small house, named it the Holy Angels School and began teaching fifteen pupils. There they passed a difficult winter, for it was not only severely cold but their stock of imported provisions consisted of one sack of flour, a small keg of sugar, as well as five barrels of local wheat, seven of barley, and some potatoes.

By this time the Church of England, which some years previously had swept on down the Mackenzie River and by-passed Fort Chipewyan, decided to establish a mission there. Roderick MacFarlane welcomed the new missionary, the Reverend Arthur Shaw, and his bride, who had recently come from England, and arranged with Peter Lutit, the company's carpenter, to vacate his newly built home to accommodate them. For the time being this became the mission. When about the same time A. C. Garrioch, a lay worker then, arrived from the Red River Settlement to teach school, he put up a log shack about a hundred yards west of the fort on a piece of land donated for church use by the company.

Mr. Shaw was a relative newcomer from England, but Garrioch, whose grandfather, William Garrioch, had come to Canada around 1791, was no stranger to the West, nor indeed to the Peace River country. His mother had been born at Fort Dunvegan out of the union of the redoubtable Colin Campbell, who had been born in Ontario's Glengarry County about 1787, and Elizabeth, the mixed-blood daughter of the famous Northwester the Hon. John McGillivray. His maternal grandfather probably knew the Peace River country more intimately than any other man of his time. As a young man in 1812 he had been stationed at the Northwesters' Fort Dunvegan from where, in 1819, he had provided stiff opposition to Colin Robertson who had wintered at St. Mary's House near the modern town of Peace River. Over the decades he had moved back and forth and up and down the Peace River, spending periods of a year or two at Forts Dunvegan, Vermilion and Chipewyan and then returning repeatedly to each of these for further terms. Finally as Chief Factor of the Athabasca District he had remained at Fort Chipewyan from 1841 to 1847. Then, after serving the company and enjoying the Peace River country for thirty-five continuous years, he retired and left the land he knew so well.

Because of his family background, Garrioch automatically became one of the aristocracy at Fort Chipewyan. For even then the community had its elite made up of hardy third and fourth generation descendants of Scots fur traders, Orkney boatmen and French or Métis voyageurs, on the one side, and of Cree, Chipewyan or Iroquois natives on the other. In this whole community, however, Garrioch could find only six Protestant families with children of school age and from these he drew twelve pupils, all boys. Despite that modest beginning the Church of England's affairs progressed to the point where in 1879 construction began on St. Paul's Church and its consecration followed on Easter Sunday 1880.

For years no white women except the missionaries' wives attended the little church. This lack of white women was an important fact at Fort Chipewyan; because of it no caste system with whites on one hand and natives on the other hand could develop there or at any other of the posts in the Mackenzie watershed. At first, to meet their domestic needs, the white traders married Indian girls, and in subsequent generations those of mixed blood. One important aspect of such marriages was that the woman assumed the rank of her man and the rest of the community treated her with the deference due to that rank. The chief factor had his lady, the white clerk his wife, and the voyageur his woman, and it could happen that all three of these females were sisters. Within a generation or two in Fort Chipewyan, or any other post, everyone was related in some degree to everyone else. Moreover, the social scale was flexible enough that in competition with newly imported clerks of white blood the male offspring of these mixed and fruitful marriages could aspire to some rank in the fur trade hierarchy.

The bulk of the positions of privilege remained in the hands of the whites, who in general were Scottish and Protestant. The recently introduced Roman Catholic and Protestant churches did nothing to change that, but did tend to divide the community into factions and into classes, with the majority of its population consisting of Métis voyageurs in the Roman Catholic camp and the influential minority worshipping at the Anglican altar. The Anglican Church registers for the first few years after 1874 indicate that even that early a band of capable mixed-bloods had become the solid core of the Fort Chipewyan community; Mowatt, Wylie, McLeod, McCallum, Gairdner, McAulay, McDonald, Garson, Sinclair, Lutit and Flett. Most of them were already closely intermarried, and from time to time new recruits, cousins of some degree direct from the Orkney Islands or the Hebrides, came to throw in their lot with their namesakes in the close-knit community. Of its members the numerous Fletts, Lutits and the Wylies were probably the ones who could have traced their ancestry farther back into Canada's fur trade days than any others, except for a few Catholic French, the Mercredis, St. Cyrs, Ladoucers and others. Many of the latter were descended from the earliest voyageurs ever to paddle the Quatre Fourches or the Rivière des Rochers.

Within a year Garrioch was sent to teach at Fort Simpson and on the trip downstream he met another man destined to become a great figure in the North, Dr. W. M. Mackay, who was in charge of the brigade. Dr. Mackay, one of the many medical men employed by the Hudson's Bay Company, had left Scotland in 1864 and four years later had been assigned to Fort Simpson. For the next thirty years as a trader and physician, he became justly famous as he moved about the North and served at Forts Rae, Dunvegan, Resolution, Lesser Slave Lake and at Fort Chipewyan from 1887 until twelve years later he retired to Edmonton.

Long before that time, however, during Roderick MacFarlane's reign, other outstanding men looked in upon Fort Chipewyan. One of these was the famous botanist, John Macoun, who toured the West in connection with the CPR surveys. When he reached the fort in 1875 he was impressed by the garden which years previously Father Faraud had created by draining a slough behind his mission. Macoun's testimony before the Schultz Commission a dozen years later is indicative of his feelings at the time.

> . . . I found growing on soil that would be of no value here whatever, sand and muck, an old swamp where they had planted wheat on May 5, and I found it in the stook on August 26, and brought away from it the grain that was awarded the bronze medal at Philadelphia, in 1876.

Macoun's description of this award as "the bronze medal" may have led to the rosy conclusions fabricated by enthusiastic reporters which over the decades have often led to the statement that in 1876 at the International Exhibition held in Philadelphia, Fort Chipewyan carried off the top prize for wheat. A study of the prize list clears up this misapprehension. It indicates that at this exhibition some silver medals and many bronze medals, of which this was one, were distributed for wheat. Perhaps the only significance we can attach to the sample of grain in question is that it was certainly a worthwhile specimen and, moreover, that it was by far the most northerly one on display. As any indication of the existence at Fort Chipewyan of a climate amenable to wheat growing or of the presence of enough arable soil, it can be ruled out. As an indication of the devotion, the perseverance and the labours of the priests in their effort to cultivate grain on the pre-Cambrian shore of Lake Athabasca, however, a gold medal would perhaps have been little enough recognition.

It was probably this medal that so excited Father Emile Petitot's imagination when in 1879 he witnessed what must have been another of the many low water periods in the Delta and stated that:

> At that time, the channels of the Athabasca were almost dry; the main current had left the central one and gone wholly to the east, and the savanna of the estuary, elevated many feet above it, was changed into the immense and perfectly firm prairie, covered with young willow copses and dotted with waterholes . . . Perhaps I should more correctly say that this basin of five to six leagues still existed with its rocky rim, but instead of water it contained grass . . ."

Strangely enough the scientist, Robert Bell of the Geological Survey of Canada, who was at Fort Chipewyan in 1882, did not comment on this phenomenon noticed by Father Petitot. By that time, of course, a year or so of high summer runoff had probably restored the Delta to its more usual condition.

But Bell did comment on the tar sands. He had been sent to make a survey of the Athabasca River and to study the oil sands with a scientist's critical eye. Many a fur trader, of course, had speculated about their value to future generations. Typical of these traders was a Hudson's Bay man named Thomas Spence, who, travelling up the river in 1878 with the

Reverend A. C. Garrioch, waxed enthusiastic over the industrial prospects of the area. He could foresee the day when ". . . in response to the miner's pick and shovel, his drill and his explosives, [they will] give up their secrets of fabulous wealth. . . . I can foresee that before very long these great rivers will be spanned by wonderful bridges beneath which steamers will pass to and fro. . . ."

Bell, the first geologist to report on the oil sands in any detail, considered them ". . . of great scientific interest and economic importance." He suggested that one possible method of extracting the oil would be to use the heat yielded by burning some of the impregnated sands to release the oil in the remainder. Bell also looked at various spots on the east shore commencing about Tar Island where the traders and missionaries collected the tar in barrels to take to the posts, where, after boiling it down, they used it for repairing their boats. In some cases they had even used it on their roofs but with little satisfaction.

Robert Bell's memoir, the forerunner of many other reports on the Athabasca oil sands, was the first significant indication to Canadians that fur was not the only resource to be found along the Athabasca River. Within a year of the publication of his report, the first of the long line of the venturesome tribe of entrepreneurs who hoped to extract oil from the sands had organized a company to exploit them. The long and baffling search for an economic way to utilize the sands had started.

Fort McMurray had been built, scowmen were beginning to challenge the Grand Rapids and entrepreneurs were pecking away at the oil sands. The mid section of the Athabasca River, dragged from its long primeval silences, was about to enter upon its new role as a highway of commerce.

CHAPTER NINE

Earliest Steamboats

The steamboats of which Thomas Spence day-dreamed were far closer to reality than he realized. In the fall of 1882, four years after his prophecy, a number of men with a strange glint in their eyes arrived at Fort Chipewyan and their unwonted activity marked the beginning of a new era in the old fort's life. For they had come to build a steamboat!

Twenty-two years earlier Bishop Clut's barges being rowed across the lake to the mission had been an all-time sensation. But here were men proposing to create an altogether new wonder, a huge boat which, it was said, would propel itself across the lake and travel effortlessly not only from Fort McMurray to the start of the rapids near what we call Fitzgerald but back again.

Although the old-timers of the fur trade regarded this encroachment of civilization with some misgivings, they welcomed the prospect of easier transportation up and down the river. As for Chief Factor Roderick Mac-Farlane, he had no misgivings. He had been one of those who at the meetings of the Northern Council had advocated this labour-saving innovation. On his trips out to Norway House he had watched the beginning of the white man's takeover as civilization extended across the prairies. First had come the Mounted Police, then the Saskatchewan River steamboats, and now the CPR, which, starting out from Winnipeg in 1881, reached Qu'Appelle the next year and was due to arrive in Calgary in 1883.

Before the railway graders had started west, however, but after the steamers had begun plying the North Saskatchewan River, the Hudson's Bay Company began sending freight for the North as far upriver as Fort Carlton. From it they had cut a hundred-mile cart road to Green Lake, whence they could float goods downstream into the Beaver River and on to Ile-à-la-Crosse, and then send them over the Methy Portage. The road proved so difficult to travel that within two or three years the company tried another route which they cut from the mouth of Frog Creek in eastern

Alberta to the Beaver River near Cold Lake. After that for a few years their northern goods followed this much longer route—up the Saskatchewan to Frog Creek, overland about fifty miles to the Beaver River and thence down it to Ile-à-la-Crosse. Though this route was easier than the one north from Fort Carlton, the company longed for the day when it too could be abandoned. Moreover, now that the buffalo had vanished, so had the pemmican which in the past had fueled the voyageurs on these northern routes and its place had been taken by more costly imported foods.

No wonder then that the company's officials, following the progress of the CPR on their maps, decided to try an altogether new route and before the steel reached Calgary had taken several vital steps to bring it into being. Their plan was to ship by rail to Calgary, get freighters to haul their northern goods the two hundred miles to Edmonton, a strung-out settlement of 263 people, and then to keep their carts rolling to the Athabasca River at what came to be called Athabasca Landing, a name which was soon shortened to The Landing. Roderick MacFarlane, one of its keenest advocates, gave the route a preliminary inspection in 1881 and the gears began to mesh. Preparations were started to improve the pack trail to The Landing, construct a warehouse there and build scows to take goods through the Grand Rapids to Fort McMurray, where they would be loaded on the steamboats the company proposed to build.

One by one the links in the chain fell into place. In January 1882 John Walter of Edmonton contracted with the North-West Navigation Company Limited, a subsidiary of the Hudson's Bay Company, to whip-saw lumber at Athabasca Landing and build three scows of eight tons capacity to be used to take supplies, equipment and machinery down through the Grand Rapids and on to Fort Chipewyan. In May he sent men and ten Red River carts over the old pack trail to The Landing to carry out the work there. When on July 8, 1882, the *Northcote* arrived at Edmonton with material for the new Fort Chipewyan sternwheeler, which was to be named the *Grahame* to honour the commissioner of the Hudson's Bay Company, all Edmontonians, all 280 of them by then, buzzed with excitement. For 25,000 pounds of its lading, including machinery and a knocked-down boiler, which accounted for 2-1/2 tons, was destined for the new boat. A couple of weeks later J. Littlebury, who was to be the engineer of the steamboat, set out with another brigade of nine wagons and thirty-one carts, taking this material to Athabasca Landing. In November the crews of Walter's scows returned to Edmonton to report that early in September they had made their way safely through the Grand Rapids and after an eight-day trip had reached Fort McMurray. These men, leaving a skeleton staff to guide the scows down the safe water to Fort Chipewyan, had walked back along the barely perceptible trail to the mouth of House River and then had come in by way of Lac La Biche. A couple of weeks earlier the Hudson's Bay Company had sent out a gang of men to convert the crude trail the machinery had taken into a proper cart road and to put bridges over the various creeks between Edmonton and The Landing.

If Edmonton was enraptured over all this activity, everyone at Fort Chipewyan was entranced when during the summer Captain John H. Smith arrived to organize the construction of this gigantic vessel, which was to be 130 feet long by 24 feet beam and to carry 200 tons of freight. His first task at Lake Athabasca was to scout for suitable timber, and he decided to cut much of it near the fort and to get the larger logs from the Quatre Fourches River not far from where three Métis had built their homes. While plenty of fascinated spectators watched, the vessel took shape over the winter. By November 10, 1883, Captain Smith was back in Edmonton, having launched the sternwheeler and berthed her on the south side of the lake in 14 feet of water.

The big day, of course, came when after all the months of hammering and clatter, it was announced that the boat was at last going to make a trial run. The natives and Métis had lugged aboard an immense pile of cordwood and watched as the sticks were shoved into the furnace. Black smoke belched out of the two stacks, and, while steam roared out, the order to cast off moorings was given, and the great splashing paddle wheel began to revolve. Slowly, at first, the leviathan of Lake Athabasca backed away from the shore. Then as the engineer poured on the steam and the vessel appeared to leap away into the lake, a hundred voices rose in wild cheering. A new miracle assembled before their very eyes had come to Fort Chipewyan—this thunder boat which drove itself!

Back along the North Saskatchewan River the *Northcote* unloaded piles of freight at Edmonton but also at Fort Carlton and at the mouth of Frog Creek. The company had wisely not put too much trust in the navigation of the Grand Rapids and had decided to send some goods by way of the Methy Portage. As it turned out, those entrusted to the rough battering of the terrible rapids also got through, so that when the spring of 1884 unlocked Lake Athabasca they were waiting for the *Grahame* to pick them up. By then, of course, the CPR line to Calgary had done the *Northcote* out of much of its former job and in June the Hudson's Bay Company advised all freighters that it had four hundred loads ready to be rolled north in their squeaking Red River carts to Edmonton and taken on to the newly built warehouse at The Landing. By that time too the company had put a ferry of sorts at the crossing of the Redwater River.

At Fort Chipewyan that spring, while Roderick MacFarlane was champing at the bit to send the *Grahame* away on its business, J. Littlebury, the engineer, and J. Favel, the pilot, were chewing at their moustaches and wondering where all the water had gone. The previous fall they had berthed her in fourteen feet of water, but now she squatted like a mud-hen in eighteen inches of it. They had witnessed a record drop in the lake level of twenty-two feet from the high stage of the year before. Soon, however, the water rose and, loaded with goods needed farther north and trailing black smoke behind her, the *Grahame* rounded the corner of the Doghead and steered for the Slave River and the outpost which had been established in 1872 but which was renamed Grahame's Landing and eventually Fitzgerald. From it, of course, the goods would have to be hauled across the sixteen-mile portage to the relatively new Fort Smith post which MacFarlane had ordered built in 1874 and named after Donald A. Smith, the company's chief commissioner.

The *Grahame* came up to the builders' expectations. She made her first trip from Fort Chipewyan to Grahame's Landing on June 15, 1884 and covered the 120 miles downstream in seven and one-half hours. Then she splashed her way back to Chipewyan in fifteen hours. The Indians along the river had been astonished at this smoking, sparking, splashing monster. She had made another trip shortly afterwards, this time up to Fort McMurray in thirty hours, and had returned downstream in fifteen hours. That summer, too, she had made two trips up the Clearwater, 60 miles to the foot of the rapids. Before long she was to venture up the Peace to Vermilion Chutes. The *Grahame* had pleased her officers.

From then on, as she thrashed up and down the Athabasca, the *Grahame* was the pride of the North. And certainly in the high water of June the trips were ideal. Navigation was a small problem. The pilot just pointed her up or down the river, dodging the islands, and all went well. He had nothing to do but to watch the fascinating forested hillsides in the freshness of their early summer garb. Here and there the greyish cliffs of oil sand showed off their wealth of black petroleum occasionally edged as at Fort McMurray with a base of white Devonian limestone. The trip along the river presented a kaleidoscope of colour, with the broad stream, the narrow band of white limestone and the darker cliffs of oil sand, softened by trees growing over them, and farther back the gently rising hills. There was little for the passengers to do but sit and smoke and relax.

The trip upstream pleased the old voyageurs most. Imagine it. From Fort Chipewyan to Fort McMurray in thirty hours, and no tracking! Gone were the man-killing days when they had pulled scows and York boats and sturgeon-heads mile after mile up the river, weary day after weary day. From daylight to dark they had pulled until each time they slipped on a slimy rock and fell they felt they could never rise again. Each time they sank in the mud and sand up to their knees, they felt like staying there —but they had to go on. On and on, forever the pulling seemed to last. An hour they dragged at the tracking line, then five minutes was taken for a rest and a smoke. Then on again. At the end of three hours, they had another meal; then on they went again. Sometimes they made ten miles, rarely twenty, and sometimes, pulling up any rapids, less than five in a day. It was the hardest kind of labour. And now on this section of the Athabasca, all that was but a painful memory.

The voyageurs and boatmen had no complaints against this new mechanical boat which relieved them of this type of toil; rather, they rejoiced. For it provided a new employment and one more congenial. The belching smoke-stacks arose from a flaming furnace whose hungry maw was never satisfied. Stokers stuffed logs in and still the fires demanded more. Every few miles they had to stop for more wood. This need for wood brought into being a whole new industry of woodcutters and wood piles which in time was to become an important one. At last steamboat navigation had come to the Mackenzie watershed. Its full flowering was to take a few years, its halcyon years were still ahead, but the *Grahame* had given it a good start.

For over a hundred years the old Methy Portage had been the northern voyageurs' *bête noire*. Now this hated Long Portage had started its decline and within a few years grass would grow over the old trail and fireweed and raspberry canes would intertwine with the spokes of cracking, useless old Red River cart wheels. For the next forty years, in separating the men from the boys, the vicious Grand Rapids and the miles of violent white water below them were to take the place of the old Methy Portage.

Just as the CPR, winding its way across the prairies, had put the Methy Portage out of business and had encouraged sternwheelers on the Athabasca, so it opened up possibilities to a hardy breed of independent traders who began looking to the North. Some time previously a few had made tentative moves in that direction, but once furs could be shipped to eastern markets by rail, many of these traders invaded the North. Some, like Dutch Henry who visited Moberly at Fort McMurray in 1870, did not stay in the country very long. Others, such as Dan Carey and Twelve-Foot Davis, had been Cariboo miners and then, starting about 1871, had descended the Peace River to trade with the Beaver Indians. As early as the 1880's and also descending the Peace River, Elmore Brothers, who had good financial backing, set up shop in the Fort Vermilion area and began competing with the Hudson's Bay Company at Fort Chipewyan.

Shortly after the Lac La Biche mission had been started another group of traders began congregating at the lake and dealing with the Crees and Chipewyans who lived along the lower Athabasca. By 1883 Myles McDermott and E. Hamelyn were drawing most of the furs from the adjacent area, and before long built posts at Heart Lake. Soon other men like J. Ladoucer and Peter Pruden were providing stiff competition for the Hudson's Bay Company's posts at Lac La Biche and Fort McMurray. Similarly, in the Lesser Slave Lake region other traders, Colin Fraser, for instance, who built a post there in 1885, began reaching back into the hinterland north and east of the lake between the Athabasca and Peace rivers. The next year or so saw an influx of independent traders into the Lake Athabasca region and by 1887 Elmore Brothers, Stewart and Bannerman, L. Pruden, J. Ladoucer, J. Tourand, W. Flett, Tommy Upee, and others, all competed with the Hudson's Bay Company and with each other. Competition was so cut-throat that within two or three years most of them were forced to close their doors.

For a while the Indians had a sellers' market, only to find how ill advised they had been to swerve from their loyalty to their old-time friend, the Hudson's Bay Company. The winter of 1887-88 was a hard one, rabbits and lynx were scarce and, perhaps lulled into a false security by the presence of so many traders, the natives had not hunted as diligently as they should have. In any event, all the Beavers and Chipewyans had a hungry winter and here and there some of them died from starvation. Those trading into Fort Chipewyan, where the missions and the Hudson's Bay Company scraped their cupboards bare, suffered few deaths. But by this time the old company, which invariably tried to provide enough rations to share with its hungry customers, found it too much of an additional task to feed those Indians who for two or three years had not dealt with it. Failing to obtain relief from the independent traders who had secured their furs, they now came looking to the Hudson's Bay Company which had not anticipated having to care for them.

The worst suffering struck a party of Beavers whose homeland was some 150 miles from Fort Vermilion. When starvation stared them in the face, the two strongest hunters went for help and after many days fell in with another group which gave them a little food to take back with them. They returned to a silent camp. In the tepees they found nineteen bodies, some of them partially eaten. Two members of the band were missing—two sisters. One of them had a husband who during the winter had attached himself to another band living a hundred or so miles away. For a long time the fate of the two sisters was unreported, but finally one of them, a near crazy, half naked, living skeleton, turned up at the Little Red River post between Fort Vermilion and Lake Athabasca.

When the others were all dead she and her sister had set out for that post, each suspicious of the other. As she finally explained, "She was watching me and I was watching her." One night her sister suddenly ordered her to sleep on the other side of their fire. Then, later on she felt a touch on her foot, so she sat up, and hours later, fearful and mentally unbalanced, she lifted their gun, shot her sister and fled. But when the cold drove her back to the fire, she found that, before she had expired, her victim had crawled hundreds of yards following her track. Weeks later, recoiling from her dreadful memories, she declared: "And she is dead. I must have eaten her or I would not be here." Thenceforth in the eyes of the community the distraught woman was treated as a pariah. When she left there and sought out her husband, he too turned away from her and refused to take her back. Finally she found refuge and understanding at the Fort Vermilion Anglican mission.

As a result of the Indians' suffering during that drastic winter, Bishop Young and others wrote the Minister of the Interior at Ottawa, pointing out that "Owing to the strong competition in the fur trade, and other causes, the Indians cannot look to the Hudson's Bay Company for help as they used to do." They advocated that the Dominion Government should take steps to bring these tribes under the protection of a treaty so that like the Indians farther south the government would help to feed them.

Another result attributable partly to that winter's suffering and partly to the intense competition amongst the recent influx of independent traders was that a number of men lost money and pulled out of the Fort Chipewyan area. By 1890, for instance, after Elmore Brothers sold out to the Hudson's Bay Company, only P. Pruden and Colin Fraser (who, although he had sold his own business, seems to have worked for Dick Secord of Edmonton) were left in the area. Memories are short, however, and during the next five years various traders began re-entering the far North and also setting up posts on the Pelican River, at Wabasca, Heart Lake, and at Gregoire and Gordon lakes. From 1892 on, however, there were always a few Chipewyans who brought their own furs into Edmonton. For these Indians who a century earlier had not quailed before the terrible trip from Lake Athabasca to Hudson Bay found little to test their mettle in ascending the Athabasca River and going on to Edmonton.

Undoubtedly these natives did not follow the river from Fort McMurray but worked their way across country to Lac La Biche by the route that some traders used in wintertime. The traders' dogs needed fish for food and the Athabasca was not generous. But by heading south from Fort McMurray to Gregoire Lake and thence keeping close to the route which years later the Alberta Great Waterways Railway took, they could stop at Christina, Wiau and Heart lakes on their way to Lac La Biche. A few Chipewyans had built shacks at most of these lakes and from them the travellers obtained the necessary fish. Similarly, the Chipewyans from Lake Athabasca could stop over with their relatives and enjoy a social evening or two before pressing on to Edmonton.

Of all the independent fur traders Colin Fraser was the most outstanding personality. The son of Sir George Simpson's Highland piper of the same name, he had been born at Jasper in 1850 and as his father had moved about he had lived from time to time at Fort Assiniboine, Lesser Slave Lake and Lac Ste-Anne, and when old enough had been taken on by his father's employer. The year 1884 found him setting out on his own on a trading venture to Lesser Slave Lake where over twenty years earlier his father had taught him many of the tricks of the trade. The next year he built a post of his own there. Two years later he turned his attention to Fort Chipewyan where for twenty dollars he bought a shack. Undoubtedly he shared the failure of so many of the traders in that area and in 1890 sold out to the Hudson's Bay Company. In 1892 he was in the midst of an attempt to settle on the Shaftsbury Settlement near the modern town of Peace River.

The call of Lake Athabasca, however, proved too strong and in 1893 he moved his family to Fort Chipewyan where he acted as agent for Dick Secord of Edmonton. A year later he was trading entirely on his own, with his headquarters on the shore about half a mile west of the Nativity Mission and with outposts at Fort Vermilion and Fond du Lac. In July of that year he brought his furs to Edmonton, and in the largest single sale there up to that time his friend Secord bought them for $20,000. Included in that deal were 36 silver fox skins, 78 cross fox, 124 red fox, 41 fisher, 72 otter, 812 beaver, 33 wolverine, 106 bear, 3,016 marten, 582 mink, 115 lynx, 7 wolf and 3,100 muskrats, as well as 48 pounds of castoreum.

One interesting featur? about Edmonton's active fur market was the way in which many traders sold their lots of pelts. A trader would come in and leave his bales in the warehouse of a dealer friend such as Dick Secord. Then when word got around, each of several prospective buyers would go over and take his time examining this particular bundle, and then make the trader an offer. A few days later, after several offers had come in, the actual sale would take place.

Colin Fraser was a busy man and wasted little time in Edmonton before setting out again with a year's supplies for The Landing, where he would make or acquire a scow or two to carry them north. On this particular trip in 1895 he returned to Fort Chipewyan with at least one unusual item—cedar shingles for his warehouse there.

During some of his best years at the turn of the century Colin Fraser brought in more valuable loads of furs and on at least one occasion he sold one lot for $35,000. Trading was big business and Colin Fraser was the man to build up and handle a big business venture. For nearly half a century he lived at his well equipped post where he was one of the leading men of the North. When he died at the age of ninety-one he owned twenty buildings at Fort Chipewyan and for many years had been the grand patriarch of the Mackenzie watershed.

By 1893 his good friend Dick Secord had become one of the largest independent traders operating in the North. That year he not only shipped 350 muskox robes to the famous dealers C. M. Lampson and Company of London, England, but had Colin Fraser buying furs for him at Fort Chipewyan, while Hislop and Nagle were looking after his interests on Great Slave Lake. In 1897 he and John A. McDougall formally joined forces in the firm of McDougall and Secord, which, amongst many other activities, continued Secord's large-scale fur trading business, and each year sent several scows down the Athabasca River.

Occasionally at the mouth of the Lac La Biche River these scows mingled with those coming from the mission at the lake, but in 1889 Bishop Faraud sent the last shipment of two barge-loads by that route. After that for a year or so the Hudson's Bay Company carried the church's goods by way of Athabasca Landing, where in 1891 the church built a warehouse. The next year Bishop Grouard sent a small steam engine down from The Landing so that it might be used at Fort Chipewyan to saw lumber for the mission's first steamship, the *St. Joseph*, which was launched the next year. Like its opposite number, the Hudson's Bay Company's *Grahame*, it was to ply between Fort McMurray and Grahame's Landing.

The sawmill at the Nativity Mission not only cut the material for the *St. Joseph* but in 1895 sawed lumber for the new church which the fathers planned to build at Fort Resolution. All these timbers, planks and shingles were loaded on a raft and topped off with the yearly supplies for that mission and the one at Fort Providence. Fathers Laity and Dupire and Brother Charbonneau boarded the scow and for two serene days floated down the Slave River. In the next morning's fog, however, they misjudged their position on the river, missed the last possible landing spot and were carried into the sixteen-mile rapids above Fort Smith. The first cascade tumbled the raft about like a cork, spun it around and finally swept off its cargo. Miraculously the three men managed to stay aboard, and when whizzing past a small island all three were able to leap ashore, with Charbonneau still clinging to the rope of a small skiff. Even there they were in a desperate plight, but almost unbelievably their luck held and somehow they managed to row to the river's left shore. Only bits of the raft, the church building material and the boxes that held the year's supplies, were ever seen again.

With blind impartiality the rapids of the Mackenzie waterway wrecked scows, lay or ecclesiastical. In mid-summer 1885 when Captain Smith, who had built the *Grahame*, was taking the boiler and two other scow loads for the *Wrigley* down the Athabasca, the second stretch of rough water below the Grand Rapids acquired its name of Boiler Rapids by wrecking it. Out of the party's three scows, the two which carried Captain Smith and Brereton, the Hudson's Bay factor from Athabasca, got through safely, but the other hit a rock, broke apart and let the boiler drop into the depths. After that, the party ran the rest of the rapids to Fort McMurray with half loads and then came back for the remainder.

After a long delay the boiler was salvaged and made its way to Fort Smith safely. There under Captain Smith's watchful eyes it was installed in the *Wrigley*, which was named to honour the current commissioner of the

Hudson's Bay Company. The *Wrigley* made her first trip in 1886 and was quite different from the *Grahame*. She was a smaller ship, only ninety feet long and having a beam of fourteen feet, but because she was intended for service on Great Slave Lake and down the Mackenzie River, she drew much more water and was propeller driven. Except for her stem and stern posts, which were imported oak, she was built of local lumber whip-sawed on the job. In her construction, one of Captain Smith's more devoted colleagues was John Sutherland, a young man from Thurso on the Scottish mainland's extreme northern coast. As a lad of some nineteen years his first job as a Hudson's Bay Company employee had been in building the *Grahame* at Fort Chipewyan. From that time on his fifty-six years with the company were spent on river boats, mainly as chief engineer.

Captain Smith, of course, was a pioneer in steamboat building and handling in the Canadian northwest. Some years previously he had helped to construct the Hudson's Bay Company's *Chief Commissioner*, the first steamer to run north of Winnipeg. Later on he had been in command of the *Lily*, the second sternwheeler to run up and down the North Saskatchewan, and during that time made his headquarters at Prince Albert. In due course he had gone to Fort Chipewyan to build the *Grahame* and later the *Wrigley*. Perhaps the high point of his career was when in 1886 he had the distinction of running the *Wrigley* down the Mackenzie to become the first steamboat to cross the Arctic Circle there.

After the *Wrigley* was commissioned the Hudson's Bay Company had a relatively easy transport system from the mouth of the Clearwater River to the Arctic over 1500 miles away. Much of the farness had gone out of the far North. The middle Athabasca, however, the short stretch extending for 250 miles below The Landing, was the bottleneck in the whole system—it was easier to take a bale of goods the 1500 miles from Fort McMurray to Arctic Red River than it was to take it the 250 miles from The Landing to McMurray.

Since the *Grahame* and the *Wrigley* were proving so successful, the company decided to build a sternwheeler at The Landing. Such a steamboat, it realized, would do little to break the bottleneck of the Grand Rapids, but what little it could do would be all to the good. Moreover, Athabasca Landing was not only the gateway to the Mackenzie waterway but was becoming increasingly important as the jumping-off place for the Peace River country. Accordingly, the company hired Captain John Segers to build the *Athabasca*, a sternwheeler, which in August 1888 made its first trial trip. Like many of its subsequent jaunts, which often turned out to be more trials than trips, this first run fell far short of being a marked success.

In high hopes the *Athabasca* set out upstream dreaming of docking at the company's post at the west end of Lesser Slave Lake where gradually the town of Grouard was coming into being. She made her way up the sixty-odd miles to the mouth of the Lesser Slave Lake River and then started up that winding little river. But as well as being serpentine and somnolent, the Lesser Slave Lake River had a few minor rapids and twelve miles upstream the *Athabasca* stove in a section of her planking on a rock and sank. Down she went, sinking with all hands, six inches, eight inches, a foot, and there she squatted. The ripples and the rocks had defeated her, and after her planks were mended and her lading piled out on the bank, she returned crestfallen to The Landing.

Several times during the next few years she repeated the attempt to get up the vexatious little river, but even though on two or three occasions the Dominion Government blasted rocks here and there, she failed to ascend the little stream. Finally in June 1892 in high water she made it and with a flourish steamed into the broad freeway of Lesser Slave Lake. Before her lay some eighty miles of wide and deep water. Unfortunately the most westerly seventy miles were blocked with ice. Once more she returned to The Landing. Later in the season and occasionally in other seasons she was able to get to the post on the west end of the lake. But navigation in that direction is another story.

Meanwhile the Hudson's Bay Company improved its facilities at Athabasca Landing. In the fall of 1885 it established a trading post there and somewhat later improved its port facilities by building much larger warehouses. In 1887 the company erected two warehouses thirty feet by forty feet on the island at Grand Rapids. In 1891 the company even built a pier there.

Heading downriver from The Landing the *Athabasca* met fewer misadventures and less frequent groundings, and although at times due to low water she failed to get to Grand Rapids, she became an important auxiliary to the scows which year after year let the current carry them down the broad river. She did her best, however, and thenceforth, supplemented by scows, the Hudson's Bay Company had such a satisfactory transport system from The Landing to the Arctic Ocean that in due course it published a table showing the passenger fare to various points along this 1,854-mile waterway—not strictly a timetable because all references to time were carefully left off it.

CHAPTER TEN

The Athabasca Scowmen

For decades after the *Athabasca* was built, The Landing was the gateway to the glamourous north country and its river was the roadway to its romance. And leading to it from Edmonton was the hundred-mile Landing Trail confronting travellers with problems which at times took a week or more to overcome.

Each year the freighters, with carts in the earlier days but later on with wagons, took the long road from Calgary to Edmonton and for an additional hundred miles north hauled load after load to The Landing. Each winter after 1891 when the railway from Calgary reached Edmonton, scores of men spent weeks on several roundtrips over the snow-packed trail taking northern goods and supplies to the warehouses on the bank of the Athabasca River. Every summer freighters rolling north fought their way through mud holes, while their horses, driven almost to madness by mosquitoes and with their flanks streaming with blood from the vicious bites of horseflies, plodded their painful way. Most freighters, of course, protected their own heads and necks with mosquito netting but any inexperienced passengers travelling without that protection suffered much as the horses did. All summer long all northerners had to endure the mosquitoes and, undoubtedly, a few men were driven frantic and perished when hour after hour swarms of these insects continued their devilish probing for blood. But, whereas mosquitoes merely pricked the skin, horseflies were not so subtle. They bit, leaving a wound oozing blood.

Despite the mud holes, mosquitoes and bulldog flies, the freight accumulated at the five or six buildings which during the earlier years lined the bank of the broad, placid Athabasca. Broad and placid it may have appeared as it flowed past to the right and then swung to the left to disappear around the first of a thousand headlands. Broad and placid it was too for most of its 165 miles to the Grand Rapids, but there the river narrowed and begrudged canoe, boat or scow safe passage through the

96

turbulent east channel. Many a scow wrecked and many a life lost bore witness to the toll taken by this savage mile of rapids. Moreover, although these were the trip's severest test, year after year the memorials of the toll taken by the lower miles of lesser but tricky rapids between them and Fort McMurray also added fresh crosses to the tally ranged along the river's banks. But the dangers and the adventures and the exultations at risks run safely brought into being a new class of brave and skilful voyageurs, the scowmen of the run from The Landing to Fort McMurray.

To avoid any confusion between the roles of the scows and the steamboat *Athabasca* or her successors, we should point out that the scows were not only the sternwheelers' predecessors but also their supplement. Before the *Grahame* was built at Chipewyan in 1883, scows were delivering their loads to Lake Athabasca. Even after the *Athabasca* was launched at The Landing in 1887 and put into service the next year, they continued to play their difficult roles. The *Athabasca* was intended to navigate the river between Mirror Landing some sixty miles upriver and the Grand Rapids 165 miles downstream. When she was built it was hoped that she could make her way up the Lesser Slave Lake River and across the long lake to its west end, and indeed some years she could do that, but her main purpose was to carry freight up and down as far as the Grand Rapids.

Since her lading had to be transferred to scows at the Grand Rapids anyway, scores of scows continued to be built at The Landing and sent off downstream. Many of them, trusting to the quiet water that far down, started off with skeleton crews and planned to pick up additional men at the dangerous rapids. Every March, the month before the river's ice broke up, saw a fresh influx of men to The Landing. For then private traders, the Hudson's Bay Company and later on the missionaries, sent crews in to build scows—a few in the earlier years but later on, during The Landing's heyday, as many as a hundred a year. In the earliest years these were made of lumber whip-sawn from timber growing nearby, but eventually from planks sawn by a regular mill. At the height of The Landing's fame the shipyards on both sides of the river hummed with activity as the men, framing, planking, caulking or tarring, turned out scow after scow, meanwhile repairing occasionally to the Grand Central Hotel for refreshment.

Scows were glorified packing boxes, flexible and capable of carrying some twenty-five tons. They were flat bottomed, about fifty feet long, eight feet wide on the bottom, flaring out to twelve feet across the top, with a square bow and stern. They were built and lined up side by side high enough up the bank to be safe from the river's clutches when the press of ice passed by in the spring or when this was succeeded by a high flood.

Meanwhile, the men who formed the famous Athabasca Scow Brigade, mainly Crees and half-breeds, began filtering into The Landing. Some, of course, wandered in from such settlements as Lac Ste-Anne, St. Albert and Lesser Slave Lake, but the majority of them came from Lac La Biche. Daring and dexterous, unruly, with little taste for civilization and its ways, these scowmen had developed in a direct line from the Hudson's Bay Company's northern York boat men and then through the pioneering stages of the Lac La Biche mission's scow service to find their life's fulfillment as members of the elite body in the most romantic river service of all, the Athabasca Scowmen. Happy-go-lucky, touchy, independent and truculent, and allowing no man to drive them, they nevertheless yielded unquestioning loyalty and gave the last ounce of their strength to the few men who could lead them. They were a hardy, adventurous corps whose heroism and mighty achievements have been left unsung. No toil was too arduous, no rapids too awesome to run for the sake of leaders who overlooked their weaknesses, understood their sensitivities and reciprocated their loyalty. Over the years on the 250-mile run from The Landing to Fort McMurray a score or so of such leaders rose to a renown that made them the talk of all the northerners from Edmonton to the Arctic. Such men were Captain Haight, Louis "Shot" Fousseneuve, Philip Atkinson, George and Billy Lutit, Duncan Tremblé, and many others.

Finally crunching and roaring, the ice ground past The Landing, and then under the watchful eyes of such men as these, loading the scows began. To any traveller anxious to get under way and to begin to see the wooded shores slipping by as his water-borne scow drifted with the current, the loading process seemed interminable. The crew, dragging their feet in a display of distaste at having to do this mundane labour so unworthy of their talents, sometimes stretched it out for two or three days. Eventually the last of a party's scows was loaded, but even then the brigade could not set off until each of its native personnel had visited each of his friends in hamlet or tepee to say a leisurely goodbye and to shake hands all around. Finally, generally late in the afternoon, the last of the crew members came aboard, and while all The Landing's transient or permanent population stood yelling "Goodbye, *nestow*" and drowning out the yelping dogs, the scows eased off into the river's current. At last mere passengers, priests and policemen, explorers and occasional tourists, felt the thrill of setting out for new adventures amidst the mysteries of the lonesome land down north. At last too the scowmen could dispose themselves comfortably on bales and boxes and relax. For, except for the pilot, ever alert, and his cohort the steersman at the sweep, they had nothing to do until they approached the nearest rapids, and they were miles ahead.

An ordinary brigade formed a significant flotilla as in a straggling line which opened or closed as the vagaries of the stream dictated, its six or seven scows, carried along by the river's three-mile-an-hour current, swept around the bend below The Landing to shut off civilization and to open up vistas of new river reaches ahead. On this broad stream, locked between its forested banks and lit by the late afternoon sun intensifying the freshness of spring's opening leaves, passengers and crew alike had entered a new world. In later years some brigades carried a cook scow, so that meals could be taken on board while the brigade wound its way ever downstream, and on clear nights on those stretches of the river where no rapids were anticipated, could float all night. Then, bedding down somewhere amidst the boxes and bales, everyone but the steersman stretched out to lie watching the awesome display of stars so thick that there was scarce room for another and so clear that it seemed possible to reach up and touch them. Finally, listening to the creak of the stern sweep or to the snores from various parts of the scow and the gentle splash and gurgle of the waters alongside, or even to the hoot of an owl over on the shore, sleep came to close another day's adventure.

When the barges could not run all night or when there was no cook scow, the craft were tied up ashore and each crew, choosing a place as exposed to the breeze as possible so that it would help to blow away the mosquitoes, lit its own big campfire and prepared its own supper. As daylight faded and nothing was visible but the various fires spread along the bank, each camp became a close-knit unit shut out from the rest of the world by the wall of darkness. As the swarthy crewmen moved about, each engaged in some cooking task, their gaudy belts and headgear added to the gaity and companionship of this little huddle of men set down in the dark solitude of the vast forest. And as they laughed quietly and told tales of former adventures with the rapids or encounters with spirits or weentigos, the soft musical notes of the Cree language murmured around the fire. For while some such as Duncan Tremblé knew several languages, English, French, Cree, Chipewyan, Beaver, etc., Cree was the *lingua franca* of the brigades. It was said of old Duncan that he spoke seven languages, thought in Cree and lied in all of them. But all cursing was in the white man's languages, English and French, because the uncivilized natives had previously never thought it worthwhile to curse.

The smoking and the talking around the fire soon died away for daylight would come early and the men had to snatch what sleep they could. All too soon came the cry from the head guide: *"Ho lève! Lève! Lève! Il faut partir,"* and soon the fragrant smoke from the newly stirred fires sifted over the camp, tea was brewed, and slithering down the muddy bank the men resumed their places on the scows. Breakfast would come at a stop some three hours later, to be followed by another stop and another meal about noon, and then another at four o'clock, and finally another night's camp.

With their poles the crew eased their craft out into the stream once more—a stream often blanketed in mist where the scow ahead became a dimly visible phantom, and the direction of the steersman or the murmurings of its Cree crew became ghostly voices floating in the blanketing void. Once more the flotilla was under way. Such conditions, however, prevailed only in good weather. Floating down the river during a three-day rain, trying to shelter under dripping tarpaulins, or camping in the mud was a vastly different story. But rain or shine, the scows must go on.

Go on they did, floating down long, straight stretches and looping around hairpin bends until the mouth of the Lac La Biche River with its two or three shacks appeared on the right and some seven miles farther the Calling River flowed in from the west. Once in a while a bear or a lynx, crossing the river ahead of them, became the target of a hail of bullets, or a contemplative moose, watching too long, fell before a fusillade of rifle shots. Eventually as meal succeeded meal and little streams flowed in from clefts in the shoreline, an elbow of the river warned the crew to prepare for the minor tussle of the Pelican Rapids. An eager tenseness rippled along the line as the pilot in the leading scow pointed his directions, and with a new purposefulness the steersmen gripped their twenty-five-foot-long sweeps, while the crewmen, lounging no longer, manned their heavy oars, all ready to obey their leaders' orders without question. Then for a few minutes the scows, speeding up and bobbing and twisting, bumped along until before anyone realized it they were floating serenely in quiet water once more. The Pelican Rapids had been passed.

With equally little effort the scows descended the minor Stony Rapids a few miles farther on and then the Joli Fou Rapids, named after some happy fool so long before the days of scows that no clear account of his misadventure remained in the voyageurs' memories. Soon the gap in the trees appeared and through it quite unassumingly the House River brought in its tribute from the east. The more devout crewmen crossed themselves and the rest, after a temporary silence, went on to tell the newcomers of the twin tragedies whose evil memories hung over this pleasant appearing flat—the murder of Brother Alexis and the more recent calamitous death of an entire Cree family. During a time when diphtheria had entered a shack at Lac La Biche, the little family had set out from there to return to their trapping ground farther down the Athabasca. One at a time but all within a few days, in their camp the dread disease had choked the hunter and his wife and all four of their children. Weeks later some acquaintance happening along discovered their fate and interred what the wolves and ravens had left.

The House River also marked the approach to the dreaded Grand Rapids with their many memories of men young and healthy swept to their doom. The most fearsome rapids on the whole river, their worst section was too dangerous for even the most intrepid crews to run. There were three separate portions to the Grand Rapids: the very rough water from Deadman's Creek—a name not idly bestowed—to the tip of the half-mile-long island; the plunge through the main drop where the river split to go around the island; and a final portion where the reunited stream still tumbling and boiling began to calm down. Guided by daring men, scows ran the first and third sections. Down the middle one, however, steered by sweep, paddle and pole, they teetered along, each tethered to several combined crews which picked their way among the rocks of the island and tried to restrain the scow's plunge down the channel.

After drifting the 165 miles from The Landing in from three to six days, depending upon the stage of the water, the sight of Deadman's Creek swept away every voyageur's laziness. Now the men, with every muscle taut and every sense alert, took their stations, ready to obey the slightest signal of command. One towering Métis braced himself as bowsman, a couple rose to help the steersman man-handle his huge sweep, and the others put the great oars in place and stood—not sat—at them. With shouts, the men bent to their work, standing up and pulling till at the end of each stroke they were squatting, and then while the spray dashed from their long blades, stood up again for a new stroke.

The trip to the head of the island took ten or fifteen minutes. Then during two to four days everyone camped on the island while the goods were moved along to its foot. In the earlier years everything had to be carried that half mile, but after 1889 when the Hudson's Bay Company built a tramway for that distance with wooden rails encased in sheet metal, the men welcomed the convenience of trundling the trucks down to the lower end of the line. Then like true voyageurs they enjoyed themselves immensely by standing in the trucks as they would have in a scow and poling them back up the track. All day long they packed or trundled but invariably at night the dark woods glowed with many campfires. Drumming, dancing and gambling, the native folk passed most of the night, oblivious of how soon daylight would bring more toil in its train.

While many of the crewmen trundled trucks, the more skilful tackled the task of working the scows down to the foot of the island through the second section of the rapids. There, while the barges were reloaded, the Mounted Police, who had stationed their first detachment on the island in 1893, inspected the lading for liquor, which, except under permit, must not be taken into the North. Then, fighting to keep afloat and to avoid the rocks in the third section, the crews finally sailed out into the calmer waters and set out on their eighty-seven-mile trip to Fort McMurray.

But no matter what care the boatmen exercised, each year saw some scow upset or run aground on the boulders of the Grand Rapids or break its back on some jagged reef and lose its valuable load. Hardly a year went by but some brave or foolhardy man lost his life, to have his body, if recovered, laid beside the row of crosses which marked the increasing tally the river had taken. Warburton Pike, the explorer and muskox hunter, told of one mishap in 1889 which his crew arrived in time to right. A Hudson's Bay Company clerk named MacKay and a half-breed companion coming afoot from Fort McMurray had run out of food and when they reached the rapids were unable to attract the attention of the man guarding goods on the island. In an endeavour to cross over to it they walked upstream two miles, built a raft and tried to pole down to the island. But their craft smashed against a rock and the two men were swept down the channel. The half-breed managed to swim to the island but MacKay, to avoid being carried into the rapids clung to a rock in mid-stream. His companion aroused the only man on the island but having no boat these two, in a brave but forlorn attempt to rescue MacKay, started to build a raft. They had worked at this for some hours when to their delight they saw Pike's party heading down towards them. Immediately after it landed everyone turned to and by means of a long rope lowered a boat down to the rock and took off the victim weakened by his long fast and chilled to the bone by sitting on the rock for several hours in wet clothes.

While the Athabasca scowmen were experts in their own field, the three Caughnawaga Iroquois brothers, Pierre, Louis and Michel French, whom J. W. Tyrrell took along as canoemen on his 1893 trip across the Barren Lands, showed them a trick or two about fast water. His party descended the Athabasca in two canoes and reached the Grand Rapids at the same time as a group of scows in charge of the famous "Shot" Fousseneuve. Seeking his advice about running the worst water, the Iroquois were told that no man could possibly survive it. But the Iroquois decided to try anyway. Shot declared that they were crazy. However, as Tyrrell relates the story:

> . . . the three Iroquois took their places, Louis in the bow, Michel in the middle, and old Pierre in the stern . . . all about them the boiling waters were dashed into foam by the great rocks in the channel. Presently it

101

appeared as if they were doomed to be dashed upon a long ugly breaker nearly in mid-stream; but no! with two or three lightning strokes of their paddles the collision was averted. But in a moment they were in worse danger, for right ahead were two great rocks, over and around which the tumbling waters wildly rushed . . . in that instant Pierre saw his only chance and took it—heading his canoe straight for the shoot between the rocks . . . with unerring judgment and unflinching nerve they shot straight through the notch, and disappeared in the trough below. Rising buoyantly from the billows of foam and flying spray, they swept on with the rushing waters until, in a little eddy half-way down the rapid, they pulled in to the shore in safety . . . without concern or excitement [they] returned for the second canoe.

In the meantime, Shot and his men were having the sort of trouble which occasionally happened to the best of the scowmen. In letting one of their craft down it stranded on a flat rock in the midst of the rapid which Pierre, Louis and Michel had just run. It took several hours for Shot's and Tyrrell's entire crews to get it off. Losing scows in the rapids was an altogether too common occurrence. In June 1894 Dick Secord, for instance, one of the prominent traders who ranged the Mackenzie watershed, had trouble with both his scows there. One was broken on the rocks and all its goods washed away, and during the excitement another broke loose from its moorings and went dashing down the rapids. Fortunately it did not break up and his men were able to catch up with it in the quiet water below and to save both it and its load.

Even getting a scow through the Grand Rapids in safety was no guarantee that its goods would reach Fort McMurray. If from The Landing to the Grand Rapids the men had been able to lounge about, the remaining eighty-seven miles to Fort McMurray kept them on the alert. For in that stretch the river dropped almost four hundred feet with reaches of quiet water alternating with ten vicious rapids; the Brule, Boiler (where the steamboat boiler was lost), Middle, Long, Crooked (where the river makes a spectacular hairpin turn), Rocky, Little and Big Cascade, Mountain and Moberly. All of them had to be run with care, but the Boiler and the Long rapids were the most dangerous and through both of them any brigade's scows were taken one at a time by concentrating a double crew of the best men on each. At these, judgment, strength and skill met their supreme test with every man aboard alert, expectant and agile as a cat.

Once more the pilot selected the channels to be taken—and at every stage of the water they were different ones. Once more, assisted by two or three extra men to manhandle his huge sweep, the steersman followed the pilot's orders to cross the current or run with it. Once more he directed the men at the four heavy rowing oars to pull or to hold. Other men with their long poles stood at the ready to thrust out to help make the sharper turns. Then, rocking back from that shove they stood tensely watching for the precise instant when again they should jab at other jagged rocks or rounded boulders. Coolness and judgment won the day—or sometimes even lost it. For the safest water, the deepest water raced towards the jagged rocks and then, curving in a flash, swirled by them. Into that millrace the scow had to be guided—not a mere slip of a canoe but the cumbersome, lumbering hayrack of a raft—and tilted for that straight, ugly reef. Broken by the wild, involuntary shout of excitement, the poles thrust out and by inches the scow avoided the almost certain fate of being shredded and sunk. Then it was time for a pause spent pulled up to the bank, and for a meal. Four, five, and on long days sometimes six times, these powerful men relaxed from their energy-draining toil and ate. The fifty or so men of a brigade consumed an amazing amount of flour, bacon and tea. But one of the main inducements of the service was the fact that during the summer the half-breeds' often hungry lot was relieved by substantial, if scarcely gourmet, food.

In such waters accidents happened frequently and occasionally claimed a man's life, but despite that, rapid after rapid was run. When the water was high, the distance from Grand Rapids to Fort McMurray was made in a day, because then the remainder of the rapids were easy to negotiate; during low water it might take a week.

Crooked Rapids, actually a smooth curving slope, was mainly memorable because there the voyageurs played a little game with any unwary passenger who was going downriver for the first time. At one point in swinging around this hairpin bend the current set straight towards the sheer rock wall and the speeding scow seemed destined to certain destruction. Then invariably and in an instant the water, recoiling from the wall, swept it off downstream. The scowmen, with no appearance of guile, encouraged any tenderfoot to move forward so as to enjoy the thrilling moment to the full. Then, unobtrusively they moved well back. As the craft swung clear, a great wave always broke over the bow and drenched the unwary victim. All considered this a hilarious joke and none more so than a passenger on his second trip.

To thread a way through the Little Cascade during times of very low water, some of the crewmen had to get out and push the craft along. The Big Cascade, one of the major obstacles of the trip, however, was a different story, as explained by Guy H. Blanchet.

At the east side of the river, the drop is a sheer six feet, but the ledge is broken into steps at the other side. Here, again, the trouble was that the river was too wide for its water at ordinary levels. At extreme low water, it was necessary to take the west side and worry the scow over, by portaging cargo and shoving over the slippery ledges. As the river rose, a fair stream gathered into a bite in the ledge, close to the east bank, over which a light scow could be run, though with some danger of breaking its back. Various conditions developed as the flood increased. A great back-curling wave formed at its foot, into which the bow plunged while the stern was so high that the sweep could not be used effectively. Sometimes a scow nose-dived and sometimes broached to, both with dangerous possibilities. The best condition to find the cascade was half-flood, when it could be jumped with full load—a moment when one seemed to be plunging into an abyss and another in a turmoil of big waves and flying spray.

103

Agnes Deans Cameron, who went north with the scows in 1908, told of what the Big Cascade did to one of them while she stood on the bank photographing it. As she described it, just as she was focussing on it she heard a crack like the shot of a pistol.

The scow has broken her back and begins to fill . . . In less time than it takes to write it, the men from our scow have launched the police canoes and make their way through the boiling water. . . . Lines are run from the wreck to the shore, other scows discharge their cargo on the bank and push out to take the water-logged goods from the wreck. The lightened craft is pulled ashore. There has been no loss of life, but it is a sorry-looking cargo that piles up on the bank,—five thousand dollars' worth of goods destroyed in three minutes!

Well, perhaps not destroyed but damaged and requiring considerable time to dry. As Miss Cameron discloses, the goods were taken the short distance to Fort McMurray where

On the long beach is strewn the water-soaked cargo of the wrecked scow. . . . All day we worked trying to save some of the wrecked cargo. Bales of goods are unwound and stretched out for hundreds of yards in the sun. Bandana handkerchiefs flutter on bushes. Toilet soap, boots, and bear-traps are at our feet. The Fire-Ranger of the district, Mr. Biggs, has his barley and rice spread out on sheeting, and, turning it over, says bravely, "I think it will dry."

From the Cascades the remaining white water of the Mountain and the Moberly rapids presented little challenge and at last the men tied the scows up at Fort McMurray, a poor place in a beautiful setting on the flat at the mouth of the Clearwater. In the summer, here and there, close to the few log buildings, tepees dotted the clearing and to these the scowmen repaired to dance, feast and gamble away the tension of the last few days. Their responsibility had ended. So did most of their scows for they were sold for about ten dollars and broken up for the lumber they contained. From here, in most cases, their loads were carried aboard the stern-wheeler, the *Grahame*, and sent off downstream. A few, those of the independent traders, would continue down the calm Athabasca and a few Hudson's Bay scows were left loaded and taken in charge by the stern-wheeler and pushed north. In either case, their crews were let go and after resting a day or so set off back upstream to the Grand Rapids to augment the crews of other scows and to relive the thrills of running down to Fort McMurray once more.

That walk back to Grand Rapids was a man's work. The barely perceptible trail was some fifty-five miles in a straight line and many miles farther than that when slogging through muskeg, dodging streams and detouring around hills along its route. One greenhorn who travelled it said: "It is a case of zig zag, up and down hill, over muskeg and into muskeg and over miles of fallen timber. . . ." By taking seven or eight rests and spelling five or six times to eat, the strongest of the scowmen could leave Fort McMurray at daybreak, carrying their food and blankets, push on till sundown, and finally arrive at Grand Rapids in twenty-four to thirty-four hours' actual travel. One noted riverman named Clark actually made the whole distance in twenty-three hours and thirty-eight minutes elapsed time.

Even at that, walking from Grand Rapids to Fort McMurray was child's play as compared to having to tow a scow from there to The Landing. Fortunately few scows had to be taken up, because the bulk of the freight in the form of heavy goods and supplies went downstream; furs, much lighter in weight, were practically all the freight that moved upstream. As a result, as compared to perhaps a hundred scows moving north each season, less than a dozen were required to return against the current. No toil was more frustrating, disheartening or laborious than tracking scows from Fort McMurray to The Landing. For tracking was the name given to the method of having men walk along the shore hauling a craft upstream by means of a long rope. The rope was attached in such a manner that the boat was almost in a state of balance between the current, which tended to force it away from the shore, and the pull on the rope which counteracted this tendency. Held in this state it was not too difficult for the steersman in a scow to direct it in or out from the shore by means of his steering oar. Tracking a canoe required considerable effort, tracking a York boat upriver was a discouraging ordeal, but tracking a great lumbering box-car of a thing called a scow up the Athabasca was a man-killing job.

As many as ten men spaced at intervals of about ten feet along the line formed a normal tracking crew and the leading man could be as much as four hundred feet ahead of the scow. Each of them wore a harness of sorts attached to a rope which in turn was fastened to the main one-inch hawser. If the water was deep near the bank the craft could be kept close to the shore and this lessened the pull necessary. When, however, the boat had to pass outside shoals or riffles, the pulling effort increased as the angle between the rope and the bank widened.

The actual pulling was the least difficult part of the work. Finding footing along slippery cutbanks, through scrub willows or over sharp rocks or rounded boulders, keeping the line clear of uprooted trees hanging over the water, or else floundering along in water or knee-deep in miry beaches, was what exhausted the men. Often a scow grounded on a bar and the men had to wade in and lift her off, and occasionally the hawser snapped and for a while the barge drifted freely—downstream, of course. When such obstacles made it impossible to proceed farther along one shore, the trackers boarded the boat and ferried themselves across to the other side. That entailed a spurt of heavy rowing, and usually they lost some headway, but at any rate it was a change from clambering along steep gumbo slopes. If practical, two or three scows started upstream at the same time so that at the rapids all three crews could combine their effort to drag up one at a time. On one occasion at the Grand Rapids in 1913, eighty men, hauling on a single hawser, could not hold their scow, which broke away and smashed up on the rocks.

On another occasion when Billy Smith, who spent over sixty years of his life along the Athabasca River, was part of a crew tracking up the river for Hislop and Nagle, they ran out of the usual food and for days had to get along with bannock and tea. Then at Pelican Rapids they used up their last match. For three days they had to carry a lighted stick with them. Six men pulled on the tracking line while two relaxed. It was their duty to keep the stick alight. At one point the line broke, and the four men in the lead fell on their faces in the mud. The other two, still straining on the line, had a desperate time before it was spliced again.

Ever so slowly the trackers progressed up the seemingly endless miles to The Landing, wading into and out of the water, creeping, sliding and often falling in the mud, fighting for every one of the more than a million feet (252 miles) they gained. Struggling from daybreak to dusk and taking from fifteen to twenty-three days to make the trip, they parcelled their time into spells of an hour for pulling and five minutes for resting. Three spells made up the time between meals and usually they had five meals a day. To fuel these human engines, each of the five meals was a heavy one. On one occasion, according to Harrison Young, a Hudson's Bay Company factor, sixteen trackers "had consumed eight bears, two moose, two bags of pemmican, two sacks of flour, and three sacks of potatoes." Only the very strongest man could eat like that, but only the strongest could endure this most brutal form of labour.

At last, however, usually pressing forward in the dark of the final day, they tied up their scow and cast off their hateful harness. They had reached *kapavnik*, The Landing, and all its joys lay wide open before them. The dreadful toil in the mud and the water, plagued by the ceaseless torture of clouds of mosquitoes and squadrons of bulldog flies was over. Though they had started at daybreak, another day was to break and to find them still drinking, dancing and gambling, for they had rejoiced the night away —often spending their summer's wages before dawn. But money was not their object anyway. For no amount of money would they have endured even one day of such toil on a farm or at any other occupation. Only the excitement and the knowledge that they played an important role which no one else could fill, and their *esprit de corps* made these descendants of generations of voyageurs endure this. For they were the elite of the waterways—the Athabasca Scowmen.

CHAPTER ELEVEN

Klondikers

The scowmen's courage and the Hudson's Bay Company's capital combined to ease the lot of explorers, scientists and just plain tourists eager to peer down the long river-traced vista to the north. Year by year it became more apparent that the vista would yield new adventures, new commercial advantages and new scientific opportunities. For that vista led to the Eskimos, to the wood buffalo and muskox; to the Yukon, oil sands and minerals. Time after time the shifting spotlight of interest played on each of these, only to move over to another, and then after a laspse of months or years to return to highlight this one or that once more.

Of perennial interest, of course, were the oil sands, the tantalizing mother lode of the western world's greatest source of petroleum. From the beginning of the fur traders' activities along the Athabasca River they had dipped into little pockets of free tar to stick the seams of their canoes. Then when the sternwheeler, the *Grahame*, began thrashing up and down the river, its firemen frequently flung chunks of the oil sands into their fireboxes to raise steam more quickly. But even before the *Grahame* had been launched a couple of Edmonton's well-known businessmen had been wondering about the feasibility of getting oil from the sands. Taking their cue from the activities of the Imperial Oil Company which had been incorporated in 1880 to refine the oil in the vicinity of Petrolia and London, Ontario, they decided to get in on the ground floor of the oil business in Alberta. So in May 1883, A. D. Osborne and T. Smith of Edmonton headed for The Landing with the announced intention of investigating the oil sands area.

For weeks little was heard from Osborne and Smith. Then in December the Edmonton *Bulletin* stepped into the picture with the announcement that:

Fifty miles of lead piping for the Winnipeg and North-West Petroleum

Company is said to be now lying at Calgary. It is proposed to lay this pipe from Athabasca Landing to the mouth of Sucker Creek on the Saskatchewan, a distance of about sixty miles. It is intended to bring the crude oil by boat from the company's claim to Athabasca Landing, refine it there and send the oil through the pipe to touch the navigation of the Saskatchewan. More power to them.

At last the oil sands were to release their treasure—Edmonton bid fair to be Canada's Oil Capital and the Athabasca River its handmaiden. Then strangely enough the venture turned out to be a pipe dream of which the fifty miles of pipe never materialized, but the dream lived on.

That fall far out on the prairies near Medicine Hat drillers seeking water for a CPR tank were repeatedly frustrated by gushes of natural gas. Within a few years that gas which the water-drillers rejected was to become the cornerstone of Medicine Hat's industrial development and was to make all Albertans petroleum conscious. Near the mouth of the Buffalo River fifteen miles below the Grand Rapids, however, natural gas bubbled freely through the water. The hissing of the breaking bubbles along that stretch of the Athabasca led to the scowmen referring to that section of the river as "The place where the water boils." Scowmen, of course, although alert to any natural phenomena, were far from cluttering their heads with daydreams of acquiring riches from petroleum manifestations. Moreover, it is doubtful if any of them had ever realized that these bubbles could be ignited.

In August of 1887 Captain J. H. Smith, making his way up the river after having built the *Wrigley*, was more curious or more knowledgeable than they. When walking along the beach, seeing the bubbles and hearing the hissing, he moved a small stone and touched a match to the emerging gas. From then on, this stretch of the river bank with its handy fuel became a favourite camping ground.

This gas bursting out of the ground near Buffalo River added its fuel to the excitement aroused by the studies of the scientists of the Geological Survey of Canada, Dr. Robert Bell in 1882 and Dr. R. G. McConnell in 1890, and led that organization to drill Alberta's first oil well in 1894 at Athabasca Landing. After deepening the hole to nearly 1,800 feet during two or three successive summer seasons and getting showings of gas and oil, the well was abandoned. In 1897 W. A. Fraser moved his rig to a spot a mile or so south of the mouth of the Pelican River. There, after obtaining showings of gas and heavy oil at various levels down to nearly one thousand feet, the well was abandoned, but to the delight of all travellers it was left to flow uncontrolled and burned for over twenty years. Except for the information obtained by the Geological Survey of Canada, these wells had no impact on the development of the oil sands.

From then on for nearly a decade the oil sands were left in relative peace as passengers on the scows and steamships merely gazed at them in awe and speculated on their richness. A handful of other travellers passed them too but hurried along because they had been bitten by the gold bug which had its lair in the pre-Cambrian rocks beyond Lake Athabasca. The earliest pair of these were both Edmontonians, Baptiste Pilon and his partner Moodie, who returned to that town in September 1886 after a trip which took them 110 days to complete. They had prospected along the north shore of Lake Athabasca and estimated that they had travelled 1,500 miles altogether. Their hopes had evidently been disappointed for they took no further action in that direction.

Two years later, however, they set their sights on the gold of the Yukon and were probably the first Edmonton-based prospectors to head down the Athabasca River for that destination. That trip too was a failure and they returned after an absence of some thirty months. For the next few years Pilon's interest in prospecting never waned and during the early spring of 1897 he announced that he intended to try the Yukon again. All the while, of course, men in small parties had been testing the gravels in that remote region and several Edmontonians, many of them ex-Hudson's Bay Company employees who were familiar with the Mackenzie watershed, also day-dreamed of trying their luck in the mountainous area west of its lower reaches. Amongst them were James Shand and his partner M. Velgue, who like Pilon planned to head down the Athabasca when the spring break-up came.

In May, while these two groups were getting ready to go and while other Edmontonians wondered about following their example, the news of the discovery on Klondike Creek flashed around the world. Immediately adventurers from all over Canada, the United States, Europe, Africa and even Australia, pricked up their ears and dragged out their maps of North America. Tracing Canada's railway system, many of their fingers followed it to the end-of-steel at Edmonton, paused there for a moment and then moved north to Athabasca Landing and on down to the mouth of the Mackenzie. To scores of would-be prospectors that railway system, combined with the line of sternwheelers running down to the Arctic, seemed to provide an easy way of getting to the Klondike. As early as July 29 the first Yukon-bound party arrived in Edmonton and before the year 1897 was out 130 adventurers had set out from Athabasca Landing and half as many again were ready to start. All Edmonton was agog and The Landing wondered what to do with this rush of prospectors.

By that time Baptiste Pilon and four of his compatriots of the Edmonton area who had left home in July, as well as James Shand and his partner who had left about a month earlier, had long since passed through The Landing and were wintering well down the Mackenzie River. Both parties had set the pattern which hundreds of other Klondikers were to follow; whip-sawing lumber and building a scow at The Landing and setting off. From time to time Shand sent letters home to his wife, which enable us to keep an eye on his progress down the Athabasca. In due course he passed the Grand Rapids and reached Fort McMurray, which he described as a place of "about three H.B.Co. buildings, two or three houses of half breeds, and some tepees and tents."

Out of a total of over 1,500 Klondikers who passed through Edmonton during 1897-98, nearly 900 came back, approximately 70 died and the rest reached the Yukon. Half of that total chose to take pack horses and cross to the Klondike overland while the remainder, the more fortunate ones, chose to descend the Athabasca. Of some 780 who did, over 560 got through to the gold fields.

The real madness of the rush through Athabasca Landing only reached its peak in the spring of 1898. All that winter the hopefuls detrained at Edmonton and after an interval went on to The Landing. All spring along the Landing Trail passed the fit and the unfit, the seasoned veterans of other rushes, and office clerks at a dead end who should have stuck to their stools. Along it passed the quiet, competent man trying to dodge the know-it-alls who, by assuming a mantle of knowledge they did not possess, revealed their inward uncertainty. Along it passed many a man whose untried resolution was doomed to dribble out before the grim reality of the trek and a few whose untested courage was destined to soar above that of their fellows. Amongst those few were eleven women who set out along the Landing Trail. After varying experiences six of them reached the Klondike and two of them bore children on the way. One of these was the unfortunate Mrs. Hoffman who was heavy with child when she stepped onto the barge at The Landing. All went well until a storm on Great Slave Lake wrecked their boat and drowned her husband. Despite that, she carried on. In due course her baby was born but died long before she reached the Yukon.

Mrs. Sam Brown of Detroit was more fortunate in that her husband accompanied her all the way. She established a novel record for the Edmonton route to the Klondike. The couple left Detroit about the middle of March 1898, and twelve months later were crossing the portage to LaPierre's House in the far North. Before leaving Fort McPherson, however, they were blessed with a baby—sex unstated—which they took on to Dawson City. This child held a unique distinction—not only was it born on the way to the Klondike but it was also conceived en route.

When day after day in the spring of 1898 this Klondike-bound mixture of hopefuls, including Mesdames Hoffman and Brown, kept pouring into The Landing, they touched off Athabasca's zaniest days. That spring an unnamed correspondent tried to depict the activity there when, after mentioning some of the launches, the *Anna, Montana* and *Enterprise*, he ended with the comment:

> Peterborough canoes are strongly in evidence here, also all kinds of punts and every conceivable kind of row boat darting here and there across the river, up and down and nowhere in particular, just trying the current and testing their boats; some out on shooting trips. Game is scarce, but poor shots very numerous. . . . It looks as though every man who ever had an idea that he was a boat engineer was here and had tried his hand and the result is boats,—beautiful, practical, pathetic, ludicrous boats, all the owners, however, with one end in view, and one man's chances are about as good as another's.

One boat this reporter failed to mention was Jim Wallwork's little sternwheeler launch the *Daisy Bell* which he purchased at Edmonton, had hauled to The Landing and slipped into the Athabasca. Young Jim Wallwork from a ranch at Lethbridge was a remarkable man who carried through a remarkable feat. On his *Daisy Bell* he conferred the unique distinction of being the only steamer to make the trip down the Mackenzie, cross the mountains and finally splash her paddle wheel in the Yukon River.

At The Landing the ice eventually went out and standing in their scows or boats, rejoicing and calling across from the *Woonsocket*, the *Minne-ha-ha* or the *Enterprise*, the adventurers waved their farewells. For at last they were afloat on the Athabasca. That seductive slap of the wash running along their gunwales and that soothing wobble beneath their feet were no longer day-dreams but realities. At last they were afloat; at last they were away. The Athabasca armada had set forth.

Down the current they swept—the greatest flotilla The Landing was ever to see—until the *Nellie, Jessie, Biddy, Emma, May* and *Squaw* and many another strange craft practically plugged the great bend where once more the willing waters swung around to the north. In such wise they travelled the first mile of their 1,800-mile voyage, a handful of women and hundreds of men. Off they went with spraying paddles clashing with awkward oars, crossing in front of each other and occasionally bumping. In their midst the smirks of incredulity playing around the silent lips of tanned pilots busily swinging their sweeps told of their amazement at this mob of unpredictable innocents let loose around them.

About the middle of May the first contingent cleared the Grand Rapids and "boats to the number of sixty-four left the rapids here, practically one fleet, bound north. Some guides had a round dozen of boats to chaperone, while others had but two, some four and others six." At last on June 3 the first Klondiker's steamboat reached Fort McMurray. Other outfits were right behind them. As a correspondent said:

> When McMurray was reached, a happier lot of men it would be hard to find, laughing, shaking hands and congratulating each other on their safe arrival . . . sixty-three boats and a crowd of men, hilarious with joy at getting safely over the rapids, yelling and dancing in the exuberance of their animal spirits.

All of this contingent reached McMurray safely even though there were enough bruises and bumps and broken ribs to keep two of the Klondikers, Doctors Buck and Dillabough, busy. After having piloted boats and scows and greenhorns through the seventy-five miles of rough water from Grand Rapids to Fort McMurray, the rivermen, mostly Métis, hurried back upstream to bring others down. At Fort McMurray itself the stream of Klondikers received an injection of some seventy hopefuls who had come across from Prince Albert by way of the old, seldom used Methy Portage. Reinforced by these venturers they set off six or eight craft at a time down the broad, placid stream and headed north like flocks of geese pushing on to their breeding grounds. During daylight hours any osprey or eagle watching from a tree atop any of the towering oil sand cliffs could note a few of this contingent loafing down the straight stretches that carried their craft towards its uncertain destiny.

In due course the flotilla of Klondikers emerged into the weird mystery of the Delta with its maze of channels. Where those of the Athabasca ended the Klondikers found themselves staring out over the broad expanse of Lake Athabasca which, depending on the time of their arrival, was calm, blue and beckoning or lashed into a wild fury of rain-swept whitecaps. Once they crossed it and stepped ashore at Fort Chipewyan they found that they had entered a new and strange world. As Ernest Corp, one of them, wrote:

> Fort Chipewyan was swarming with hungry, howling Indian dogs. Fish seemed to be the chief diet for both Indians and dogs. The Indians had nets out all the time, and would go out and bring in a boat load of fish when they felt like it and toss them to the dogs. Between times, the dogs were more like a howling pack of wolves, and boats had to be watched all the time or the dogs would soon clean it out of anything eatable.

It was not only the fish-fed dogs that found a godsend in the Klondikers' boats. The native boys likewise living almost wholly on fish, muskrats or moose meat, also found those scows a source of hitherto untasted delicacies, especially bread. My friend Joe Mercredi, a man well over eighty now, recalls the arrival of this spate of Klondikers and how much he and his companions enjoyed their short stay. He, of course, was familiar with the *Grahame* and the previous year had seen an occasional bargeful of Klondikers stop on their way north, but this sudden arrival of scores of scows in the spring of 1898 was the noteworthy incident of his boyhood. It appears that during a period when the lake had been rough for a few days more and more scows accumulated on the south shore and then when the storm died away they had all headed across to Fort Chipewyan in a body.

"We were playing down here by the bay," Joe explained, "and one boy said 'Look, there's a scow coming.' When we looked we saw them all coming around the end of the island there, so many it looked as if one could cross the lake by walking from scow to scow. When they landed we stood back but they were very friendly and one man beckoned us to come down to the edge of the water. We all ran and the bigger boys got there first, and that man handed them a loaf of bread."

As Joe tells it his eyes light up as once more he sees that afternoon more than seventy years ago when the man gave them bread—*pain*, he recalls. "*Pain*—we had never seen *pain* before. Bannock yes, but not much of that—we lived mainly on fish. It was wonderful, and all of us learned the magic word 'bread,' and as each boat landed we ran to it shouting 'bread, bread' and most of those bearded strangers laughed at us and gave us things. We were sorry when they left to go north."

"But Joe," I say, trying to lead him on, "Joe, you saw many Klondikers going north. Did you see many coming back later on?"

"Oh yes, that fall and the next spring lots of them. The north had been too much for them—wrecked their boats, drowned and froze and starved them. When they came back they were not smiling and laughing, they had no food to give away, and at the mission and the fort they gave them food.

My father, too, he gave them fish. Sometimes they went into our houses when we were out and stole things.

"Yes, they stole things. My father tell me of his cousin, not here but farther north. His cousin see some Klondikers get into their boat and go down the Slave River. After a while—maybe a couple of hours—his cousin go where they had camped and he find a whip-saw they had left behind. He get into his canoe, paddle like crazy two, three hours and catch them and give them the saw. Then he come back south again.

"But he not live there, he live at Fort Resolution and two, three weeks later he go home—him, his wife and two children and what you think he find? His cabin door open, his pots stolen and some dried meat gone. Some Klondikers had slept in his shack. And when he go outside again and look up at nail on the wall—what you think?—his own whip-saw is stolen. Some Klondikers took it. Maybe not same fellows but by gar maybe so same fellows."

As Charles Mair who was at Fort Chipewyan with the 1899 treaty commissioners reported, some of the Klondikers were still returning as late as August that year. According to him, the *Grahame* which arrived from Grahame's Landing had 120 defeated Klondikers aboard her and they claimed that even then there were still another 60 who were making their way back. Only about 30 per cent of those Klondikers who chose to descend the Mackenzie waterway failed to measure up to the rigours of the North and turned back before reaching the Yukon. A few of those were scoundrels but not many—just enough to give all Klondikers a bad name in the North. Incidentally, the Hudson's Bay Company, glad to get them out of the country, provided them with free passage south on its steamer.

CHAPTER TWELVE
Paddle Wheels

For some years after the rush to the Klondike the route down the Athabasca continued to be the only practical one. Until 1904, in spite of falling short of its builder's expectations, the Hudson's Bay Company's *Athabasca*, bruised by sandbars, bedevilled with boiler problems and blocked by the shallow rapids of the Lesser Slave Lake River, remained the only steamboat operating between Mirror Landing and Grand Rapids. Year after year the *Grahame*, plying between Fort McMurray and Smith's Landing, continued its more or less tranquil trips. Occasionally it encountered the Catholic missionaries' *St. Joseph* which was based at Fort Chipewyan and travelled the Athabasca and Slave rivers and once in a while it made a trip up the Peace as far as the Vermilion Chutes. There, at times, it met the missionaries' other steamer the *St. Charles*, the first sternwheeler on the upper Peace River. Built at the St. Augustine Mission it made its first trip to Fort St. John in the fall of 1903. By 1905 the Hudson's Bay Company's *Peace River*, which had been built at Fort Vermilion, had started regular trips from Hudson Hope to Vermilion Chutes. By that time a few hardy pioneers had been wondering about the agricultural possibilities of the Peace River country and it became obvious that settlers would soon rush in there. In anticipation of that, Jim Cornwall launched himself into the steamboat business.

J. K. Cornwall, variously known as "Peace River Jim" and the "Apostle of the North," was probably the greatest booster the North, and particularly the Peace River country, ever had. A man of tremendous talents and a flare for salesmanship, he aroused mixed feelings in his contemporaries; many regarded him as a sham, but the majority fell under his spell and became his loyal supporters. The year before the Klondike rush, at the age of twenty-seven, he had come west from Brantford, Ontario, and had fallen in love with Canada's northland.

In 1898, in partnership with Fletcher Bredin, Jim Cornwall started a

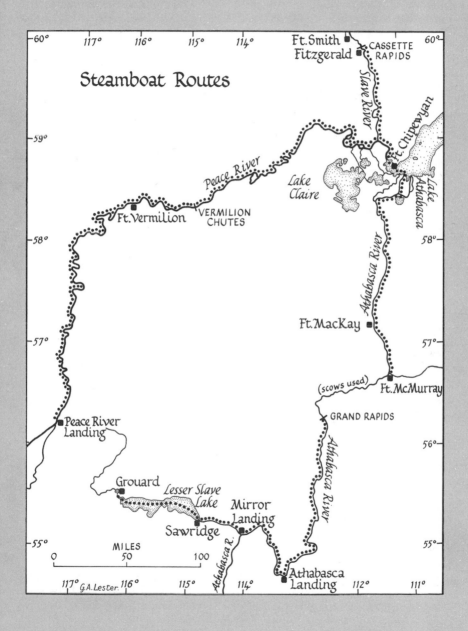

Steamboat Routes

60°   117°   116°   115°   114°   Ft.Smith   60°
                                       Fitzgerald   CASSETTE RAPIDS

Slave River

59°   Peace River   Lake Claire   Ft. Chipewyan   Lake Athabasca

Ft.Vermilion   VERMILION CHUTES

58°   58°

Athabasca River

Ft.MacKay

57°   57°

                                              (scows used)   Ft.McMurray

Peace River Landing   GRAND RAPIDS

                                                                              56°

Grouard   Lesser Slave Lake   Mirror Landing   Athabasca River

55°   Sawridge   55°

MILES
0   50   100

117°   G.A.Lester.   116°   115°   Athabasca R.   114°   Athabasca Landing   112°   111°

trading business in the Peace River country. By 1903 the partners sold out to Revillon Frères and in association with J. H. Woods he formed the Northern Transportation Company and turned his attention to building a steamboat which he hoped would ascend the Lesser Slave Lake River.

Just as the *Athabasca* had disappointed the Hudson's Bay Company, so in 1904 Cornwall's first steamer, the *Midnight Sun*, failed to ascend the Lesser Slave Lake River to its source in Lesser Slave Lake. She could not get over the shallow water of the worst set of rapids. To overcome that disability, however, he soon built his *Northern Light*, a sidewheeler, and by 1907 was in business on that lake. Then he was able to carry freight and passengers as far as Mirror Landing on the *Midnight Sun*, whisk them over the sixteen-mile portage to Saulteau Landing and re-embark them on the *Northern Light* for the trip to Lesser Slave Lake town at the lake's west end. By 1909 the Northern Transportation Company had put another sternwheeler, the *Northland Sun*, on the run from Athabasca to Mirror Landing. At the same time, because of a conflict of names on official registers, it changed the name of the *Northern Light* to the *Northland Light*. The next year Cornwall completed construction of a new sternwheeler of very shallow draft which he called the *Northland Call*.

By 1912 there were so many steamers operating upstream of Grand Rapids that it is hard to keep track of them. By then the old *Athabasca*, the relic of Klondike days, seems to have been taken out of service and the Hudson's Bay Company had set to work to build two new steamers. One, the *Slave River*, launched in June 1912, was to be used on Lesser Slave Lake. The other, the *Athabasca River*, launched about a month later, was to run up and down to Grand Rapids. She was 130 feet long and her engines and boilers had come from the old *Hazelton* which for several years had worked up and down the rapids of the Skeena River. About the same time, the Northern Transportation Company added further vessels to its fleet, the *Northland Echo* and the *Northland Star*.

But the same Jim Cornwall of the Northern Transportation Company whose steamers had done so much to boost Athabasca Landing also cast his eyes on bigger game. As early as 1905 he had formed the Athabasca Railway Company by means of which he had hoped to run a railway from Edmonton to The Landing. While on paper his railway company remained in existence for a few years, the actual railroad which came to be built was the Canadian Northern Railway line which started regular passenger service to The Landing in September 1912. By that time scores of settlers were flocking into the Peace River country and during the few summer months when they could operate, Cornwall's steamers and those of the Hudson's Bay Company, did a good business. With all this new found prosperity Athabasca Landing rapidly grew into a busy town.

The Landing's reign was of short duration, however, because other men with railroads on their minds had been looking north from Edmonton. Before long two of these lines started grading their way north; the Edmonton, Dunvegan and British Columbia (nicknamed the Exceedingly Dangerous and Badly Constructed Railroad) headed for Peace River Crossing—otherwise known as Peace River Landing, and finally as Peace River town—on the one hand and on the other, the Alberta and Great

Waterways through the muskegs from Edmonton to Fort McMurray.

By the fall of 1914 J. D. McArthur's E.D. & B.C. building on a course which took it some thirty miles west of The Landing had crossed the Athabasca River at old Mirror Landing and was running trains to Sawridge at the east end of Lesser Slave Lake. Its arrival brought many changes. Mirror Landing lost its importance and steamers to that point were no longer necessary. It gradually disappeared after the railway created on the opposite side of the river a rival town for its divisional point and named it Smith, after one of the famous railway-building engineers, Rathbone Smith.

By 1916 when the E.D. & B.C. had descended the long hill to Peace River Crossing and provided an end-of-steel on the Peace River over a hundred miles closer to the Arctic, Athabasca Landing began to lose much of its former business. Now goods could be shipped to Peace River Landing by train, taken in hand there by Peace River steamers and carried down to the barrier of the Vermilion Chutes where they could be reloaded into sternwheelers such as the *Grahame* plying from Fort McMurray to Fitzgerald. If they now followed a more circuitous route to Fort Smith, it was a much easier one than that which forced them to fight the Grand Rapids.

While the residents of Athabasca Landing had been watching the E.D. & B.C. on the west take business away from them, the Alberta and Great Waterways to the east gave them fresh cause for alarm. For its primary purpose was to strike the navigable portion of the Athabasca River at Fort McMurray and thus circumvent the Grand Rapids and the rough water for eighty-odd miles below them. Its builders chose a route through sand hills and muskeg north to Lac La Biche and thence, more or less following the old trail, headed north near Heart Lake to Wiau, Christina and Gregoire lakes. Athabascans watched uneasily as this railway straggled its way across the muskegs north of Lac La Biche. Nevertheless they had until 1917 before the AGW, having come within striking distance of its final terminus, put the finishing touches to what the E.D. & B.C. had started and deprived them of their steamboat business. Before that, of course, the downriver steamboats had deserted them.

No one had ever taken a sternwheeler down the Grand Rapids but in 1914 the time had come to try that desperate venture. During high water that year the Hudson's Bay Company ran its *Athabasca River* and the Northern Transportation Company took two of its steamers through that dangerous passage. For the run through the Grand Rapids Jim Cornwall took command of his company's *Northland Echo* and with Joe Bird as pilot successfully made the leap through the foaming millrace. Eventually at Fort McMurray he replaced her with a new steamboat which was given the same name. Some of these steamers which had considered Athabasca Landing as their home port were put into service on the run from Fort McMurray to Fitzgerald and at least one was transferred to the Peace River. With new railways reaching out to new railheads, Athabasca's days as the gateway to the North were over.

Only its freighting teams stuck by it, although, because of the advancing railways, they too suffered. For a twenty-year reign the freighters heading their teams out from Athabasca or returning from some far-off place came and went purposefully but with little commotion. Their success depended much on sobriety and steadfastness but little on showmanship. During the era of freighting teams no town in Alberta saw the continual entry or departure of so many freighters as Athabasca, which was the headquarters of scores of these men who made their living by hauling from its end-of-steel.

Their point of departure, of course, was Athabasca Landing but their destinations were often hundreds of miles away along the few winter trails chopped out of the heavy forest or upstream or downstream along the river's ice. Their longer trips were to Peace River Crossing, 250 miles away, or occasionally to some point far beyond that. Their shorter ones took them to Calling Lake, Pelican, Sandy, Wabasca and even to Trout Lake, which later on, because its lake trout excelled all others, came to be called Peerless. The oil camps at Pelican Portage and at the mouth of the House River were other destinations and after 1914 when George Mills, the foreman of the government crew, cut the winter road from House River to Fort McMurray, they carried freight to the oil derricks near there or Fort MacKay. Although scows still swept their loads through the Grand Rapids during the summer, the sternwheelers had practically stopped running out of Athabasca Landing. Much of the freight, therefore, had to be left until winter when the teams could operate. As Athabasca's paper, the *Northern News*, stated in February 1914: "During the last week 200 teams have gone down the river."

Out of the hundreds of freighters, old-timers vividly recall a score or so. High on that roster are men like William Carson, Raynor Whitley, C. Anderson, the Taylor brothers, Roger Ferguson, Jack the Ripper, Jack Rice, Ran Gibbons and J. R. Leith. And a hardy lot of men they were. Unfortunately not even these men, colourful enough as individuals and steadfast in their loyalty to Athabasca, could recapture the aura of romance the town lost when the sternwheelers left for rivers farther north.

Perhaps nothing else had contributed to that aura so much as had the names of Jim Cornwall's steamers, the *Midnight Sun*, and the various *Northlands*—the *Star*, *Light*, *Echo* and *Call*—names filled with the allure of the magic lands of caribou and muskox, white fox, polar bears and white whales. Yet the *Midnight Sun*, *Northland Call* and the others were no pampered darlings; each steamer's charm lay in its smell of wood smoke, fish and greasy bacon, for it had work to do. No tall, lithe yacht was she slicing through the water but a work horse, short, broad and flatbottomed—a scow with a superstructure. And like a scow, when nightfall found her, she tied up to a tree along the river bank where she waited out the few hours of darkness. Her fires burned low, her boiler rumbled and muttered uneasily, in accompaniment to the variety of snores arising from the weary, sleeping crew, and all the quiet night sounds of the forest floated out to her.

Soon—too soon for the vocal sleepers—the myriad stars faded out and the Milky Way vanished. From out of the morning sky dropped the soul-stirring cry of the wild geese beating their way north, the "unseen flight of strong hosts prophesying as they go." Cooking pots clattered. Scorching bannock and frying bacon assailed awakened nostrils. With a bang someone opened the furnace door and noisily pitched huge logs onto the fire. In no time, it seemed, the mooring place was disappearing behind the bend as the paddle wheels splashed off downstream.

Short of having enjoyed a voyage on one of the Athabasca steamers, the best way to get some conception of such a trip is to quote from the writings of some of the lucky or ardent souls who travelled down the Arctic-seeking waters. Warburton Pike, the hunter and explorer who boarded the *Athabasca* at The Landing towards the end of June 1889, was one of these. Among his few fellow passengers was Mr. Flett, who "was just returning from a visit to his native country, the Orkney Islands, after an absence of forty-four years in the service of the Company, all of which time was spent in the wildest part of the North. He was full of the wonderful changes that had taken place since he was a boy, but finding himself completely lost in civilization, had hurried back. . . ."

Because of low water that season, after snagging on sand bars off and on for three days, the *Athabasca* was forced to tie up at the mouth of the Pelican River and to send a skiff down to Grand Rapids asking the company's men there to bring up sufficient scows to carry the boat's load onward. After a wait of ten days they appeared and while the sternwheeler made her way back to The Landing Pike went downstream with them.

Three years later, Miss Elizabeth Taylor, the first woman tourist to tackle the far-flung waterway, boarded the *Athabasca*. She was fascinated as she watched the load of supplies it took on board for all the northern points. "Such a variety of packages addressed to such interesting places, tobacco put up in parcels of 65 lbs. each stitched up in dull red painted canvas, boxes of 'Old Honesty' oysters from Mobile, Ala.; strong, polished kegs of sugar for the Catholic Missions, plainer unpolished ones for the H. B. Co.; bales of blankets of 95 lbs. weight from England, sacks of flour, great flat greasy sacks of bacon, boxes of apricots and canned peaches, and boxes of evaporated fruit."

In due course after going through the Grand Rapids in scows, Miss Taylor boarded the *Grahame* at Fort McMurray along with "Bishop Young, who leaves us at Fort Smith; Bishop Reeve, and Bishop Clut, the Catholic one who goes to Fort Good Hope, I think. Dr. Mackay from Chipewyan is on board," along with the oxen destined for the portage near Fort Smith.

On June 19 they reached Lake Athabasca, but because of the danger in crossing it during a period of high winds, they were held up for four days. During the delay the oxen ran out of hay and since there was no grass on shore, the "captain took up a contribution for the oxen in the shape of pink calico bags of hay which are the only furnishings of the bunks. As I had a rubber bed [air mattress] my tick was among the first to go." She had some consolation, however, at Grahame's Landing where the oxen pulled them across the portage to Fort Smith in a lumber wagon. It was no joy ride, however, because the "mosquitoes, gnats, and bulldogs were quite up to my expectations. I have never seen anything like them. Even the half breed carters wore head nets." On the way they stopped for a meal at what she described as a picturesque camp around a great open fire. "A long line of 'bannocks' or galettes, standing on end, propped up by sticks, cooked before the fire and a big HBC kettle was slung on a small sapling."

Bishop Reeve told her how on one occasion hunger had caused him to interrupt his preaching. ". . . he stopped in the midst of a service once to snatch up his gun, which was close by, and bring down a goose from a flock which was passing over. But he said he did it instinctively, and his wife and children were literally without food at the time."

One of the more graphic accounts of embarking on the *Grahame* at Fort McMurray and eventually going down to the Arctic is that of Agnes Deans Cameron who did so in 1908. Later in the season when the water was low she made the return trip south from Fort Chipewyan and in mid afternoon the *Grahame* ran hard and fast on a sand bar. Reversing the engines did not pull her off and she remained there all through the night. As daylight returned the crew set to work to carry much of her lading to some scows. Meanwhile, the captain set out a kedge-anchor and by fastening a line to it winched her off and reloaded.

While Miss Cameron's descriptions of matters affecting the various craft in which she travelled are full of interest, her references to many of the characters she met are doubly so. At Fort Chipewyan she talked with one of the grand old men of the North, William Wylie, the Hudson's Bay Company's blacksmith. As a lad in 1863 starting his employment with the company he had arrived at Fort Chipewyan straight out from the Orkneys. In all his days he had never seen a city, for from his home he had boarded the company's ship which carried him to Hudson Bay whence up the hundreds of miles of forested rivers he had travelled with the brigade until after crossing the Methy Portage he had descended to Fort Chipewyan. During nearly all of his long residence there he had been the company's blacksmith. Around 1872 the nails and ironwork which had gone into Roderick MacFarlane's rebuilt Fort Chipewyan had been his handiwork. So had much of the metal work that went into the *Grahame* when she was built in 1883. In all his years at the fort, he had never been farther away than the limits which the steamer could navigate, Fort McMurray to Grahame's Landing north and south, and from Fond du Lac at the east end of the long lake to Vermilion Chutes west up the Peace River. Nevertheless, he had become one of the outstanding men of Fort Chipewyan and of him as an old man Miss Cameron said:

To him these are innocuous days of ease, in which we are falling into luxuriousness with all its weakening influence. "It was much better in the old days when we had only dried meat and fish-oil. Nowadays, when we have flour and tinned meats and preserved fruits, all my teeth are coming out!" . . . Talking with the old gentleman, you are conscious of the innate moral strength rather than the mechanical skill of the craftsman. Instinctively you feel the splendid power of his presence and come out from his forge murmuring, "Thank God I have seen a *man* this day."

A month or so later when she returned to Fort McMurray on the *Grahame*, she found that just as the Fletts had done some twenty years earlier, William Wylie and his family had decided to make a trip home to the Orkneys and were on their way out. But the old gentleman never reached his homeland. Catching the train at Edmonton, he and his family went as far as Winnipeg but, possibly because he was feeling unwell, they returned to Edmonton, where on January 3, 1909, he died.

Having come to know many of the aristocracy of Fort Chipewyan, the Mercredis, Fletts, Wylies and Frasers, Miss Cameron also met some of the Lutits (sometimes spelled Loutit), a family of which she correctly said, "There were Lutits in Chipewyan as far back as the old journals reach. The Scottish blood has intermingled with that of Cree and Chipewyan and the resultant in this day's generation is a family of striking young people. . . ." She said that the patriarch of the family "tells of the days when as a young man he served the Company, and 'for breakfast on the march they gave you a club and showed you a rabbit-track!' " Speaking of the younger men of the family, she went on:

George Loutit without help brought a scow with four thousand pounds from Athabasca Landing to Chipewyan through the ninety miles of rapids. His brother Billy, carrying a special dispatch of the Mounted Police, ran with a hand-sled (and no dogs) from Chipewyan to Fort Smith and back in three days—a distance of two hundred miles at least. Once, when the river rose suddenly in the night, Billy unloaded nine tons from one scow to another, astonishing the owners, who snored while Billy was toiling upward in the night. The rivermen tell of George Loutit quarreling with a man one afternoon in a saloon at Edmonton and throwing his adversary out of the window. When he heard him slump, George immediately thought of the North as a most desirable place and started hot-foot for Athabasca Landing, a hundred miles away. He arrived there in time for noon luncheon next day.

While stories of such prowess never suffer in the telling, my friend Raynor Whitley, an old freighter whose rippling mind bubbles over with memories of the early days, is the authority for one of Billy Lutit's adventures. In the forenoon of the day when the Athabasca River broke up in 1904 an ice jam formed just below the town about where the modern bridge is. Within hours the pent-up waters rose and flooded the lower edge of the town—the river bank business section of that time. The water rose until it was four feet deep over the threshold of the main entrance of the Grand Union Hotel and a canoe could have floated in through the hotel windows. The Hudson's Bay Company's warehouse somewhat lower down the bank was hopelessly flooded. Thousands of dollars worth of the company's supplies piled there waiting for the ice to go out so that they could be sent down on the waiting scows were covered by water and in danger of being utterly destroyed.

Leslie Wood, the company's factor, needed help and sent two messengers speeding off with letters asking for men to be sent from the company's Edmonton headquarters a hundred miles away. At this point Billy Lutit and Raynor Whitley came in. One of Wood's messengers was Billy and the other, whose name is forgotten now, galloped his horse to Whitley's stopping place at Stony Creek some twenty miles south along the trail to Edmonton. Arriving there about 3 PM, he handed a note and a letter to

Raynor's father. The note asked Mr. Whitley to rush the letter to W. T. Livock, the company's factor at Edmonton. Turning to Raynor, then a strapping lad fifteen years old, his father said: "Get your horse and go—and hurry up."

So, bearing the letter and a sandwich or two, Raynor galloped off on his eighty-mile ride. Some ten miles along his way as horse and rider trotted around a sharp bend in the trail they came face to face with two black bears. The three startled animals reacted automatically. As Raynor says: "The bears snorted, tumbled over backwards and ran south, the horse reared, swung around and galloped back north. But I stayed right there—I fell off."

After back-tracking a mile or so, he caught his horse, turned him around and resumed his ride. All through the night he rode, stopping once in a while to get off and ease his aching buttocks and to let his horse drink at a brook and relax for a minute or so. His pony had to swim the Vermilion River, so Raynor slid off, hung on to his tail and thus crossed the icy water. At eleven o'clock next morning he rode up to old Fort Edmonton and delivered his letter to the factor.

Mr. Livock took immediate action and ordered twenty-five men to make all the speed they could to The Landing. When they arrived they set to work carrying the goods out to dry. The sugar, of course, was ruined, the salt a soggy mess, but the bags of flour as they usually did had allowed water to penetrate about an inch only and form a crust while inside that the rest of the contents had kept dry. Clothing and calico and blankets had been saturated and were in danger of mildewing. Raynor says that for days every available fence, building or toilet for three hundred yards along the bank of the Athabasca post flaunted gaily coloured cloth goods drying out.

In Fort Edmonton, of course, after Mr. Livock had issued his orders, he turned to Raynor, congratulated him upon his remarkable ride and handed him five dollars. On his part, the fifteen-year-old lad went out to untie his horse, lead him to some stable and get breakfast for himself.

But just as he strode through the gate of the fort's picket fence, who should he meet but Billy Lutit bearing Leslie Wood's second letter. All through the night also without stopping except to drink at a rill or a brook, he too had jogged continuously. Having left Athabasca Landing about noon the previous day on foot, he had run all the way—a hundred miles in twenty-three hours. The Lutits, all of them, were justly famous men and we shall meet them again, but we are not yet through with Agnes Deans Cameron.

Miss Cameron arrived at Grahame's Landing, as she said, "on the heels of a tragedy." A few days earlier a new priest, Father Brohan, a young man fresh from a seminary set amidst the peaceful fields of France, had reached the mission at Fort Smith to take the place of Father Bremond, who after serving there for ten years was going back to France for a holiday. The younger man, entranced by the majesty of the mile-wide river at the point where its placid waters started their surging swirl into the Rapids of the Drowned, persuaded the older man to take him across the river in the mission canoe. On Sunday, June 14 they crossed without incident, but on their return trip steered a course perilously close to the rapids. Probably all would have been well had not Father Brohan, becoming alarmed, made a nervous movement and capsized the canoe. As an old Indian woman, the only eye-witness, said, "One arm lifted out of the river, the paddle pointed to the sky—a cry came over the water, and that was all." Two more names had been added to the roster of priests whom the northland had claimed.

Strangely enough Miss Cameron's book fails to comment on the fuel the sternwheelers used. For decades all of them were woodburners and since they fairly ate up cord wood, scores of men earned their livelihood cutting and piling it at strategic points along the rivers. The pile had to be at the very edge of the bank and at a point where the rivers' scouring had left deep water so that the boat could be pulled hard against the shore to make it possible for the crew to cross a gangway in carrying the fuel on board.

Bill Burns, an ex-boxer who had chosen to live in the North, spent several years as a wood-cutter. In the fall of 1924 Captain McLeod of the *Athabasca River* dropped him off at a fine stand of spruce about three miles south of Embarras Portage and promised him $3.50 per cord for all the wood he could pile within fifty feet of the bank and $3.00 a cord for all piled farther back. Bright and early next morning on the highest spot he could find nearby, Bill started to build his log cabin and a few days later when his partner joined him he had it almost finished. By spring when the other man left, a long pile of neatly stacked wood stood as witness to how hard they had worked. At times, of course, they took a day or so off to visit trappers or other axemen within walking distance of their shack. The two trades fitted together nicely and by cutting wood many a native added $500 a year to his income.

Few men have columns erected to their memory. Of those who do, scarcely any are men of the labouring class. And yet where the 60th parallel of latitude, the north boundary of Alberta, crosses the Slave River immediately south of Fort Smith stands a concrete monument to a wood-cutter!

To the Memory of
Edward Martin
Died June 13, 1928

The Best Woodcutter
of the North, He Supplied
Fuel to Steamboats

A Silent and Lone Man
Who Took Pride in His
Work and Built an
Honest Pile

Ed Martin was a "loner," a taciturn man with no real cronies, who lived in his tiny shack across the Slave River from Fort Smith. No one knew anything of Ed's early history. Everybody, however, knew him as a man of integrity. Unlike many a man who cut his wood carelessly and stacked it loosely in an effort to defraud the company, Ed cut only the best wood and piled it carefully and symmetrically. Occasionally he would cross the river to the Hudson's Bay Company's store to pick up his pay and buy some supplies and with scarcely a word would return to his cabin and his cord wood.

Then one day a native tending his nets heard a single shot and along with a Mounted Policeman went to Ed's shack to find that he had killed·himself. No papers of any sort in his shack threw any light on his background or indicated any relations, but a suicide note referred to a sum of money he had in a tin box—$1,182.10.

The publicity attendant on his suicide and the interest aroused by the relatively large amount of money in his estate brought letters from a variety of men and women in Canada and the United States all alleging kinship, but none could substantiate their claims. In due course the money in Ed's tin box was lodged with the Public Administrator of the Northwest Territories, where to all appearances it seemed likely to remain for all time. But many men who had admired the integrity of the woodcutter were moved by generous motives and they, including a judge, urged the administrator to use part of the unclaimed money to erect a monument to the faithful worker who few really knew but all respected. It cost some $500 and the rest of the money remained with the administrator.

And there the story should have ended.

But it didn't. Some years went by and finally an aging lady from the United States arrived in Edmonton with indubitable proof that she was indeed Ed Martin's mother and therefore heir to his $1,100. Moreover, she went to see the remains of his shack and the monument which sentimental hands had erected to his memory. Neither grateful nor sentimental, she declared that she would never have spent the money so foolishly and demanded the full $1,182.10. She got it too. In the end, out of his own pocket, the administrator had to repay the money spent on the memorial. As for the monument itself, it remains still dedicated to the man "who took pride in his work and built an honest pile."

The piles themselves and the men who built them were an essential part of the complicated system of northern transport which employed so many men of varied skills. It supplied the livelihood of wood-cutters and roustabouts, famous pilots like Johnny Berens who served the Hudson's Bay Company for fifty-nine years, Joe Bird, Louis Bourassa and Julian Cardinal, as well as canny engineers like William Hay, John Sutherland and "Judge" Johnson. In supreme command of each sternwheeler, of course, was the captain and in this capacity a long line of men far above the common stamp served their companies on the Athabasca and on the other rivers.

In the early days to start the long procession came J. M. Smith who built the *Grahame* and J. S. Segers, both of whom ran steamers on many of the continent's rivers. Later on others operated out of Athabasca Landing; G. D. Barber, skipper of the *Northland Call* and manager of the Northern Transportation Company, C. W. Riddle of the *Northern Light*, and the famous E. B. Haight of the *Northland Sun* who at one time took turns with John Gullion in commanding the *Peace River*. Before coming to the Athabasca Haight had led an adventurous career, having gone to Egypt in 1884 as one of the Nile Voyageurs and then taken part in the North West Rebellion a year later. Other men better known on the river below McMurray and on the Mackenzie were Captain Matheson who rebuilt the

Northland Echo after she ran the Grand Rapids, and Captain J. W. Mills. He it was who built the *Fort McMurray* at McMurray in 1915 and a few weeks later near Vermilion Chutes suffered with her when she struck a rock and for some weeks squatted waist-deep in water and mud. And there were many more, including Captains Cowley, McLeod, Myers and Thompson, all men who had to know everything about ships, shoals, sand bars and navigation.

It was men like these who watched the prospects of the river towns—the end-of-steel towns—Athabasca Landing, Peace River Landing and Fort McMurray, wax and wane. As we have seen, Athabasca Landing's comparatively long reign ended when in 1916 the E.D. & B.C. Railway reached the Peace River. Thenceforth for a brief span northern freight went down from Peace River town. Perhaps the most noticeable shift made to capitalize on this Peace River route was that of the Hudson's Bay Company's *Athabasca River* which had been built at The Landing in 1912, ran the Grand Rapids in 1914 and thrashed her way down the Athabasca and then up the Peace to the Chutes. There during the ensuing winter she was dragged around that waterfall and then replaced the old *Peace River* in the service between there and Hudson Hope. Subsequently, when she brought northern freight down to the Chutes her lading was transferred to the recently built *Fort McMurray*.

Peace River town's brief burst of serious participation in transshipping freight to the far North ended when about 1921 the AGW became capable of carrying goods to Cache 23 a few miles south of McMurray. During that period which saw much activity, the famous *D. A. Thomas* was launched at Peace River. Eventually the Hudson's Bay Company bought her and decided to transfer her to the McMurray-Fitzgerald route and this involved toppling her down the Vermilion Chutes, a vastly more risky operation than that accomplished by the *Athabasca River* which during a winter many years previously had been dragged upstream over the Chutes.

The *D. A. Thomas* was a big boat, 167 feet long with a beam of 40 feet and few men would have dared to try to coax her into the exact spot in the mile-wide, rock-strewn rapids, from whence she could make the hazardous plunge down the sheer thirty-foot drop of the Chutes. When, however, Captain Cowley and his pilot Louis Bourassa manoeuvred her to that spot her hull completely filled the gap they had chosen to descend and then on the hidden lip of the fall she grounded. But luck was with her. The rushing water, piling up behind her, raised her enough so that she slipped over the crest. Her bow dropped and her stern rose until she was canted at such an angle that she must plunge or perish. A whirling backlash at the foot of the falls dropped tons of water over her bow but she withstood it and nosed her prow up through the wave. At the same time, of course, her stern went down and the hidden rocks ripped off half her madly thrashing stern wheel. Before anybody could cry out or cheer, she had floated clear of the danger and edged forward calmly into the bubble-flecked water below. Then after minor repairs she was able to make Fitzgerald under her own power.

Running down the Vermilion Chutes or through the Grand Rapids or ramming rocks, grounding on sand bars or being frozen in drifting ice were only part of a steamboat captain's life. In times of favourable water, while ever vigilant, a skipper did little but watch the river winding ahead or observe the wildlife in the water or on shore. Squirrels swam the great river, so did lynx and once one of these big-footed cats misjudged a boat's speed and found himself lifted in a wild circle by the terrible thrashing wheel. Unbelievably startled, he landed in the water again and made double quick time for the far bank.

Bears and moose frequently stood watching the big boats approach and in doing so invariably risked their lives, as revealed by Charles Mair, who on ascending the Athabasca on the *Grahame* in company with a lot of disillusioned returning Klondikers, related that:

Next morning, upon rounding a point, three full-grown moose were seen ahead, swimming across the river. An exciting, and even hazardous, scene ensued on board, the whole Klondike crowd firing, almost at random, hundreds of shots without effort. Two of the noble brutes kept on, and reached the shore, disappearing in the woods; but the third, a three-year-old bull moose, foolishly turned, and lost its life in consequence.

A skipper generally looked on such activities with a benign eye. Captain McLeod of the *D. A. Thomas*, however, was said to be more wary of larger animals and to keep a rifle at hand in the pilot house to ward off any possible attacks by swimming moose. In case they should turn on his ship and gore it, he was ready for them. Indeed, it is alleged that once when he saw a moose high up the hillside apparently pawing the earth and looking as though it might charge down and attack the steamer he stopped his craft and shot it. One of his predecessors was said to have taken even greater precautions to safeguard his ship and his passengers. Watching a moose which they had already left about a quarter of a mile behind, this captain landed, climbed hundreds of feet up the steep hillside and crawled along till he shot it. He had noted that the big black animal seemed to be getting his dander up and might attack the boat on its return trip. They took no chances, those steamboat captains!

And indeed they carried a heavy responsibility. But none of them would ever quit his fascinating work until advancing years dimmed his vision which for so many summers had read all the information that various currents and colours of water could convey to squinting eyes that at times would not lift from watching the water for half an hour at a stretch. Demanding their work may have been, but above all their life on the Athabasca, Peace and Slave rivers had an appeal that could never be measured by the pay they received.

CHAPTER THIRTEEN
Mainly Mounties

During the short, balmy summer months the steamers carried any mail destined for the North. All through the long, bitter months of winter, however, the mail carriers and their dog teams brought their prodigious powers and their hardihood and reliability into play along the winding, lonesome bush trails. They came of a long line dating back before the days when in 1821 George Simpson and his rival at Fort Chipewyan had relied on their winter expresses to keep themselves and their associates posted on the happenings up and down all the great frozen waterways. During open water, of course, canoes passing and repassing carried these couriers back and forth, but in winter, lashing on their snowshoes and shouting to their dogs, the mail carriers set out on their weeks-long journeys.

In more recent times the Hudson's Bay Company, as well as carrying its own mail, extended its service to help the missionaries, the Mounted Police and the few other people in the area. By 1908, well after an official post office had been established at Athabasca Landing on January 1, 1901, but before Fort Chipewyan got a regular post office in 1912, the government had entered into a contract to have mail carried from Edmonton to Fort Resolution. By 1911, one of the famous Lutits, George, was the official mail carrier on this 750-mile run. In October that year the government announced a new schedule for the winter mail. It was to leave Edmonton on November 29 and at monthly intervals until February to carry letters only and to take the route across country to Lac La Biche and thence by the old trail which was later to be followed by the Alberta and Great Waterways Railway. Later on, in 1915, after the winter road had been cut through to McMurray and after Joe Bird had piloted the *Northland Echo* down the Grand Rapids, he undertook to deliver the mail during the summer by scow and then to return to House River by pack horses. For the rest of the year mail deliveries were made back and forth over the winter road. North of McMurray steamers and dog teams carried on as they had for many years. In 1915, following this road, the telegraph line reached McMurray.

Winter after winter the famous travellers, Joe Bird, Billy and George Lutit, one or more of the Bourassas and many another mail carrier snow-shoed from post to post, urging their five or six dogs forward on their week-long trip to the next spot of white human habitation. For most of the winter, with the temperature about thirty degrees below, these jaunts were more or less routine. But when the wind howled and the relentlessly sifting snow beat into their faces, only the drivers' determination and the dogs' courage kept them going. When the temperature dropped into the forties or fifties below zero and the sleds pulled hard on the sand-like snow, few but the most hardy men could face these trips.

For driving dogs, such an exhilarating exercise when all conditions were right, entailed many a difficulty when the weather was bad: the terrible, tendon-tearing pain of mal-de-racquette, when the driver's snowshoe harness was ill adjusted or when even the strongest man had been too long on the trail; the ice balling up between the dogs' toes, necessitating moccasins for their feet, and many another wearying hardship. A night's camp in the snow, a routine matter in fair weather, was an endurance test in foul. Making a fire, setting the dogs' moccasins on sticks to dry, standing their fish in the snow before the flames, making a windbreak and a bed—all this was no lark even for the hardiest man.

Even when travelling was not unduly difficult an occasional accident befell some of the best drivers. Joe Mercredi of Fort Chipewyan told the writer of one time when the Hudson's Bay Company's express from Fort Dunvegan never reached Fort Chipewyan. He could not remember the names or the year because it was in his father's time, but the details were clear. The express, carried by two men, had been expected about Christmas but that season slipped by past New Year's and on into January and still neither the men nor the dogs nor any news of them came in. Finally the factor sent another pair to go as far up the Peace as Fort Vermilion to search for them and to see if they had called there.

For some weeks the weather had been calm but not until they were nearly to the Vermilion Chutes did the searchers find any sign of the express men's passage downriver. Then, following their half-obliterated tracks which led them up the river's bank into a clump of trees, they cleared up the mystery. There lay their sled and the bodies of the two men. Unfortunately the writer, intent upon the fate of the men, did not think to question Joe about the fate of the dogs. The trippers, however, had evidently eaten their evening meal in peace and had tucked themselves into their blankets. Then during the night, probably in a high wind, a rotting poplar tree had broken off and fallen right across the two men either killing them instantly or injuring them so that they could not get free.

While a mail carrier's life was made up of hard, lonesome treks, the steamboats provided scores of adventurous men with easy, companionable access to many of the places the carriers visited. As the years went by more and more of them loaded their gear and supplies on the *Athabasca River* or the *Grahame* and set forth. Every boat had its quota of traders, missionaries, Mounted Police, oil or mineral prospectors, scientists and an occasional screwball. Once in a while one or two of them perished but most were of a hardy sort who met the North on its own terms. One of its most pleasurable terms, however, was the tingle that suffused each one of them when the steamer's thrashing paddle wheels began churning the water of the first bend below The Landing or slipping past the tar sand cliffs at the end of the snye at McMurray and they were starting out for the thrilling world of the northern rivers. At last they were off, some for the first time, some merely returning to a well-known shack on some far-off river, creek or bay, but all of them striving to hide their excitement behind a thin mask of nonchalance.

In the case of the Mounted Police, their nonchalance was more a mark of the constables than a mask. In 1893 to keep tab on the many trappers, natives and sometimes even criminally-minded men, the Mounted Police began establishing small detachments—sometimes of one man only—all over the vast Mackenzie watershed. That year Inspector D. M. Howard was posted to Athabasca Landing. Before long he had stationed some of his men at Mirror Landing, Lesser Slave Lake and the Grand Rapids. High on the list of the duties of his eight constables was that of preventing the illegal flow of liquor into the area where at the time its sale was prohibited. The many seizures they made and the host of tricks by which bootleggers tried to, and frequently did, outwit them would fill a large volume.

With extremely rare exceptions, every Mountie was a splendid specimen of a man and of a peace officer. Just as the original NWMP had soon mastered the technique of making their way amidst the hardships of the open prairie, soon these men had learned all the tricks of life on the great rivers, in the endless forests and amidst the howling blizzards of the ice-locked, sea-like northern lakes. Of all their activities none was more spectacular than the long patrols they made whether on inspection trips or to bring in some criminal or crazed trapper. Names prominent in the roster of famous patrols were A. M. Jarvis, W. H. Routledge, A. Pedley, R. Field, E. A. Pelletier, "Nitchie" Thorne and "Denny" LaNauze.

Early in January 1897 only months before the Klondike craze, the police sent out the first of their long northern patrols, consisting of A. M. Jarvis and Staff Sergeant Hetherington. They were provided with three teams of four dogs each and two spare dogs. J. Gullion and P. Lutit, Jr., another of the famous family, went along as guides and drivers. Setting out by way of Lac La Biche, they called at Heart Lake, McCallum's post on the Clearwater River and Fort McMurray. Going on from there, they stopped at the Métis settlement at Little Red River and two others between there and Fort Chipewyan. The white and half-breed population there totalled about 150, not counting some thirty lodges of Chipewyan Indians and twelve lodges of Crees, who seemed to be more or less permanently in residence. Jarvis was told that during the summer six or seven hundred Indians came in to trade.

Continuing the trip, the patrol found Campbell Young of Edmonton and a George Martin trapping along the Slave River, and in due course reached the head of the rapids at what was then called Grahame's Landing but which we now call Fitzgerald, where some twelve Indian and half-breed families lived. They reached Fort Resolution, the northern extremity of their trip, on February 13, some six weeks after they had headed out from Fort Saskatchewan into the most severe of the winter's weather.

Setting out south again Jarvis retraced some of the route he had taken but turned off to the west and ascended the Peace River. At Little Red River, near where navigation was interrupted by the Vermilion Chutes, he found a small Hudson's Bay Company post and then went on to the Fort Vermilion area where W. D. Wilson supervised the company's main establishment. Included in the straggling Fort Vermilion settlement were the Anglican and Roman Catholic missions and the prosperous farm operated by the Lawrence family, as well as trading posts owned by Twelve-Foot Davis and Fred Brick. On the whole, Fort Vermilion was a substantial settlement of 168 people keeping an eye on 159 horses, 297 cattle and 54 hogs.

From there the party continued upstream to Peace River Crossing and reached Fort Saskatchewan on April 15. Jarvis and his companion had accomplished a remarkable trip of over two thousand miles in the very heart of the winter. On his return from that first NWMP patrol into the North he made recommendations covering the Indians and the protection of the game animals in the area he had traversed. One result was that during the following summer the police opened an outpost at Fort Smith under Corporal Trotter.

Inspector W. H. Routledge who left Fort Saskatchewan on December 16, 1897, with three men, three sleds and thirteen dogs and went down the Mackenzie watershed as far as Fort Simpson and back in a hundred days elapsed time, was the next policeman to make a long patrol. As he said on his return, ". . . the party all in good health and without the loss of any dogs, completing the round trip of 2,172 miles in 80 days of actual travel. The hours of travel each day averaged from 5 a.m. until 5:30 p.m. with 4 'spells' for meals, &c." Though he had to share the credit with his experienced dog drivers, his trip was nonetheless a remarkable achievement.

By 1902 the police had established a three-man detachment at Fort Chipewyan. Before long two of its outstanding men, Sergeant R. Field and Constable A. Pedley, became involved in dramatic and indeed traumatic patrols. Fate seems to have chosen Field to deal with men whose reason had become unhinged. News of his first case reached him from the Anglican mission at Hay River.

An entry in the mission records on January 2, 1902, revealed that "Poor A. L. Willson who has been helping us in the mission service for nearly two full years . . . shows unmistakable signs of insanity." By the time Field arrived on February 15 the man was "hopelessly insane" and one of the mission staff using the missionary's dog team helped take the man to Fort Chipewyan. From there in the dead of winter Field took the crazy man along the lonesome route to Fort Saskatchewan, over five hundred miles away, and returned to his detachment.

The next year Field got involved in another dangerous episode when from Black Lake—some one hundred and forty miles east along Lake Athabasca to Fond du Lac and then a further seventy miles east along the Black River, and far into Saskatchewan's rocky pre-Cambrian shield —word came that a Chipewyan there was in trouble. Paul Izo Azie had abandoned his family and as a result two children had perished. When he was able, in 1904, Field went to Fond du Lac by canoe, arrested Azie, rounded up the necessary witnesses and started out for Edmonton some seven hundred miles away. Ahead in one canoe went Field, his canoemen and his manacled half-crazed prisoner. Following freely in another canoe came the witnesses. At Fort Chipewyan Field paused to advise Pedley of how he was getting along and then started south up the Athabasca River. At The Landing he procured wagons and the prisoner and the witnesses rode in to Edmonton where poor Azie was sentenced to two years confinement. Then doubling back on their route, Field stopped at Fort Chipewyan, while the witnesses, having lived all summer at government expense, paddled the length of the magnificent lake to tell their homefolk of their exciting visit to Edmonton, the incredible city of ten thousand people.

Since Azie's case was far from being exceptional, it may be wondered why the police went to such effort and expense to subject him to the white man's justice. Their trouble was felt to be justified because it provided an object lesson to demonstrate that no place was too remote and no crime too insignificant for the law to reach out and lay its hand on the criminal.

Soon after he had rejoiced at Field's return, Pedley found himself involved in a much more harrowing experience. During 1904 a Presbyterian minister having travelled into the far North had returned to spend the winter huddled up with Anton Ribeaux, a half-breed, in a dimly lit hut on the banks of the Peace River. The gathering dark of winter, the educational gap between the two and the fact that neither knew more than a few words of the other's language, bore most heavily on the minister, and Ribeaux feared for his sanity. When word of his worries reached Fort Chipewyan, Sergeant Field sent Pedley to look into the matter.

When Pedley reached the shack the depressed missionary had frozen parts of his feet and had become a raving madman. Strapping him onto his sled, poor Pedley returned to Fort Chipewyan and then set out with his charge on his bitterly cold trip to Fort Saskatchewan. In all, the return trip of some thirteen hundred miles occupied some forty-four freezing winter days.

He left Fort Chipewyan about December 10 taking plenty of provisions, blankets and a small tent. He wrapped the mad missionary in warm furs, bundled up his frost-bitten feet in large moccasins, placed him in a sleeping bag and then lashed him to the sled. Soon after starting up the long reaches of the ice-clad river, Pedley ran into a heavy snowstorm and after that the weather turned bitterly cold, at times dropping to nearly fifty below. At dusk each day he camped, fed the dogs and his prisoner who at first ate sparingly and then refused to eat. Day after day the monotonous grind went on—tramp along behind the sled, camp and feed the dogs, let the missionary loose to exercise and sit by the fire and eat, watch him constantly and then sleep lightly.

Before reaching Fort McKay a gale so vicious it would have torn a tent to pieces confined them to a shelterless camp for two days and two nights. Going on the next morning Pedley was able to shoot a caribou and the fresh meat raised the spirits of dogs, Mountie and madman. Looking forward to meeting some other white men at Fort McMurray, he was disappointed to find that its population that winter was one lonely half-breed family. They received the party hospitably and for two days the head of the family assumed charge of the missionary.

After leaving there along the trail heading south to Lac La Biche, Pedley reported:

> Fresh troubles were at hand, however. The missionary grew sullen again and refused to eat. When food could no longer be forced down his throat I became alarmed, and concluded to once more loosen his fastenings to give him exercise, hoping thus to restore his appetite. While I was gathering fuel for a fire he became violent, picked up a stick, and attacked the dogs. Then, seeing me with my arms full of kindling wood, he made a dash for the open prairie. With all his fasting and confinement he gained speed and soon outdistanced me. But I kept on running, and found that he was too weak to go far. In the end I overtook him, and fastened his legs and arms so that he could not do any injury to himself and me.

He then carried the man back about a quarter of a mile and continued until he reached Cheecham's Lake where he met some natives and engaged a guide to accompany him to Lac La Biche. There he hired a team of horses and the rest of his trip to Fort Saskatchewan was fairly restful. Pedley and his prisoner had been nearly a month on the way. The doctor there treated the madman and before long was able to report: "His mind and speech were as good as ever. His life was saved."

After relaxing a few days, Pedley returned to Lac La Biche to pick up his dog team and to hurry home to Fort Chipewyan. But his grim month-long trek had been too heavy a load and at Lac La Biche he broke down and became violently insane. Once more he returned to Fort Saskatchewan by horse and sleigh, but in the hands of friendly traders who delivered him to his comrades whence he was sent to the asylum at Brandon. Fortunately, after six months, he was cured and discharged and went back to further duty with the police force. Eventually at the expiration of his term of service he re-enlisted.

When Pedley was weeks overdue at Fort Chipewyan, Sergeant Field, of course, worried about what misadventures must have befallen him. But he too had his problems. While resting after his return from a long and arduous routine patrol farther north, he looked out over the ice of the broad lake and, making its way past Potato Island, he saw a dog team approaching. Driving it was Joseph Bouchier who explained that his son had gone insane. Because his own dogs were practically exhausted from the recent patrol, Field hired others and accompanied Bouchier south to Fort McKay. At that place another of his arduous trips started in earnest when through another snowstorm he started south with young Bouchier and faced a gruelling trip with a wild man who kicked and growled and bit like a mad dog. On his seventeen-day trek through the wintry woods he hoped he had had all he was ever going to have of taking mentally sick men to hospital.

There were, of course, other cases of mental unbalance which did not end so favourably and of which the police never heard in time to take action. For instance, there was the case in the spring of 1911 when on going their rounds the police called at a cabin along the Salt River near Fort Smith and discovered the decomposing bodies of Pete Melland and W. S. Oliver. In the shack they found a note saying:

Cruel treatment led me to kill Pete. Everything is wrong. He never paid one cent. Ship everything out. Pay George Walker $10.00. I have been sick for a long time. I am not crazy, but simply goaded to death. He thought I had more money than I had and he tried to find it. I tried to get him to go after medicine but could not, he wanted me to die first. So good-bye—W. S. Oliver.

I have just killed the man that was killing me, so good-bye and God bless you all. I am awful weak and have been down since the last of March, so there is nothing but death for me—W. S. Oliver.

That was one instance where through no fault of their own the police arrived too late to help. Another interesting case was that which after its occurrence the Anglican bishop of Athabasca brought to the attention of Inspector Griesbach at Fort Saskatchewan and which the Mounties appear to have decided not to pursue further. In 1896 it reached its tragic conclusion a mere 150 miles from Athabasca Landing, at what was then known as Trout Lake but which is now called Graham Lake (an arm of Peerless Lake).

On January 3, Napanin, accompanied by his wife and child, reached the Hudson's Bay Company's post there and told Frank Beaton, the trader, that the night before the devil had appeared to him and commanded him to eat his child. His wife had talked him out of it and they had come in to Trout Lake where Beaton gave him something to eat and sent him over to the nearby Indian camp where his father and a prominent medicine man named Yakwemoo lived. That night, according to Beaton's journal, the Indians beat drums and sang over him. "I expect they will try and drum the devil out of him. I hear that he told the Indians that he had to kill and eat them. He says he sees the devil often since then." For several days Beaton kept going to see how he was getting along and every day he seemed to become more violently insane. "He is always saying that he is going to be a cannibal. The Indians are terribly frightened. He told them that two men would arrive from Lesser Slave Lake in a few days, that is the devil told him so." As Napanin predicted, the men did arrive and after they left he said: " 'You must look out for me for I think I shall kill some of you.' "

On January 19 the sick man's father came over to see Beaton, saying that his son was getting worse and that they thought they would have to kill him. A day or so later the Indians asked the trader to come and read some prayers for the patient and he did so. At the same time he observed that Napanin looked much worse. "He does not look like a human being. He seems to be terribly swollen in the body and face. I do not know how this will end, the sight of him is enough to frighten any person. The poor Indians slept very little here for the last 19 days. Since he arrived they have been watching him all the time."

"January 20. I am going to go and sit with the crazy man tonight and see how he is."

Beaton suggested tying him up, but the Indians averred that "no rope could hold a cannibal. The sound of him was terrible. He was calling like a wild bull. We tied him with the ropes and I left them to come and get more rope, but could not find any that was of use. I went back again about 3 a.m. in the morning. When I got back the lines were breaking that was on his arms. The Indians asked me what we should do. They said that when he got up he would kill us all. I told them if they was to do anything to do it as I had no more lines to tie him with."

By this time nearly three weeks had elapsed since his arrival, three weeks during which every moment of each night and day they had watched him. He was getting worse and everyone in the camp had been tried almost to the breaking point. The moment of decision was at hand. Napanin's father said: "I give him to you to do what you want to do with him. Only I do not want to see them hit him," and he went out.

The Indians decided that poor Yakwemoo, the medicine man, would have to do the deed. "But Yakwemoo did not want to do it. He wanted me to do it. I told him that I would not do it and that I did not want to see them do it. He asked me again. I told him to do it himself. And then he asked his son to do it, but he would not. He told his father to do it himself. And then his two brothers-in-law got hold of him and told him that they would all be killed if he did not strike the cannibal. At last Yakwemoo said: 'You all want me to do this, I will try and do it.' He then took the axe. I went to the door. I not knowing how it was, I seemed terribly frightened. I came back again. He had already struck him on the head once with an axe. He struck him again and the man was going to rise. Yakwemoo said he would yet get up, that he could not kill him. I told him to try and put him out of suffering. He hit him again and the man did not move. Yakwemoo now turned round and told them 'I have done what you told me to do.' "

Except for such cases of mental illness to which the remoteness and isolation of the area contributed, there was very little actual crime in the vast forests of the North and, therefore, these cases of insanity occurring among both whites and natives, the most difficult with which they had to deal, loom large in the police records. At some time during his service in the Mackenzie watershed every Mounted Policeman invariably played a part in taking some unbalanced soul to the asylum.

One of the outstanding northern police, a man who rose rapidly to assistant commissioner of the RCMP. was C. D. "Denny" LaNauze. At various times he was stationed at Athabasca Landing, Peace River, McMurray and Fort Smith. As well as playing the leading part in one of the most difficult and famous patrols of all, he also had his share of lunatics. During the summer of 1912 while stationed at Fort Simpson he had to take an insane Sikanni Indian some four hundred miles upstream to be placed on the train at Athabasca Landing.

The next year he opened the new police detachment at McMurray but remained there only a year before being replaced by "Nitchie" Thorne and being promoted to inspector in charge of Hay River in 1914. It was while he was there that he received his most challenging assignment and one on which he started with only twenty-four hours' notice. He was to take two constables and go to Great Bear Lake and the Arctic coast to look for the two Oblate priests, Fathers Rouvière and Le Roux, who had been unreported for some time and who, it was suspected, might have been murdered.

It took a year after he had left Hay River to lay his hands upon the killers and it was to take another year before he could bring them back. In the meantime, his party wintered at the police post on Herschel Island and then in the spring of 1917 made its way south. The final stages were made on the sternwheeler *Fort McMurray* which called at Fort Chipewyan on its way to its southern port. The prisoners had given no trouble at all and were probably as willing to oblige as were the only two Eskimos who had ever preceded them at Fort Chipewyan nearly a hundred years earlier —Hoeootoerock of Franklin's expedition and his companion, the unfortunate Tattannoeuck who later lost his life trying to reach Back at Fort Reliance.

In spite of LaNauze's noteworthy modesty, the remarkable feat which he and his two companions had carried through successfully caught the public's attention. Another patrol, however, an earlier one which commenced in June 1908, when Inspector E. A. Pelletier and three constables embarked at Athabasca Landing, was no less a test of courage and endurance. Eskimos were involved in it too, but its purpose was not to arrest any of them but to lead the way for the Mounties in exploring a vast territory to discover how best to police the southern edge of the Barren Lands. Because upon its successful completion the patrol did not produce any strangely garbed Eskimos, the newspapers devoted little space to it and the public barely noticed it. It was, nevertheless, an outstanding achievement.

By canoe Pelletier and his companions left Athabasca Landing, but from Fort McMurray to Fort Resolution were able to ride on steamers. From there they paddled east across Great Slave Lake and eventually after many mishaps reached Fort Churchill by dog team. Leaving there on February 7, driving dogs, they walked to Gimli on the west shore of ice-bound Lake Winnipeg where they were able to board a train. Few men could have endured their strenuous 3,347-mile trip of which with typical laconic praise Commissioner Perry wrote: "of the many long and arduous patrols performed by the force, this has been the most extended and difficult."

Besides making long patrols such as Pelletier's, cracking down on shady characters, trying to keep illicit liquor from entering the North, and making bitter trips to bring in lunatics, the police also had the difficult task of looking after the wood buffalo. They had to enforce the law passed in 1893 which forbade killing the last remnant of the wood buffalo herds which had once been so numerous in the North but by that time were only to be found at the west end of Lake Athabasca. To this duty the men stationed at Fort Chipewyan and at Fort Smith devoted considerable time. Their intervention on behalf of these majestic animals came just in the nick of time. Even then by 1900 a reliable estimate indicated that their numbers had been reduced to some 250 animals. Due to their efforts, however, when by 1911 government game guardians took this duty off their shoulders, this last herd of wild buffalo had increased considerably. By 1914, when scientific investigators went in to study them, they found two separate herds totalling some five hundred animals in the same general area.

One of the most interesting reports of the many policemen who concerned themselves with the buffalo was that of Inspector A. M. Jarvis, who in the spring of 1907 went down to Fort McMurray with the scow brigade. From Fort Chipewyan on, Jarvis questioned any natives he met about the state of the buffalo and one and all shook their heads gravely and declared that packs of wolves were decimating them. Jarvis became suspicious of all these tales.

At Grahame's Landing he met Pierre Squirrel, a leader in the area, and arranged to meet with the various chiefs and hunters to explain that he had come to see how bad the wolves were. He wanted some of them to pack for him and to guide him here and there over the areas which the buffalo frequented. In his report he stated: "Countless objections were raised to my plans; the whole country was under from one to five feet of water now; they said we would not get a dry spot to sleep in; we should be devoured by flies; we would die of rheumatic fever; it was impossible to find the buffalo; they might be hundreds of miles off now." Jarvis announced his determination of going anyway but "Next all the horses were lost—wives were sick—contracts and promises elsewhere were remembered, and on the following day the chiefs were gone."

Only Sousi Beaulieu was left and he guided Ernest Thompson Seton and Jarvis. Here and there they saw some buffalo and indeed saw tracks of a wolf or so, but in spite of the stories which declared that packs of wolves had left numerous buffalo skeletons to bleach in the sun, they could find little evidence of wolf depredation. As Jarvis said: "The wolf is a mere ruse to divert attention from the two legged predators . . . the buffalo are in danger of extermination, not by wolves but by poachers. These poachers are all known and live in the village of Smith Landing in summer time."

Throughout the summer Jarvis made other circuits of the buffalo range and recommended that more police be stationed in the area. "Without such protection," he reported, "the buffalo will not last five years longer." The natives' prevarication to Jarvis, though natural enough, did little to raise his opinion of them. Sergeant A. H. L. Mellor, whose 1913 patrol took him into the Fort Smith-Fort Providence, area, also commented caustically on his experience at Fort Providence, saying: "We were met with a harrowing tale of starvation, which, however, lost considerable of its horrors when, on investigation, it turned out to be merely an absence of tobacco and flour. I have never before seen such prosperous-looking starving people."

The Sousi Beaulieu of whom Jarvis spoke was, of course, a descendant of old François Beaulieu who had settled along the Salt River before 1790. The transformation of the younger man's name to Sousi throws an interesting light on the Chipewyans' inability to pronounce his baptismal name. He, like many another of his stock, had been baptised as Jesus or Jesu, which on Chipewyan tongues became Sousi. For generations the Beaulieus, physically powerful men and perhaps mentally strong too, have been guides to scores of travellers heading into the North.

About sixty years ago the late Fred Seibert, who carried his surveying instruments over much of the north country, employed one of the clan to whom we shall ascribe the fictitious name of Jake. According to an article which Fred wrote in one of Canada's famous magazines, he managed to endure if not to love Jake's eccentricities. Although in the article he pointed out many of poor Jake's faults, he also praised him—but only in the field where he said his ability excelled that of all other men. For Fred said that wherever he met them the tall, strong and personable Jake was inordinately fond of the opposite sex and unusually successful in more or less immediately getting any of them into bed.

After writing the article Seibert went off to the First War and on his return resumed his surveying practice in the North. When he was on his way to Fitzgerald again he began to worry about how Jake might greet him and to wish that his writing had not been so caustic. There was no chance, of course, that Jake would have been able to read the article but Fred knew that others would have read it to him and feared that the fat would be in the fire. Fred stepped off the sternwheeler and almost the first man he met was Jake, and yet strangely enough a Jake who was not at all angry but in an extremely happy mood.

"Fred," he said, "Fred, you my good friend—you write story about me. Everybody up here hear about me. All the women up here hear about me too and all of dem want me. You my good friend—you say me one grand stud horse."

But the Beaulieus of the Fitzgerald area have diverted us from the subsequent history of the buffalo. By 1922, when the government of Canada set aside the Wood Buffalo Park and installed a park warden service, the number of animals had risen to between 1,500 and 2,000. The park took in a vast area north of the Peace River and west of the Slave River and extended into the Northwest Territories. Within a few years it was enlarged to include much of the area surrounding Lakes Claire and Mamawi as far south as the lowest reaches of the Athabasca River. With its present 17,300 square miles, of which 3,625 are in the Northwest Territories, it is nearly as large as the province of Nova Scotia. The Ottawa government's move in establishing this sanctuary was to prove successful. In it today some 14,000 buffalo fare well.

So too did the bulk of those adventurers who rejoiced as the great rivers carried them north. Most of the missionaries, Mounties or mail carriers, having had their first look at the North when they embarked at Athabasca Landing, Peace River or sometimes McMurray, went on to success or fame or both.

Up to 1921, of course, most of them had been swept down into the magic land from Athabasca Landing or Peace River. Those who remained in the North and only occasionally "went out" for a visit were able to watch the shifting fortunes of these end-of-steel towns. When by 1915 the E.D. & B.C Railway reached Peace River and Athabasca's sternwheelers vanished, it had nevertheless grown into a thriving town with other irons in its fire. Peace River town, to which Jim Cornwall had moved Twelve-Foot Davis's body so that from his grave the pioneer trader could watch over Jim's interests in selling the lots he had subdivided on the flats below, had entered its heyday in 1916. As a port catering to the North, its brief, colourful reign practically ended by 1921. That year the AGW Railway was

137

completed to old Waterways on the Clearwater and the sternwheelers which had largely forsaken McMurray's old port during Peace River's short reign returned to the berths they had left a few years before. Thenceforth Waterways, the handmaiden of McMurray, was to be the jumping-off place for the North.

CHAPTER FOURTEEN

McMurray's Slow Growth

When in the spring of 1878 Henry John Moberly left James Spencer in charge of Fort McMurray it was a poor huddle of a post. For the next forty years until about 1920 when the whistles of shunting AGW locomotives began drifting down to its river flats it made remarkably little progress. Not that it was lacking in resources: its port pointing the way down the Athabasca River; thousands of square miles of valuable timber surrounding it; thousands of these same square miles underlain by oil sands bearing billions of barrels of oil and these in turn underlain by beds of table salt hundreds of feet thick and spread over hundreds of square miles.

Neither had it ever lacked enterprising men always trying to utilize these riches—indeed few towns in the West have been crammed with such a succession of them. While over these decades most of these resources defied extensive exploitation and many of those who had tried to develop them gave up and went away, nevertheless the resources remained and so did many of the men, so that Fort McMurray had more than its quota of interesting characters. Unfortunately we have space for only a quick summary of the untold number of attempts at exploiting these resources and for only a few tales of the type of men who made Fort McMurray and the surrounding area so fascinating.

When in 1884 the newly built *Grahame* called there on its first trip up from Fort Chipewyan and even made two trips up the Clearwater to its first serious set of rapids, Fort McMurray was a forlorn spot. Even during Isaac Cowie's sojourn starting in 1886 it made such little progress that in 1899 when Charles Mair of the treaty party paused there, Fort McMurray "consisted of a tumble-down cabin and trading store on the top of a high and steep bank."

Discouraging as its appearance was its prospects were to be even bleaker because the Hudson's Bay Company had decided to dismantle its store and move the logs to a new location down the river some thirty miles to the mouth of our Mackay River, which at the time was called the Little Red River. The company had decided to name the new post Fort Mackay after the esteemed Dr. W. M. Mackay who at Fort Chipewyan was in charge of the whole area. The new Fort Mackay (now spelled McKay) was or less on the same site at which in the spring of 1821 Robert Clouston had started a short-lived company outpost.

Dr. William Morrison Mackay was another of the Hudson's Bay Company's rugged Scottish characters. As a qualified physician he had entered the company's service and sailed for Canada in June 1864. After working at York Factory, he had been sent into the North in 1868 and stayed at Fort Simpson for four years. Remaining in the Mackenzie watershed, he had become associated with another of the company's Scots, William Flett, formerly of Kirkwall in the Orkneys, and in 1874 he married his daughter Jane. From then on Dr. Mackay's life had been bound up with the vast territory drained by the Mackenzie River and was in charge of such posts as Fort Rae and Fort Resolution. At Fort Simpson when he heard of the 1869-70 smallpox epidemic, he set out with a train of dogs and hurried over the Methy Portage to Fort Carlton on the Saskatchewan River to lend what assistance he could and returned to his Mackenzie River post in March 1870. Starting in 1882 he had been in command at Fort Dunvegan for five years, had then assumed charge of the Lesser Slave Lake post for a further five years and in 1892 had become Chief Trader of the whole Athabasca District, when for five more years he resided at Fort Chipewyan. In 1898 he retired and moved to Edmonton and spent the rest of his life still practising medicine, becoming in 1902 the first president of the Northern Alberta Medical Association. Fort McKay, which was to remain a viable settlement from 1898 forth may well bear its name proudly.

For a few years Fort McKay put a crimp into Fort McMurray. But not for long. Because even though there were relatively few Indians in the immediate trading area of Fort McKay, other traders began visiting the site of the company's former post and within a few years decided to build posts of their own. The first of these was William Gordon, a Scot, who about 1900 had been trading at Athabasca Landing where, with the help of his sister Christine, he operated a restaurant for a few years. By 1905 he had made his Fort McMurray post his headquarters and during his frequent absences had left it to his sister to operate. Christine Gordon thus became the first white woman who really made her home at Fort McMurray. Other white women, traders' and missionaries' wives and Grey Nuns, had been passing through ever since 1859, and Mrs. Segers, the famous steamboat captain's wife, had died there in 1887, but Miss Gordon was the hamlet's first white permanent female resident. That distinction, however, was her least claim to fame, because throughout all the decades till her death during the 1940's she was in many ways the town's most esteemed citizen.

As evidence of the respect in which she was held, her first name, erroneously spelled, was bestowed on the large Christina River and on one of its large headwater lakes some one hundred miles south of Fort McMurray. Moreover, with her brother William she shared the honour of the naming of Gordon Lake, a huge body of water covering an area of over fifty square miles. Prior to being renamed, the Christina River had been known to the traders by the ubiquitous name of Pembina or Summerberry—both referring to the large, lustrous pembina berries (viburnum) which grow so profusely along it.

Not long after the Gordons' arrival at Fort McMurray the Catholic church established a permanent mission there under Father Laffert who had come from Fort Chipewyan. Humble as his mission was, it lent an air of permanence to the hamlet. This was augmented in 1907 when the Hudson's Bay Company returned and erected a new set of buildings and installed as their factor one of the long line of Lutits, and one who eventually was to become another of the rugged old characters of the North, J. J. Loutit, who spelled his name with an "o."

The Reverend J. C. Barford, who as a young man joined the Mounted Police, has many a fond recollection of this trader whom he recalls as a grand gentleman of the old school and one with a marked Scottish burr in his tongue. A martinet in his devotion to the company's discipline, punctilious in his observances of the company's orders and integrity, and meticulous in his dress, he ruled his staff and his customers. One of his concessions to his modicum of native blood was the moccasins which he always wore. His only other concession was perhaps some undue deference every few weeks to his Scottish ancestors' fondness for whisky. Aside from his moccasins, his attire was always sartorially perfect and every year he made a trip to Edmonton where one of the best of the city's tailors catered to his strict requirements.

Young Jack Barford, reared in the softness and comforts of a cultured family circle, will never forget his first meal in J. J.'s home when, as a great favour, the kindly older man insisted that the newcomer partake of dinner at his family table. In due course, after Mrs. Loutit and their five or six children had assembled at the table and the platter had been brought in from the stove with eight or ten cooked rabbits on it, J. J. commenced a long, earnest grace. Jack, devoutly as befitted a choir master's son, bowed his head but could not close his eyes for within a foot of his face, staring at him from the platter, were untold rabbits' eyes. For the rabbits had been skinned and cleaned and boiled whole and the very sight of the staring eyes nearly turned his stomach.

When J. J. had finished his grace a restrained but definite outcry arose from several of the children all clamouring for the boon of each being served a rabbit's head. With a stern look and a wave of his carving knife, Loutit silenced the outcry and, deliberately ignoring his children's requests, turned politely to Barford and said: "Jack, how many heads will you have?"

With the quick thinking and tact which was later to serve him well as an Anglican minister and which at the time made him a fast friend of the children, Jack, turning his head to avoid the platter full of eyes replied: "Please, as a favour to me, let the children have the heads!"

But the Gordons and J. J. Loutit were not the only traders to set up in the revivified Fort McMurray. When in 1908 Inspector W. H. Routledge made one of his northern patrols by way of Lac La Biche, he found another fur trader at Fort McMurray in the person of Joe Bird, a representative of yet another family famous in the annals of the North. On that trip he found conditions throughout the area changing. In one Indian cabin he had noticed two gramophones which he thought must have cost not less than a hundred dollars each. In several others he saw musical clocks, cheap jewelry and watches. To keep up with the changing times the traders' stocks had taken on a new character and included "hand sewing machines, ladies' trimmed hats, Stetson hats, Huntly and Palmers tinned pound cake and such like." Not only was the Hudson's Bay Company facing competition, but the independent traders were changing the tenor of the trade. Without competition the company had restricted its merchandise to goods that were necessary in the natives' lives and, although paternal in its attitude, nevertheless did not entice them to fritter away the produce of their year's work for senseless geegaws. The independent traders, not paternal but practical in a dollar sense, gladly sold the natives impractical luxuries.

But Routledge noted another change that had come to Fort McMurray's horizon—oil derricks. On the way down to Fort McKay he had passed two oil boring rigs, one twelve miles below McMurray near Tar Island and another on the left bank of the river half a mile below Fort McKay. Actual drilling aimed at capturing the oil from the Athabasca oil sands had started in what was to prove to be a struggle dogged by decades of discouragement. In that struggle scores of men played their part and passed unrewarded from the scene—honest promoters, swindling hucksters, small investors who got stuck and persistent scientists who by their efforts fed the clear flame of hope. High on the roster of the better promoters stood J. K. Cornwall, R. C. Fitzsimmons and A. Von Hammerstein.

J. K. Cornwall we have met before and will meet again. R. C. Fitzsimmons came to the oil sands scene somewhat later and was the only one of the trio who lived to see the start of their large-scale successful development. A. Von Hammerstein in a move designed to find the pool of oil from which the sands had been saturated, was the first to start drilling in the Fort McMurray area and it was two of his wells which Inspector Routledge saw on his 1908 trip. Records of Von Hammerstein's wells are scanty but he drilled about nine of them between 1906 and 1910, of which one appears to have reached a depth of 1,150 feet before he abandoned it. His wells were north of Fort McMurray and mainly at Ruth Lake and at the MacKay settlement. Hard on his heels came J. K. Cornwall who with his Fort MacKay Oil and Asphalt Company drilled near Mildred Lake in 1910 and two or three miles south of MacKay in 1912. The Athabasca Oil and Asphalt Company in which he also had a finger drilled two wells in 1908 within ten miles north of Fort McMurray and a third well the following year in the same area.

During the next ten years to 1917, exclusive of Von Hammerstein's holes, some fifteen wells were drilled in the Fort McMurray-Fort McKay area, one of them deliberately looking for salt. The companies which actually drilled included Athabasca Oils, Athabasca Oil and Asphalt, A. B. C. Oil & Refining, Alcan Oil, Fort MacKay Oil & Asphalt, McMurray Syndicate, Northern Alberta Exploration, N. W. Company, and Tekoa-Athabasca. These were only the companies which actually drilled in the ground. Many other companies were formed to exploit speculators instead of sands.

In those days before World War I the Fort McKay-Fort McMurray area, however, did not see all the drilling which took place along the Athabasca River. The flare from the 1897 Dominion government well about a mile south of the mouth of the Pelican River kept luring men to that area. The fact that on various occasions the government sent crews to shut off the escaping gas and to put the flare out only to find that in spite of their persistence it broke out and burned again, helped to encourage investors.

In 1912 more or less across from the flare, Santa Barbara Oils drilled an unsuccessful well some 2,100 feet but abandoned it. In the same vicinity and about the same time, Pelican Oil and Gas drilled several wells. For decades one of them at Lower Pelican supplied a trapper with his heat and light, while another well a few miles farther down the Athabasca helped to make his competitor comfortable during the long winters. Another pair of trappers named Bartle and Bell down at Buffalo River, however, did not have their fuel supplied to them so easily. They had to rustle for it. At the same place where in 1887 Captain J. H. Smith had first set the gas bubbles on fire, these two dug a cellar about ten feet deep. When they had covered it and mudded up the cracks of this reservoir they led the gas to their cabin through a rubber hose.

In 1916 all these showings of gas led the Northern Production Company to drill a well just north of the haunted flat at the mouth of House River. Despite the company's sometimes frantic publicity efforts, drilling on the site progressed very slowly and when the hole was abandoned in 1921 it had reached the depth of 693 feet.

Up to 1917 while the boom had lasted the Athabasca River had resounded to the echoes of men coming and going with the wild glow of prospective oil riches in their eyes and the wild words of promotion in their mouths. For some of them their trip was to end in disaster as was the case with two of Von Hammerstein's men when in 1909 a scow load of his machinery struck a boulder in the Grand Rapids. It turned turtle and threw Von Hammerstein, young V. Volksooky and a half-breed named Bonneau into the raging waters. Von Hammerstein made it to the shore but his two men drowned. Two more crosses joined the others on the bank.

While many men were risking their money in oil wells nearby and some were losing their lives in the rapids upstream, Fort McMurray's progress consisted of the addition of only two or three shacks on the point of land between the two rivers. Nevertheless, all the signs were propitious and Fort McMurray's handful of pioneers were ambitious. To start a campaign which would lead them on to success, they decided to discard the "Fort" from their name. The very word smacked of backwardness and suggested to outsiders that their town might be merely a collection of log shacks. So in 1910 they had their post office changed to a one-word name— McMurray—symbolic of tar sands and wealth.

The same year fortune appeared to smile upon McMurray by presenting it with yet another resource. Over near the mouth of Horse River at the edge of the McMurray townsite the Northern Alberta Exploration Company drilled two wells 155 feet apart looking for salt. They were amply rewarded for, at a depth of roughly six hundred feet, each well drilled through a band of table salt some one hundred feet thick with another layer of about the same thickness less than a hundred feet below it. McMurray's future seemed assured.

Shortly after finding enough salt to season all of Canada's porridge, the old-timers were saddened by news which came out of the North on the *Grahame* on her first trip south in 1911. Sergeant F. J. Fitzgerald had perished on a patrol from Fort McPherson to Dawson. The pioneers all the way down the Mackenzie watershed held him in such affection that to honour his memory it was decided to bestow his name on the hamlet at the head of the Slave River rapids and to change its name from Grahame's Landing to Fitzgerald. Henceforth the two terminii of the *Grahame's* run both received new names.

By that time, however, other events were afoot in McMurray. That summer in a rush of sorts, all the river frontage for the thirty miles from there down to Fort McKay was staked as oil leases and many a man was busy cutting down spruce trees to erect into derricks. This time too the promoter Jim Cornwall not only dealt himself a handful of derricks but with the other hand was busy subdividing the flat at McMurray into a townsite. In addition, he made sure that the citizens of Edmonton, the rapidly growing city of some thirty thousand people, heard of the new townsite. Furthermore, he saw to it that they should also hear of and even stand and stare at some of McMurray's oil sands, then called tar sands, pounded into pavement in their city. Arranging for the MacKay Oil and Asphalt Company to have a party of scowmen drag a batch of his tar sands upstream to Athabasca Landing, he sent it on to Edmonton where in the fall of 1911 he paved a piece of sidewalk in front of the Windsor Hotel (corner of First Street and Jasper). Grass rarely grew on a street Jim had an eye on.

While his tar sands' scow was making its laborious way up the Athabasca, other scows passed it carrying Dominion government property downstream. And when they tied up at McMurray everyone turned out to stare. For they contained not tar sands which were old hat, but reindeer —reindeer headed for the Barren Lands. In 1911 the federal government purchased fifty head of domesticated reindeer from Dr. Grenfell in Labrador, who a few years previously had imported a small breeding stock from northern Europe. The animals purchased consisted of "6 four year old stags; 4 gelded stags, trained as sled-deer; and 40 three-to four-year old breeding does." They were destined to spend the winter at Fitzgerald.

By the time they emerged from that winter, deaths, mainly in transit, had reduced their number to thirty-one. After that all went well until the end of June 1912 when the corralled newcomers, driven to frenzy by Fitzgerald's ferocious flies, broke down their stockade and scattered in the bush. Twelve were recaptured but because some escaped again and some died, presumably of a dietary deficiency when moved to Fort Smith in 1914, the herd was reduced to two. Even then Ottawa would not acknowledge failure and ordered this remainder of two animals to be moved farther north to an island near Fort Rae, where, hopefully, the flies would be less ferocious. So Billy McNeill, their herder, moved them and spent the winter of 1914-15 with his two does, promising them that he would go out and capture a wild caribou bull. When after a month he returned empty handed, one of the does died.

During the spring of 1916, while one doe, grizzled with age, licked salt from Billy's hand and waited outside his cabin door to greet him each morning, he talked to her and wondered what would come of his letter sent to Ottawa suggesting that they call the experiment off. Finally the answer, couched in proper civil servant caution, arrived agreeing to his suggestion, and the $62,000 attempt to domicile reindeer in the Northwest Territories ended in what Billy McNeill called the most high priced feed of meat he had ever eaten.

After watching Billy McNeill's high-priced meat float down the quiet Athabasca, the people in McMurray settled down to a somnolent winter. During February 1912, Charles Eymundson, whose son had been the first white child to see the light of day in McMurray, reported the local population—probably the non-native people—as adding up to sixty-nine, including thirty-four children. He also reported that several men had come in to take up quarter-section homesteads and that there was considerable competition for favourable land both on the flats and on the higher land above.

Most of these, whether they were prospective farmers or speculators looking to a near and hopefully assured future, had reached the townsite by the risky route through the Grand Rapids. Even though, as it had done sporadically for a decade or so, the Dominion government kept sending crews out during the winter to blast the last obstructing rock out of the Grand Rapids channel, they made little improvement in navigation. During the summer of 1912 William Gordon and his sister Christine, both well versed in getting their scows down that stretch of rough water, added another wreck to the toll it took. Miss Gordon was on her way back home from a visit to Scotland and along with her brother and two men rode the only one of the three scows which hit a rock. Grabbing a canoe, she got to shore but the men who stayed with the craft a little longer had to swim to safety. The scow and the $3,500 worth of goods which Gordon had been going to send to his other trading posts at the Methy Portage, Fort McKay and Fort Chipewyan, were complete losses.

Fortunately the sawmills which, anticipating a boom in McMurray, William Biggs and Roy Field each brought in that fall came down the river safely. In due course they were put into service in timber stands up the Clearwater and supplied lumber to McMurray and downriver points. The year 1913 was marked by milestones of which the opening of the hamlet's first school, taught by Mrs. D. C. McTavish, was the most important. Others were the building of the RCMP detachment and the arrival of S. C. Ells, a geologist who came to map the tar sands and who for decades was to adopt the sands as his special project. To take charge of the police detachment came Sergeant Denny LaNauze, a stalwart Irish gentleman who previously had been stationed at Athabasca Landing. By this time he was already familiar with life along the northern rivers and in due course was to become one of the best known policemen between Edmonton and the Arctic Ocean. Coincidentally or not, McMurray's first lawyer, Cecil Potts, arrived about the same time but while LaNauze soon moved on to other fields, Potts stayed to become one of the hamlet's interesting characters.

So as to be a bit removed from the hectic activity of McMurray's grass-grown main street, Potts chose to build his bachelor home on the west side of the Athabasca not far from the foot of Moberly Rapids. There he cultivated a garden which because of its floral display was renowned all over the North. In the leisurely enjoyment of his books, his flowers and the magnificent scenery, his time passed pleasurably and nearly effortlessly. Indeed, one of his main efforts concerned itself with measuring the passage of time and for this purpose he devised a unique system. Convinced that an outdoor toilet would be incongruous in his primeval surroundings, he solved his sanitation problem in a way that not only served that purpose but also served to record the passage of time. Digging a row of seven shallow pits, he used each in turn as a repository for his daily offerings. Then, after shovelling some clay into that pit, he advanced the shovel to the next one so as to have it ready for tomorrow's contribution. Thus, daily, Monday, Tuesday and Wednesday, the shovel moved along the line of pits until finally on Saturday night he carried it back to the first of the pits and the start of another week.

Shortly after his arrival in McMurray, Potts was appointed a justice of the peace and in that capacity he came into close contact with Sergeant Denny LaNauze and with his successor Hubert ("Nitchie") Thorne, who took over the detachment in 1914. Up to that time police matters in the area had run an uneventful course but upon Thorne's arrival the pace quickened. About ten o'clock on October 28, Paul Miller came to Thorne alleging that Otto Bushner, who lived across the Clearwater River, had come to his house and assaulted him with an axe. As Miller was running away leaving H. J. McColley, his guest, with Bushner, he heard a shot fired. Taking Special Constable Janvier and two civilians, Thorne made his way to Miller's buildings and found them in flames. Two of them were too far burned to save but before it was completely destroyed they were able to put out the fire in the third. Next morning Thorne organized a party to search for Bushner. It included Jim Cornwall, his partner J. Violette, Paul Miller and others, and when they went to Miller's property they discovered bones lying amongst the charred wood. When a physician, who happened to be passing through, examined them he declared that two men had been killed; McColley, and a man who was thought to be named Reis.

During the hunt for Bushner, Mickey Ryan, a newcomer to McMurray, was pressed into service and he and a couple of constables were sent out to search along the survey line for the proposed AGW Railway. After a few days they came face to face with Bushner, who, instead of opening fire on them, put a bullet through his own brain.

Bushner, Miller and McColley were all trappers who made their head-quarters in McMurray during the summer. While most of the white population in the area were employed by the oil well drilling rigs, the previous two or three years had seen a considerable influx of white trappers who fanned out into the muskegs and timbered hills well to the north of the hamlet. Typical of one variety of these was Harry Sykes, a farmer from Alberta's baldheaded southern prairies who, after three years of crop failure, decided to recoup his fortunes by trapping. In the fall of 1914 with his uncle and a couple of friends he headed up the Firebag River where the party built its base camp. For a while they found the fresh greenery of the pine forests enchanting and by the time the snow came had begun to consider themselves capable woodsmen.

They had much to learn, however, and poor Sykes was to learn it the hard way. On November 10 when they were out to look at their trap lines he saw a moose, and hoping to kill it within a few moments took after it. But the moose proved too wise for him and after a couple of hours when his first rush of excitement had cooled and the diminishing afternoon's light had turned the forest into a grey directionless gloom, he decided to return to camp. By that time he realized that he was alone in the forest, without food or bedding and that he had no idea which way the camp lay. With that realization came panic. He was lost.

Next morning his companions started an intensive search for him. For five days, while a moderate storm bringing fresh snow hid all traces of even recent tracks, they tramped through the trees but each night returned to camp without having found any trace of him. Upon their return on the evening of the sixth day, however, they found Sykes sitting in the cabin weak from lack of food and with one hand and both feet badly frozen.

For a week they did what they could for his painful feet and then persuaded a nearby Indian to load him on his dog sled and take him to McMurray where they hoped he would find a doctor. Two or three days later, because there was no doctor in the hamlet, the Indian stopped his team in front of the recently built NWMP detachment shack and banged on the door. When Constable Thorne opened it, he explained:

"Got white man on sled—can't walk—both feet frozen—bring him from up Firebag River."

In a minute Thorne had carried the trapper in, laid him on his bed and began to examine his feet while he set the Indian to making more tea and heating up some soup. At that point Thorne, who was already known as a sturdy traveller and who later was to become famous for some of his other long patrols, began the endurance test which was to be remembered down the decades as the Saga of the Frozen Trapper. He set out the next morning to take his patient by the older more practical 300-mile trail by way of Lac La Biche to hospital at Athabasca Landing. But the story can be told best by using extracts from Thorne's laconic report.

. . . he was in great pain, his toes being shrivelled up and black, half his right foot black and two of his fingers frozen, thus rendering him absolutely helpless.

December 3—Left Fort McMurray with detachment dog train and ten days' rations for three men and two days' dog feed accompanied by a half-breed, Emil Shott, with his dog train. . . . I put Sykes in my sleigh and Shott took rations, dog feed, bedding, etc. The first day we made Willow lake, about 28 miles out, and camped at an Indian shack. Trail was very bad being very rough and heavily encumbered with windfalls. I had to ease the sleigh over all rough places as Sykes was in agony day and night. On camping I prepared supper and dressed his feet. . . .

December 4—Made Cheecham lake. . . . At this camp Emil Shott left me as he could not accompany me further, and I hired Indian John Cheecham with his dog train. . . .

December 5—Weather dull. Made Jackfish lake about 40 miles. Camped twice en route; the second time to wait for the moon to rise as it was essential to make a house of some description. Reaching the lake we travelled until 11 p.m., and finally reached the shack which was our objective. . . .

For the next two days they averaged about thirty-five miles a day and by December 9 reached the police detachment at Lac La Biche where Dr. Sabran dressed Sykes's feet and reported that gangrene had set in. There Thorne paid off Cheecham and hired a team and, loading the trapper into a sleigh, took three days to reach Athabasca Landing. Meanwhile his dog team trotted along behind the sleigh. At Athabasca Dr. McDonald reported that it would be necessary to amputate some toes. Eventually the patient was able to go back to his home near Lethbridge. Thorne concluded his report by saying:

The trail between Fort McMurray and Lac La Biche is mostly muskeg with ten large lakes en route. In the muskeg the trail is very deep and narrow and the dog sleigh was riding on one side or the other most of the time which made it very uncomfortable for Sykes who was helpless all the way and had to be lifted everywhere, the tops of his fingers being frozen and he was in great and continual pain. The pain was a great mental and physical strain upon him and this with the added loss of sleep made him very despondent toward the end of the trip.

The report never mentions the constable's own physical and mental strain.

By the time Thorne reached Athabasca with Sykes, that town had staged a remarkable recovery from its disastrous fire of August 5, 1913, which, as well as many residences, had wiped out thirty-two places of business. Several new buildings, including the Grand Union Hotel with its 58-foot-long bar, lent a look of optimism to the town but Thorne could sense that the bloom had gone from Athabasca's boom. The first sod of the new AGW Railway had been turned nearly a year previously and its route had been surveyed as far as what would soon become the town of Boyle, some twenty-five miles east of Athabasca. With many strikes against it and particularly the new AGW Railway, Athabasca's role was changing. Symbolic of that change had been old Shot's death the previous spring.

Shot had been the very epitome of scowmen. Standing six feet three he towered over the courageous companions of his craft. His dark complexion and scraggly white beard, his piercing eyes and hawk-like features denoted his domination over his wild crews. But he was also a generous man and they and all northerners mourned him. His life had corresponded with that of the Athabasca scows. He had been the first man daring enough to cross himself and run a scow down the Grand Rapids. For nearly fifty years during the heyday of the Athabasca scow brigades, he had risked his life running the rapids to Fort McMurray and then walked back to pilot other scows down, stopping fights with his great fists and calming tempers with his laugh. Finally when the glorious days of the brigades were closing Shot had died in a hospital bed.

In 1841 Shot, whose name was Louis Fousseneuve, had been born in St. Boniface. As a boy he had listened eagerly for the squeal of Red River carts returning from the annual buffalo hunts; if they came quietly, a hungry winter would haunt the Red River settlement, if the axles squealed loudly from their heavy loads, the cooking pots would bubble with plenty. As a husky youth he had gone far out onto the prairies with the carts and eventually he drove an ox cart to Lac La Biche for Bishop Faraud. He fell in love with Lac La Biche's great expanse and its swans, pelicans and cormorants, and a few hundred yards around the small bay from the mission he built his home. There he raised his brood—strong boys like their father and girls with piercing eyes and laughing glances.

Instead of running buffalo on the prairies, he snowshoed through the willows after moose and hauled in his nets laden with eight-pound jumbo whitefish with dark backs and golden sides. For he was an adaptable man. And when in 1867 Bishop Faraud was ready to take his nuns to Fort Providence, Shot, taking his life in his hands, worked the first scow down the furious Grand Rapids. Thenceforth, by hunting, fishing or freighting and navigating scows and eventually combining these activities with some trading at a little post he built along the shore of the magnificent lake four miles west of the mission, he and his family lived well.

Almost invariably from then on the priests looked to him to take their supplies down the great river. When about 1892, after Athabasca Landing had become the jumping-off place for barges, mission or lay, he merely moved his point of embarkation to that place. Every spring he rounded up his crews from Lac La Biche, Saddle and Whitefish lakes. Promising to pay them forty-five dollars for the trip to Fort McMurray and the walk back and giving them half of it in cash with the balance to come when their jobs were completed, he led them to Athabasca Landing on foot. And wild men they looked, large, dark and fierce men, adorned with head-dresses of fox tails or feathers, but men who once on board stripped to the waist. Each fall Shot's hardy men returned to their homes while he went back to his family at Lac La Biche.

Occasionally some articulate traveller employed him and wrote of his might and his skill. The Klondikers praised him as trip after trip he conducted some of them to Fort McMurray. One noted traveller, Casper Whitney, who in 1895 hired Shot and his dog team to take him from Lac La Biche to Fort McMurray fell out with him and wrote disparagingly. Fault may well have lain with Shot, but by then he was fifty-four years old and probably felt little inclined to tolerate the lack of understanding and the whims of a city-bred scientist.

Shot not only piloted scows; he built them too, mainly at Athabasca but in later life at a sawmill at Bald Hill upstream from the town. Then one day in 1914 some trifling injury broke the skin on one of his feet. The next day it itched and he rubbed it and by the following morning could not walk because of the swelling. A day later one of his companions was seen driving him up to the hospital at Athabasca and word spread that the indomitable Shot was ill—blood poisoning, a disease fatal in those days. They set off post haste to bring his wife from Lac La Biche sixty miles away, but the time was too short. On Saturday, May 16, 1914, long before she arrived, Shot died.

When the news flew round the town a quiet settled alike over old-timer and school boy—Shot was dead and his wife was expected soon. While they waited for her, however, Athabascans were busy arranging the largest funeral the town of two thousand people had ever seen. When it took place everybody turned out to accompany a squad of Mounted Police, the town band and a hundred and fifty fellow Métis. As the team carrying old Shot turned in at the cemetery, the end of the mile-long procession was just leaving the town. For they had come to say goodbye to a leader among men and a great gentleman. As the town paper, the *Northern News*, said, referring to his integrity, "He was often cheated but he never cheated."

Some men outlive their usefulness, but Shot was lucky. His life ended at the close of his era. Even as they carried him to his grave the new railway was brushing out its right-of-way around the shore of his beloved Lac La Biche—the AGW which was eagerly reaching out towards McMurray with the avowed purpose of doing away with the scows and scowmen of the middle Athabasca.

CHAPTER FIFTEEN

The Alberta and Great Waterways Railway

The AGW! The Alberta and Great Waterways Railway! Ah, there was a railway.

Its construction through such improbable terrain as the sand hills and muskegs north of Lac La Biche posed many a problem for its engineers. But to those difficulties were added political, financial and operating dilemmas. By the end of the twelve years it took for the steel to stretch the 294 miles from Edmonton to modern Waterways no other railroad had been held up to such scorn or provided the basis for so much levity. Like nearly all other northern transportation ventures, J. K. Cornwall had a hand in it. So did J. D. McArthur who in 1913 promised to finish the line to McMurray by the end of 1915.

It is with its earlier days that we want to deal; its juvenile pranks and the touches of humour, fantasy and sheer lunacy which even in the heyday of its youth turned the "Muskeg Limited" from a source of laughter —sometimes bitter laughter—into a legend. And yet it never had much youth; it was born old with old locomotives, old coaches and old flat cars.

From end to end it was about three hundred miles long with Lac La Biche near its halfway point. In its youth it scorned schedules. Once indeed, due to wash-outs, it took thirty days to run from Lac La Biche to Waterways. On most trips, however, it was able to cut as much as three weeks off that time and sometimes a couple of days sufficed. In winter, snow blowing over the tracks stopped it, in spring, mud flowing from the sides of cuts, in summer, water flooding over the grade, and in the fall, sand swirling across from the dunes and filling the cuts. And even if none of these threatened it and nothing was blowing or flowing, flooding, swirling or filling and everything was propitious, moose, fish and ducks and even weasels and blueberries stopped it.

By late 1915 its trains wobbled their way as far as Lac La Biche, even though it was to be July 1916 before it was declared open for traffic that far.

151

By that time J. D. McArthur had brought into being his pretentious, turretted, four-storied resort-type railway hotel which, in its opulence, stood looking out over that magnificent island-studded lake. Uniformed bell-boys, sleek rugs and electric lights, however, accorded ill with Lac La Biche's forests, fur traders and fishmen and its one-year reign was soon over. Financial depression and World War I joining hands with a tragic accident defeated it. During its short summer season a few teachers and tourists enjoyed its luxury until one of the lake's sudden storms smashed its windows and capsized the hotel launch out on the lake. When the storm broke, it caught the hotel-sponsored picnic party halfway back from the nearby big island and three men and four women drowned.

Before spring break-up in 1916 work trains were rolling as far as the gravel pit at Mile 197 (near the point now known as Devenish). That spring J. D. McArthur announced that by the end of the year he hoped to see the grade completed to Waterways. After considerable difficulty, the steel reached Cache 23 at the station called Lynton, on the lip of the descent into the valley of the Clearwater River and a mere fifteen miles short of Waterways. There, for many a year, the AGW stopped. Even at that, although steel had been laid that far, railway service was theoretical only. Because of the treacherous conditions of the grade and the track, trains could only run that far in winter when the ground was frozen.

That spring Dr. Walter Morrish, who at the time was a medical student, accompanied his superior, Dr. McDonald, to the end-of-steel, whence they walked forward along the tote road. As Dr. Morrish's memoirs say:

> On the banks of the Christina River we set up our hospital; a large tent for the hospital, another for the personnel, and one for the doctor. . . . Having opened up the camp, I left Dr. McDonald and moved north to see what was necessary to supply the men with some sort of medical services.

Thus he started his itinerant medical practice along the survey line of the AGW. Much of that practice consisted of pulling teeth.

> I remember coming into a small work camp where a big Swede had a bad toothache. I sat him on a stump, and in the twilight he showed me his aching tooth. I put my forceps on and extracted a tooth. You could have guessed the language when he realized I had pulled the wrong tooth. However, thinking quickly I threw the extracted tooth into the bush, argued that the one I pulled had a hole in it too, and without waiting for a breathing space I pulled out the real offender. It apparently gave him so much relief that, in spite of my mistake, he didn't beat me up.

By 1917 an occasional train reached Lynton but no more construction took place. The crews were called off and many of the engineers and other prominent men went to war—Jim Cornwall, Nitchie Thorne, P. Debney the chief engineer, Dr. W. Morrish and others.

Jim Cornwall emerged in 1918 as Lieutenant-Colonel Cornwall, DSO. For him the war was another adventure in a life full of adventure. Born in

Brantford, Ontario, in 1869, he had sold papers in Buffalo and had sailed on vessels on the Great Lakes and even on the Atlantic. Then he had come west and worked on the construction of the Crowsnest Pass Railway. Eventually the North had called and he soon became a leading spirit in promoting its enterprises. Moreover, from 1909 to 1913 he served one term as a provincial MLA when he sat for the constituency of Peace River. He then went on to organize the 218th Battalion—a railway unit—which was authorized in February 1916 and sailed for Europe a year later.

Meanwhile, the AGW, one of his pet projects, stagnated. Its progress during these years can be seen best by watching that of another famous figure, Mickey Ryan, who also became rich by supplying service to northerners. At one time a boxer of some standing, he had taken his first look at the North when about 1915 he had gone to McMurray with his nearly deaf brother Pat to labour on the building of the *Fort McMurray*. Having worked for the famous Captain J. W. Mills, who with the well-known engineer "Judge" Johnson and E. J. Williscraft, built her, he hired on as a roustabout on her first trip north. He was aboard her when near Vermilion Chutes less than two months after starting on her first voyage she ran on a rock and sank. From then on in many ways he played a leading role in improving transport facilities as far as Fort Smith. Like all men who see an opportunity before their fellows do and then work tirelessly to improve it and finally because of their foresight and their perspiration become rich, Mickey Ryan had many detractors.

Not long after returning to McMurray from the refloated *Fort McMurray*, he took the contract for carrying the mail to Athabasca Landing and by using dog teams in winter, boats in summer and horses in the in-between seasons, he made several successful if arduous trips. Then during the winter of 1916-17, after the AGW grade had advanced much closer to McMurray, the authorities routed the hamlet's mail by way of Lac La Biche. Using his horses for part of the trip to the end-of-steel, he used an abandoned speeder to rock him the remaining miles over the otherwise unused track to Lac La Biche.

His next step in 1917 was to take on the job of repairman along the little used railway telegraph line. With it came the use of a speeder and before long, because trains failed to run, he was carrying passengers and express. When in the spring of 1918 no locomotive whistles disturbed the wilderness between Lac La Biche and McMurray, he obtained a Hudson Six passenger car with flanged wheels and permission to run it on the AGW tracks. Taking his passengers to Cache 23 with his horses and loading them on his car and trailer there he whisked them about their business. Before long the money poured in. But by ingenuity and sheer industry he had earned every dollar. Perhaps never too popular with the people of McMurray anyway, he found his increasing prosperity adding to his unpopularity until a time came when, because of the slanderous rumours some of them spread about him, he felt he had good cause to sue some of them for libel.

He won his case and doing so added to the wounds the defendants suffered. Their unkindest cut of all, however, came when they had to pay their passage to and from the court in Edmonton—and pay it to Mickey to ride the trailer of his Hudson Six. Mickey's legal fees were considerable and the damages he was awarded were negligible. But in the fare he extracted from his persecutors lay a handsome profit and a great source of satisfaction.

About this time the Hudson's Bay Company appointed Philip Godsell to take charge of one of its Mackenzie River posts and in due course he went out to Edmonton's Dunvegan yards to board the "Muskeg Limited." Waiting there for the nondescript train to come from the yard he mingled with his fascinating fellow travellers. There were about fifty, all of them frontier types or those who would soon be such. There was Jim Cornwall recently returned from the war and a pair of red-coated Mounties, likewise back from the holocaust, as well as trappers and traders. Mingling with them were black-frocked priests and white-hooded nuns, together with four other white women. Several of their stoical native sisters bedecked in tartans and with their papooses slung on their backs stood watching glumly. Many of the motley assemblage had imbibed freely and continued to do so.

Finally after a long wait this museum's mixture of dirty red box cars and battered flat cars backed into the station. A moth-eaten old passenger coach partitioned so as to leave fourteen seats in service ended up two or three hundred yards past the station's plank platform. Twice too many hopeful passengers piled into it. The others, more used to roughing it, threw their possessions onto the nearest flat car and clambered aboard it, planning to use their bags and bedrolls for seats. With a wheezy whistle and a clashing of couplings, the optimistic train began its swaying crawl out through field, fallow and marsh. They were off.

But not for long. Here and there for no apparent reason the muskeg express stopped and, after a pause, set out again. Winding its way through forest and fen, it soon ventured out onto a muskeg some five miles wide. Crossing it was always a test of the crew's courage. Parting the swimming ducks and mudhens, they eased their locomotive along rails invisible beneath the slimy waters. Here and there as they crawled along in slow motion they passed shattered box cars immersed in the green scum of ditches—mute evidence of former wrecks. For miles at a time, the passengers in the caboose watched the rails' reaction to the weight of the passing train as briefly they rose and became visible directly behind the train before once more sinking out of sight. Eventually, along some dry expanse of terrain the train stopped again and it was time to light campfires, heat kettles and break out the corned beef. Finally, as dusk came and the tracks were too risky to trust during the dark, the tired crew stopped for the night.

Before dark on the second night Godsell's train, outbound 120 miles and thirty hours from Edmonton, reached Lac La Biche. So far so good, but the real trials began at Lac La Biche. McArthur's luxurious railway hotel staring uselessly over the lake was abandoned and locked when the travellers were greeted with the news that because the recent rain had washed out some of the track ahead, their stay might be somewhat prolonged. Despite the lake's magnificence when the summer sun shines, the passengers' stay in the raw, new hamlet, a stay that eventually lengthened to ten days, soon became irksome. The only operating hotel, a primitive affair sided with warping green shiplap, divided into rooms by dirty grey blankets hung from the rafters and supplying meals of canned pork and beans alternated with boiled whitefish, eventually palled.

On the tenth day Mickey Ryan's flange-wheeled car rescued Godsell. Not without much discomfort, however, and not without a struggle. When it arrived at the station thirty-seven angry passengers with a total of a ton of baggage fought for a place on it. To avoid having his car wrecked, the driver, "Gasoline Gus," refused to make the trip. That night by pre-arrangement, Godsell and a chosen few sneaked out of the hotel in the darkness and, walking a couple of miles east, found Gus and his car waiting. Godsell was the last passenger to climb on the trailer and through two days of pouring rain he had to sit on the top of a bulky load of mail sacks.

During those years nobody was ever sure whether or not the AGW would operate north of Lac La Biche. When the ground was frozen, it sometimes made it all the way to Cache 23. Otherwise it merely gave up and stayed at Lac La Biche. Mickey Ryan, wondering whether to use his car or not, was never very certain what the train would do. One time during the winter of 1918-19 after the train had made several trips, Mickey wanted to go to Edmonton on urgent business and decided to catch it at Cache 23. When he arrived there the engineer stated that because the coal which had been supplied to them had been so poor they had used up nearly all of it and could not take a chance on trying to pull a train south and that in order to get more coal he, the fireman and the brakeman were going to drive the uncoupled locomotive as far as Lac La Biche. To do even that he felt that they might have to resort to firing the boiler with wood. So with Mickey aboard they set out, but the engine coughed and spluttered along for a few miles until the exasperated engineer decided to fall back on using wood, a desperate resort but the only one. From there on the four men fed the engine by sawing up any piles of ties they came to and when these gave out they stopped in a grove of fire-killed spruce forest, cut all the fuel they could load on and started once more. The engine, used to a diet of coal, made short work of their spruce logs and as Mickey said, puffed cords of them up the smoke stack. Three days later the four tired wood-cutters pulled into the station at Lac La Biche.

Another traveller who fared a little better than P. H. Godsell was Mrs. C. Hoare, a missionary's wife, who in 1920 as a bride going north with her new husband, seems to have had a comparatively easy trip. The couple arrived in Edmonton on June 2 and then had to wait twelve days before the next AGW train headed north. Their stay at Lac La Biche only lasted four days. From there on, watching the track behind them rise to the surface of the water after the train passed over it, fascinated Mrs. Hoare, while "Occasionally the ties snapped under the strain. We were bounced up and down and from side to side. In one spot the track was so bad the cars kept uncoupling. Once we were off the track altogether."

Mrs. Hoare's food gave out before, on their ninth day out from Edmonton, they reached the point beyond which the train refused to proceed. "One day we travelled five miles; another day, three."

Fortunately Mickey Ryan showed up with his car and trailer, met the reluctant train and whisked the Hoares along the remainder of the track. On crossing a high, shaky trestle the bride shut her eyes. Her husband, who had gone north on the AGW the year before, told her of how he had crossed this trestle when the train, having less experience with the northern end of the track, had dared to cross it. He said that he and his companions were ordered to walk across the trestle in single file. Then they turned around to watch the train. One brakeman walked across the jittery structure and waited while the engineer started the train crawling forward and then jumped out to watch it make its way across alone. As the locomotive crawled by the brakeman he climbed aboard and stopped it.

During the war years McMurray grew slowly. Conflicting forces beyond its control worked for it and against it. On the darker side, the war slowed down civilian activity all over Alberta, interest in the tar sands waned and the E. D. & B.C., reaching the Peace River in 1915, had temporarily stolen McMurray's claim to being the gateway to the North. As a reflection of that fact, even though the *Fort McMurray* had been built in McMurray in 1915, she had been launched mainly to carry Peace River borne freight from Vermilion Chutes to Fitzgerald and Fort Chipewyan. The sight of the old *Grahame*, her predecessor, ending her days as a silent hulk on the river bank did nothing to cheer McMurray citizens through their depression.

By this time, however, in addition to some score of bachelors, ten white families were living in McMurray and a correspondent to the Athabasca *Northern News* had reported that ranged in order of their first appearance in the hamlet those on the distaff side were Miss Gordon, Mesdames Eymundson, Morrison, Laberge, Forman and others. In the spring of 1916 McMurray's first druggist, a man named Bannantyne, teaming up with John W. Tay, brought in a line of drugs and sundries. About the same time, one of the hamlet's strangest commercial transactions became the talk of the town. Most of the "farmers" who had chosen homesteads on the bench lands above the junction of the two rivers leaned more heavily to speculation than to cultivation. With his shack surrounded on all sides by unlimited wood available for the cutting, one of them—who shall be nameless—sent some ten miles into town to have a load of firewood delivered to his forest-locked residence. So with some business available to hustlers, McMurray's prospects were far from desperate.

Amongst the hustlers, of course, were Mickey Ryan, who was making money with his horses, the Hudson's Bay Company with its varied interests, and the Lamson-Hubbard Fur Company. Like the others, Jim Cornwall's Northern Transportation Company, with its well-known employees Frank O'Coffey and Angus Sutherland, looked forward to the day when finally the AGW would reach the town and to the time when the tar sands would develop.

All of them were also there in the spring of 1918 to play a part in one of McMurray's disastrous floods. Usually a docile, sluggish servant, the Athabasca River could change in a few hours into a ruthless, roaring monster piling great blocks of ice all over the flats at its junction with the Clearwater and pushing man and his works out of its way. At its break-up that spring, observers hearing a muttering where the modern highway bridge is, turned to look and suddenly like a volcano erupting in midstream a great mound of ice rose. Tumbling, clashing, breaking and roaring, the huge blocks piling high on top of each other moved forward relentlessly, crumbling the old, level, winter ice before them. Growing in height and width till it spread from bank to bank, the jam ground to a stop a couple of miles below the hamlet—a huge immovable dam. Against this dam more ice piled up and the water finding no escape rose quickly till it backed up over the island between the snye and the Clearwater. It reversed the flow in that river until for two or three miles upstream it covered the townsite of McMurray with a temporary but devastating lake bobbing with ice blocks. Tepees folded up and floated away, log houses hit by islands of ice collapsed and even the sturdy Northern Transportation Company warehouse was jarred askew on its foundation, and most of its contents, largely perishable foods, were washed away or ruined.

When the waters receded, McMurray was a muddy mess of logs and debris. The Northern Transportation Company had suffered the largest loss, while the Hudson's Bay Company and the Roman Catholic missionaries' northern supplies were hit heavily. Of all the warehouses, only Lamson-Hubbard's, a former AGW building up near the mouth of the Christina River, had not suffered extensively. Fortunately their goods were available to go north to stave off hunger. Fortunately, too, for the missionaries and the other traders, more goods could come in by the AGW.

The flood, while disastrous, was the most excitement the people of McMurray had known for some time. Even though an oil well was drilled near Cache 23 in 1917 and followed the next year by another one near Cheecham and still another near Anzac, nothing came of them. More success attended a provincial government salt well drilled in the subdivided part of town. One month's drilling took the hole to a depth of 685 feet and encountered a bed of salt some thirty feet thick. Following that up in 1922 the government drilled another well right in the new hamlet of Waterways but failed to find a satisfactory showing of the crystal mineral. Before that time, however, actually in March 1921, the AGW had laid its steel down the treacherous side hill to a terminal it called Waterways (Sec. 31, Twp. 88, R. 8). At last the railway had reached the Clearwater River and after spending $100,000 clearing the forest off its new townsite, sat back to rest on its laurels.

A month or so before trains were actually running to the new terminal, Nitchie Thorne, now a sergeant, made another appearance in McMurray. On February 26, 1921, he hired a team to take him and his latest prisoner the twenty or so miles to Cache 23. His long trip had begun at his post at Fort Simpson on January 11 when word had come in to the effect that at Fort Providence some 160 miles upstream a Slavey Indian, Albert Le Beau, had murdered his wife. All Thorne told his own wife was that he and his dogs expected to be away not more than a couple of weeks. It was to be over two months before he returned and when he did it was without his dog team. Had he waited for it, he would have arrived well over a month later.

Urging his dog team along some thirty-five miles a day, he met one or two parties of prospectors heading north towards the scene of the recent oil strike at Fort Norman. Pressing forward, sometimes into a headwind and sometimes under favourable conditions, his party soon covered the 160 miles to Fort Providence. On January 17 "Left Fort Providence with 4 dog trains and patrolled to Bluefish river, dug up body of Adelaide Le Beau. Weather 40 below, trail bad. 18 miles." Next day he and his dog drivers took the body to Fort Providence where for nearly a week he remained for Albert Le Beau's preliminary hearing for murder.

Because it was necessary for a coroner to see the body, he had to take it over to the nearest one, Dr. McDonald at Fort Smith, three hundred miles to the east. Consequently, on January 25, driving his dogs and accompanied by two other dog trains, Thorne started the next leg of his trip. Running along with the party came prisoner Le Beau, helping to keep the sleigh bearing his wife's body from toppling over. Thirteen days later the party reached Fort Smith.

After some delay there, Sergeant Thorne started south with his prisoner. Since he was no longer encumbered with the body, his entourage was reduced to two dog trains. By February 17 through stormy and fair weather, but usually over a bad trail, the party reached Fort Chipewyan. Leaving there two days later in company with some Hudson's Bay Company dog trains, Thorne's group travelled forty miles and "camped for night at mouth of Embarras river. Feb. 20, weather cold. Left camp 7 a.m., travelled to Poplar Point, camped for night at H. B. outpost, trail bad. 35 miles. Feb. 21, weather fair. Left camp 6:30 a.m., travelled to Sled Island, trail good, 35 miles. Feb. 22, Weather stormy, Left camp 6:30 a.m., travelled to Tar Island, trail bad, 40 miles. Feb. 23, Weather fine. Left camp 6:00 a.m., travelled to McMurray, arr. 10:30."

At Edmonton on March 1, Thorne's diary for that part of the patrol ends with the heartfelt comment: "Handed prisoner over to APP [Alberta Provincial Police] guardroom." During January and February he had travelled some 850 miles by dog team and 270 by train. All he had to do now was to get home to Fort Simpson.

In due course, after Albert Le Beau's incarceration at Edmonton, the authorities ordered that he should be tried near the scene of his crime, that is, back at the point whence after so much tribulation Sergeant Thorne had brought him. Accordingly, he left Edmonton on June 16 along with the judicial party which was to try him. Judge, jury and the defendant, travelling together and utilizing the services of the E.D. & B.C. to Peace River and the *D.A. Thomas* and the *Distributor*, reached the unfortunate man's former home point at Fort Providence on June 27. There, two days later, he was tried and sentenced to be hanged at Fort Smith on November 1, 1921. So once more, poor Albert Le Beau returned to Fort Smith to find a grave in the same cemetery which contained his wife's remains.

While in June, by railway and steamboat, it had taken Le Beau eleven days to travel from Edmonton to Fort Providence, Sergeant Thorne, who left Edmonton the previous March, took a mere four days to do so. Moreover, when two days after his arrival Thorne left Fort Providence for Fort Simpson, he covered the intervening 160 miles in one hour and forty-five minutes as compared to the five days which his trip in the reverse direction had taken him by dog train the previous January. For a new miracle had come to the North, its first aeroplane, and Nitchie had established a new record; he had made the first aeroplane journey on duty in the annals of the RCMP. While the trip from Peace River home to Fort

Simpson, a distance of 640 miles, had taken six days, his actual flying time had been a mere eight hours.

Before leaving home to arrest poor Le Beau, Sergeant Thorne had kept in touch with developments down the Mackenzie River near Fort Norman and before the outside world heard of it he had known that in the summer Imperial Oil Limited had struck oil there. Thereafter that company began arranging for aeroplanes to take supplies and men to Norman Wells. In March 1921, while Thorne was relaxing in Edmonton after his long trip south, he discovered that pilots Elmer G. Fullerton and George Gorman, along with two mechanics, were getting ready to fly two old wartime German planes north. Fortunately, along with Imperial Oil's geologist, Thorne was able to accompany them as a passenger. About four days later, after some intermediate stops, the two planes landed in three feet of snow at Fort Providence.

Cutting across the terrain which the sergeant knew so well, the next leg of their flight took them to Fort Simpson in one hour and forty-five minutes. Unfortunately in landing a mere hundred yards from the policeman's house the propeller and one ski of one of the planes were badly smashed, and though the second aircraft landed safely, it smashed its propeller when taking off to continue to Fort Norman. Thorne could rejoice that he had reached home safely but the two pilots now stranded at Fort Simpson faced the prospect of sitting twiddling their thumbs for the next five months until with the opening of navigation a new propeller could come from the factory.

But they were resourceful men in a land where the few residents were likewise resourceful. Although, when first conceived, the idea of making a new propeller seemed too preposterous to consider, between them Bill Hill, the mechanic, and Walter Johnson, a Hudson's Bay Company steamboat engineer and a one-time cabinetmaker, went to work to make a new one. Mustering all the hamlet's resources, using oak sleigh boards donated by the mission, laminating them with glue which they boiled up from moose hides, the new propeller took shape. When finished, it proved its reliability by enabling one plane to fly back to civilization.

As Sergeant Thorne watched the successful departure of the plane with its sleigh-board and moose-hide-glued propeller and thought of all the possibilities aircraft held for northern travel, he also contrasted it with his own remarkable trip. As stated in his superintendent's concise official report, it had been "accomplished by dog-train, horse sleigh, railway and aeroplane, the record being: 850 miles with dogs, travelling 28 days; 590 miles by train, travelling 5 days; 20 miles by horse sleigh, travelling 1 day; 640 miles by aeroplane, 8 hours' flying."

By that time the AGW, encouraged by the prospect of carrying passengers and machinery destined for the new Imperial Oil Limited's Norman Wells oil fields, began upgrading its road-bed and improving its service to McMurray. That was to prove a long, hard struggle, but eventually that railway lost its listing as a freak and came to be regarded as a reliable railway. By 1926 the railway had built another three and a half miles of track and moved its original Waterways to a new site still two or three miles short of McMurray. In moving, Waterways carried its name with it, while in honour of a pioneer oil sands promoter the old site, nearly stripped of its buildings, was renamed Draper. For some fifty years Waterways served as the great jumping-off place for the far North.

But though the days of the AGW's difficult gestation were over, its youthful aura of eccentricity clung to it. If on a trip the locomotive failed to plunge off the track and head into the muskeg or none of the freight cars smashed themselves against nearby trees, many another incident came along to amuse or irk the weary travellers. During duck-hunting seasons each fall the train crews stopped so that they and the passengers could spend a couple of hours filling their bags with mallards. In the dead of winter when silhouetted against the snowy hillside an uncautious moose browsed on adjacent willows, crew and passengers alike, seizing their rifles, spent a happy interval which ended by cutting up their victim and stowing his steaks and prime ribs aboard. But the blueberry season was the time when for two or three hours at a stretch, while the wheezy locomotive stood muttering in its slumbers, everybody bearing pails and sacks picked the tasty blue fruit before slowly resuming their interrupted journey.

One conductor, who for over twenty years served on the muskeg special, profited greatly on each of his winter trips. At every bridge or culvert along the 200-mile stretch beyond the station of Newbrook he stopped the train, climbed down, set a weasel trap underneath and went on. Stopping again on his way back some days later he checked his traps, took out any victims and reset them.

Ah, the old AGW—what a railway! What an era!

CHAPTER SIXTEEN

McMurray Marks Time

When in 1926 the AGW advanced its end of steel the new Waterways became a rival of the older McMurray. With the peninsula's salt, tar sands and shipping, everyone expected the two villages to develop rapidly. Unfortunately their salt disillusioned them and their sands disappointed them. Even the shipping business grew slowly with peak years now and then followed by a string of depression years. The coming of the steel had not brought the prosperity everyone had looked forward to and not until a further thirty long years had elapsed did the area's population reach one thousand.

Nevertheless, it was its shipping business that kept it alive and much of its history is the story of tugs and sternwheelers, wood-fired at first and later diesel operated, pushing or sometimes pulling barges of freight destined for the far places often hundreds of river miles away. The story of its water transport, of its fascinating characters and captains or of its difficult or heroic incidents could fill volumes. So too could the tales of Waterways' frantic years when the docks were expanded and modernized to take care of one rush after another—Imperial Oil Limited's Fort Norman wells, Gold-fields, Yellowknife, Eldorado, Uranium City, the Canol Pipeline and the Dew Line. Each of these rushes deserves a long story in its own right. And yet while heroic men strained mightily to handle rushes of freight borne in by the AGW their stories must be left for detailed treatment by other writers.

Even before the AGW had extended to the new Waterways the Union Bank had started business in McMurray and it, along with the Hudson's Bay Post, O'Coffey's hotel and the drug store Angus Sutherland built in 1921, became the nucleus of the town's main street. A year or so later, during one of his prolonged illnesses, Walter Hill, a young pharmacist, came in to run Angus's drug store and eventually became his partner. On Sutherland's death in 1951, he completed taking over the venture which

161

over the years has grown to the very extensive business now known as Hill's Drugs Limited. Today, over fifty years after he cast in his lot with the area, Walter Hill has become a veritable encyclopaedia of Fort McMurray history. For of all men he has come to know the vast wilderness that is the watershed of the Athabasca River and the unique breed of people it nurtures.

During Walter Hill's earlier years the basin at the junction of the two rivers was a busy mixing bowl of diverse characters and races. As well as the usual varieties of so-called Anglo-Saxons, sturdy Jewish traders came in to seek their share of the profits or to fret over the losses to be endured when trading with the natives who produced the area's only saleable commodity. So did several Syrians or Lebanese, as well as Moromoto, a Japanese. And, depending upon their courage, tenacity or luck, most of them succeeded and stayed to add character to the little settlement that was McMurray.

Mingling with these were a few speculative "farmers" who had filed on several of the surveyed quarter-sections surrounding the hamlet. For the few whose land holdings happened to be near it, a brief boom provided plenty of excitement. Here and there a forest-covered acre changed hands at $20,000. The discouragement caused by the long delay in oil sand development, however, finally killed that land boom.

Years elapsed before anyone followed up the 1910 discovery of beds of salt near the mouth of Horse River. In 1919 the Alberta government drilled a well in the same general area and found a bed some thirty feet thick but abandoned it in favour of another well which they completed at old Waterways in the fall of 1923 and also abandoned. Some years later John Gillespie, possibly in association with Von Hammerstein, decided to have another look at the area near the mouth of Horse River. There, by forcing steam down a well and dissolving the mineral, he produced salt for a number of years. Though he was promised that a railway spur track would be run to his plant, that promise never materialized and he was forced to cut a wagon road around the base of the big oil sands cutbank in order to haul his product to Waterways station. With the shifting and the crumbling of the sands his road has long since disappeared. After a few years this salt producing operation was discontinued.

Perhaps equally discouraging were some of the problems met by the pair of scientists who were doing their best to solve the poser presented by the oil sands. Upon his return from the army, S. C. Ells, the Dominion government geologist, came back to McMurray to continue his experiments with them. Cooperating with him was Karl A. Clark, a young scientist employed in the fall of 1920 by the recently established Research Council of Alberta and immediately presented with the challenge of finding some way to unlock their secrets. Because of the limited funds available to them and the incredible intricacy of the problem, their progress was necessarily slow, so that the small community, while wishing them well, had to turn to whatever other employment was available.

Part of that employment during 1921 consisted of constructing a new Hudson's Bay Company sternwheeler, the *Athabasca River*. She was built by the famous shipwright, Askiw, powered by engines taken from the beached *Grahame* and captained by the well-known E. B. Haight, and was

162

launched in the spring of 1922 to run between the end of the railway steel and Fitzgerald.

About the same time Mickey Ryan kept busy planning a new venture. Convinced that men, freight and mail could move north from McMurray during the winter, he had been getting ready to start a horse-drawn transport along the ice to Fort Chipewyan and Fort Smith. During the previous summer he had sent crews to cut hay or to send it down river by barges to cache at strategic sites en route and had brought in several teams of horses from Edmonton. In January 1922, as soon as the ice was safe, the first of his freighting teams set out. Though not by any means the first horses to go as far as the Fort Smith portage, these teams and their drivers performed some of the toughest hauling on record, through drifted snow, over teacherous ice and in the bitter cold of northern winters. At first Mickey used conventional sleighs but after a couple of years' experience he redesigned his vehicles by shortening and widening them. After that Ryan's freighting not only served the North well but made a profit. Much of this profit he poured into building the first sixteen-mile road around the rapids between Fitzgerald and Fort Smith, completing it by 1925. In 1929, however, aeroplanes out-moded his freight haul north from McMurray. That winter, his teamsters muffled to the eyes and making eighteen miles a day, could not help envying the intrepid aeroplane pilots who in their rickety craft made the flight from McMurray to Fort Smith in a couple of hours.

Though Ryan's teams moved considerable freight, the sternwheelers carried the bulk of the tonnage, which included supplies for mines and missions and even a herd of buffalo. During the years 1925 to 1928 the Northern Transportation Company's steamer heading north out of McMurray carried its quota of the 6,673 plains buffalo destined to be set free in the Wood Buffalo Park. Jim Cornwall and the federal authorities dreamed up this venture and Peace River Jim—Colonel Cornwall now —took the contract for shipping these animals from Wainwright Park so that they could mingle with their wild cousins along the Peace River. For four summers, every AGW mixed train—and all the trains were mixed —took its quota of buffalo north to be unloaded into the sturdy corrals erected at Waterways. For four summers, in lots of a hundred or more the animals were driven from these pens and prodded aboard barges so that the *Northland Echo* could take them under its wing for the trip down river.

Although McMurray grew very slowly, the summer months, the shipping season, found it a busy and a fascinating port. Every few days the mixed train delivered its load of goods of all sorts and its quota of hunters, traders and trappers. When, as often happened, the train pulled in from the south at the same time a sternwheeler from the north puffed in, the interchange between the two was a sight to behold. Cattle and sometimes buffalo would be loaded on barges to mingle with wood-cutters' horses and various sets of sled dogs going north. Packing them on till they filled still another scow a gang of men carried empty whitefish cases destined for Lake Athabasca. From another barge other men carried fish caught in that lake, to be packed in ice at the Waterways plant and sent off on the AGW destined to Chicago.

But even then times were changing. For one thing, one-way communication with the North had come about when in 1922 Edmonton radio station CJCA began broadcasting. Away in the North, at Fort Vermilion, Fort Simpson and Fort Resolution, with bated breath, fur traders listened to their crystal sets which brought this new magic all the way from Edmonton, the first real rent that was to cleave their ages-old curtain of isolation.

About the same time, diesel engines installed on several of the newer boats displaced some woodpiles and wood-cutters. Moreover, internal combustion engines in another guise, installed in aeroplanes, had already come in to complicate the carrying trade. Perhaps it was natural that the first plane to head down towards Lake Athabasca should lift from the surface of historic Lac La Biche which had seen the first Roman Catholic mission scows set out for the North. Over the rails of the AGW in 1926 the Dunne Syndicate of Calgary had sent their recently acquired but dismantled Vickers Viking amphibian. There it had been reassembled and with intrepid "Jack" Caldwell in its cockpit it had taken off with a load of company mining prospectors who were to try their luck among the previously inaccessible pre-Cambrian rocks of the Great Slave Lake area. During that summer Caldwell flew his "Bouncing Bruno" some five thousand miles and on his return brought the very first (even if unofficial) sack of airmail from Fitzgerald to Edmonton.

In its way the sack of mail was important enough, but of far more importance was the fact that by this new means of transport prospectors were once more looking at the mineral-rich pre-Cambrian shield which some Klondikers had peered at but forsaken nearly thirty years earlier. With aeroplanes a new age of exploration dawned. When in 1928 pilot "Doc" Oaks confirmed this by using McMurray as his base and flying out from there to the Barren Lands, the hamlet's citizens knew that they had another string for their bow. Speeding engineers and prospectors back and forth for the Toronto-based Northern Aerial Minerals Exploration Company his plane inspired all northerners with a new vision.

Before that year was over, in fact starting on its last bitter December day, a plane based in Edmonton demonstrated another service that the hardy bush pilots could carry out—mercy flights. Far off in the northern wilderness at Little Red River, near Fort Vermilion, diphtheria broke out. By dog team and telegraph the doctor at Fort Vermilion requested Edmonton to fly in a supply of antitoxin. Almost immediately, in thirty-three below weather, Wop May and Vic Horner left Edmonton in their rickety excuse for an aircraft on their dangerous mission, involving hours of exposure in the cramped seats of their open cockpit. In three or four days, they returned to Edmonton to discover ten thousand citizens waiting to give them a hero's welcome.

In 1929 James Richardson's Western Canada Airways of Winnipeg announced that with pilot Punch Dickins based at McMurray it was to start a regular air service between that point and Fort Chipewyan, Fort Smith, Fort Resolution, Hay River and Forts Providence and Simpson. Extending his territory on July 1, 1929, Dickins set his plane down on the Mackenzie River at Aklavik.

Punch Dickins and his Western Canada Airways soon had a rival, however, when the Commercial Airways Company obtained an official contract to carry mail from McMurray to the Arctic. When in the winter of 1929 this company set its two Bellancas and a Lockheed Vega down on the snye, McMurray citizens, counting these three planes as well as four of Western Canada Airways all resting in a row on the ice, knew that their end-of-steel town had also become the air terminal for the North. When next morning they watched two of the red Bellancas laden with mail for Fort Chipewyan and piloted by Wop May and Cy Becker soar off north along the river and then less than five hours later saw them return empty, they realized that for them the air age had begun. "So you've been to Chipewyan for lunch, have you?" said an amazed old-timer.

When later in the season Captain T. F. Smellie, coaxing his stern-wheeler around sand bars in the river, looked up at one of the Bellancas and observed that this wispy plane could carry more goods into the North in a year than his wallowing warehouse, few thought the matter through far enough to believe him. Yet it was so. Strangely enough, however, instead of robbing the steamers of all their carrying trade, the planes indirectly provided them with increased business by enabling prospectors to fan out all over the North and to start the mining era. In the early thirties the discovery of radium around Great Bear Lake and gold at Goldfields, about one hundred miles east of Fort Chipewyan on the north shore of Lake Athabasca, and also at Yellowknife, brought on a flurry of transportation activity through Waterways.

The first mining hotspot to be developed was at Goldfields on Lake Athabasca, less than three hundred miles from McMurray and therefore practically at its back door. In 1937 Consolidated Mining and Smelting Company began development work on its Box mine there and two years later brought it into production. For a while the town of Goldfields, which had been incorporated in 1937, boomed. By 1941, out of a thousand or so men in the area it had a population of 276. A year later when the Box mine closed down the town closed with it and most of the miners moved on to Yellowknife. During the height of the mining boom five steamboat companies operated out of Waterways: the Hudson's Bay Company's Mackenzie River Transport, the Northern Transportation Company Limited, McInnes Products, McLeod and Sons, and Goldfield Transportation Company.

For those few exciting years the hillsides looking down upon the Waterways docks resounded to the busy clatter of freight loading for the North. During the five-year stretch ending in 1941 the population of the combined McMurray-Waterways region doubled to 974 more or less permanent residents. Some of this increased population had come in to work in Dominion Tar and Chemical Company's salt plant which had started during the thirties but most of them gained their livelihood from some phase of the shipping industry as warehousemen, sternwheeler employees or boat and barge builders. A few of them put their hands to developing McMurray oil sand deposits and such ventures as Alcan, Abasand and Bitumount were afoot. In spite of such minor setbacks as fires and faltering train service, McMurray was forging ahead.

The fire of 1934 was a serious setback when most of McMurray's main street, including O'Coffey's hotel, Hill's drug store and other buildings were swept away, but the optimistic citizens rebuilt their establishments in a more commodious manner than before. Another fire in the forest through which the AGW wandered burned out a score or so of railway bridges and for a month no trains pulled into Waterways.

About this time, Industrial Minerals started a salt plant at new Waterways where the company drilled two wells in 1936 and 1937 and found a bed of salt some two hundred feet thick. In due course Dominion Tar and Chemical Company had a hand in this venture which continued to operate until in 1950 a salt plant at Lindbergh on the North Saskatchewan River put it out of business.

During its life, floods, recurring features of the local scene, took their toll and at times washed away some dock facilities at Waterways. Occasionally even the Tar Island shipyards some fifteen miles downstream came in for their costly share of flood damage. If once in a while, however, floods were bothersome, low water also had its disadvantages. During low water periods such as that of 1938 all forms of river craft—and by the thirties there were many varieties—had their problems. For then the sternwheelers could not get up to the Waterways docks and goods had to be lightered down to the yarding area commonly known as Lehman's Landing eight miles below McMurray. Various power boats, tugs and barges had to be used in this shuttle service. Similarly, in low water years there was a yarding area in the Athabasca Delta whence goods had to be lightered across the end of the lake.

All of these problems, however, were insignificant as compared to the task which faced Waterways in 1942. For that year World War II was at a desperate stage. The Japanese were threatening Alaska, and the American army, leaping to its defence, decided that it needed oil from the Norman Wells field and over mountains and muskeg started to build the 500-mile-long Canol Pipeline to supply a refinery at Whitehorse. A mountainous pile of drilling and producing equipment had to be rushed to the oil field, as well as miles of four-inch pipe for the line to Whitehorse. On top of the normal freight heading north all of this material, thousands and thousands of tons of it, had to pass over the Waterways wharves.

There in 1942 the ice went out on May 12 and the navigation season commenced. All the companies looked forward to a busy year anyway but on May 27 the U.S. War Department dropped a bombshell on their decks by advising them of its top secret war job, the Canol project. It asked them to take on the additional load of transporting thirty thousand tons of Canol material. All of the companies buckled down to help. But even by their utmost efforts, and even though the U.S. army undertook to supply troops, equipment and help in transporting the four-inch pipe, they could not handle all of it and the army had to carry some of its own. To supplement the shipping already in use on the Athabasca River—tugs, steamers and barges—the army as well as building many a barge at Waterways, hauled in countless "pontons," small duralumin barges used normally for building bridges, and many tugs from the United States. The pontons were strung together to make large rafts propelled by small motor boats and on these rafts the miles of pipe set off for Fitzgerald. Typical of a more normal setup was one of the loads the *Athabasca River* handled in July 1942 when she left Waterways hauling or pushing six hundred tons of freight. These staunch sternwheelers and their sturdy skippers did a magnificent job for the Canol project, as did everyone in Waterways or McMurray who in the frenzy that was the Canol summer worked from early daylight to late dusk.

After subsiding a little from the peak years of the Canol rush, the tonnage shipped out of Waterways increased year after year. The planes had not killed the steamers after all. In fact, when in 1946 world interest in uranium soared to fever heat, the tonnage carried climbed to new records. Following the discovery of pitchblende at Great Bear Lake, hopeful prospectors started searching with their new-fangled geiger counters along the shores of Lake Athabasca and particularly in the Black Bay and Beaverlodge Lake areas until by 1949 Eldorado Mining and Refining (1944) Limited became interested. During 1952 that company started large-scale workings at its mine and by April 1953 its multi-million-dollar separation plant came into operation.

Meanwhile the new town of Uranium City flashed into life. It got its start during the winter of 1952-53 when all the abandoned buildings were moved the few miles over from the now deserted town of Goldfields. Moreover, some twenty miles away Gunnar Gold Mines Limited made its monumental discovery of uranium ore which it worked by a vast open pit operation. Uranium City quickly grew to a town of some four thousand population and continued to exist through the ups and downs of the uranium market until today it is the headquarters of mining development on the north shore of Lake Athabasca. That the mines of the Beaverlodge area made a significant contribution to Canada's economy is evident from the fact that in 1958, for instance, they produced $58 million worth of uranium.

Unfortunately we have no space to deal with the vastly interesting story of the miners and the towns they built on Lake Athabasca's northern shore. Neither can we go into the feats of so many flyers who buzzed in and out of Fort McMurray. Regretfully too we must leave untold so much that should be said about the river-men and their trials with low water in the river or ice or storms on the vast lake. And yet there are two stories which must be told. During one of the many low water years when normally full loads could not be taken across Lake Athabasca the captain of the *Radium Cruiser* had to split his tow and move his barges out of the delta one at a time. All went well with the first two but trouble struck when the *Radium Cruiser* was ploughing along slowly pulling the third. One of the deck hands standing on the after end of the vessel was so intent on looking back at the following barge that he did not notice that the *Radium Cruiser* was turning until the heavy hawser swept him off into the lake. One of his mates sent up the time honoured cry of "Man overboard." The busy captain, repeating the cry "Man overboard," stopped the engines and seizing the nearest life ring ran and threw it to the unfortunate man who seemed to be floundering in the waves. The victim caught it and then, standing erect in waist-deep water, carried the life ring back to the vessel.

The other story had a vastly different ending and illustrates the fury of some of the storms which could lash Lake Athabasca into a frenzy of menacing rollers. "It was a hell of a night late in August 1956," said Captain Julian A. Mills when he told of one of his scores of trips across Lake Athabasca. He was heading his *Radium Queen* east to Crackingstone Point and the port of Bushell which served Uranium City. As his barges bobbled about and groaned as the waves broke over them, all of his crew were alert, listening and watching.

A mile or so behind us came the *Clearwater*—Tiny Holden, skipper—and every ten minutes or so after it got dark we kept in touch by flashing our lights at each other. You can feel pretty lonely out there in a storm and there is something reassuring in knowing that someone else in the same straits is keeping an eye on you.

Anyway, everything was going well as we came abreast of Beartooth Island and the old diesels were pounding away steadily and Tiny kept flashing his light and we answered.

The next time I flashed my light back—perhaps ten or fifteen minutes later—Tiny didn't answer. "Must have passed around the other side of Beartooth," I thought and turned my light off as we kept pounding and bumping along.

Ten minutes later I turned my light on again and left it on but still there was no answer from Tiny or the *Clearwater*. "Should have passed Beartooth by now," I figured, but in the darkness there was nothing to see and nothing we could have done anyway, so we kept on to Bushell.

Next morning the weather was clear and the storm had died down but there was no sign of the *Clearwater*. Captain Mills and two or three others going back to look for her found the barges but the *Clearwater* had disappeared—apparently she had sunk suddenly taking Tiny Holden and her crew of eight with her.

A few days later one floating corpse was found. But how, except that it had happened suddenly—how she came to her end no one ever knew. Eventually the wreck was located in 135 feet of water and salvaged without revealing what had caused her to sink.

"The only thing we could guess was that in the darkness she had run up on the sloping shelving rocks of Beartooth Island and canted over enough that a yank from the tug lines had capsized her. But no one will ever know—the lake keeps its secrets well. But nine fine men went to the bottom with her."

In spite of all their love for the North and their reverence for its old Emporium, all the skippers and their ships inadvertently treated Fort Chipewyan shabbily. Passing it at close range on their trips from Fort McMurray to Fitzgerald a few of them pulled in to the old landing but most were too busy even to nod in her direction. On their trips to Bushell they swung to the right as they emerged from the Delta and unless the weather was very clear Fort Chipewyan seldom saw them. Unwittingly her downfall had started when in 1883 Captain Smith built the *Grahame*.

Steamboats passing by a mile or so off shore brought little cash to her coffers and added precious little to her peoples' resources. The dog-days had descended on Fort Chipewyan; bad years when only her most valiant stood by her—only her long-time natives, her trappers and sturdy fisher-men and her core of many-generationed aristocracy such as the Frasers and the Fletts, the Loutits and the Wylies.

For weeks on end in good years, whole families camped out in the Delta, working long hours trapping and skinning "rats" and living almost entirely on their tasty carcasses spitted and roasted around their fires. Traps, of course, provide the bulk of the yearly take, but during the mating season—and muskrats are frequently ready to mate—hundreds are taken in another way. For then native ears, ever attuned to the calls and cries and whisperings rising from the wide marshes, eagerly await the signal that another muskrat mating season has started—the first plaintive mewing of a female pleading for a mate. That is the time to run the boats into the bays and bayous, to shut off the motor and at the edge of the reeds to sit motionless with a twenty-two rifle handy and at short intervals to imitate the bewitching love moan. Stillness, alertness, patience and frequent calling do the trick as one by one the males twitching their whiskers rush to the seductive call and venture to within almost arm's length of the boat and the ready gun.

Trapping the muskrats is only part of the game; selling them is where the hazard lies. For prices are unpredictable and may go up or drastically down. My old friend, K. C. McDonald batching in his cabin at Fort Chipewyan in spite of nearing the century mark, spoke of the ups and downs of prices. "Just after the war" (and for fear of interrupting him I didn't dare to ask if he meant the 1900 Boer War or the 1914 Great War), "Just after the war, long before there was any radios or telegraph lines, I hit the jackpot. Me and my wife—she was old Ed Smith's daughter—me and my wife were the first to come in from the traps that spring and we had a boat load of rat pelts. And I carried 'em over to Tom Woodman of Lampson and Hubbard."

"They're good rats," said Tom, "a good lot. I'll give you three dollars each for them."

"OK," I said, "you give me a few groceries for now and I'll leave 'em while you count 'em. I'll be back next week and you can pay me." And I walked down to the lake shore, two hundred yards away. And as I was unhitching my boat who should I see but Tom McLennan, the trader from McMurray aheading for shore, the first stranger from outside that spring. So I waited. "How's business, Tom?" I said, and a funny look came over his face.

"Dunno. It's all right with me I guess but with you Ken, you and the trappers, it's going to be bad. The price of rats is all gone to hell."

"What price are they now?" I asked.

"A dollar fifty for the best," he answered.

"A dollar fifty—phew!" But then I shut up and went about my business.

Didn't go back to Tom Woodman for a week—was afraid to. But Tom was a man of his word—all them old traders were. He never let on and he never welshed—just paid me the rest of the money for them three-dollar rats.

But if the price of rats sometimes went up, Fort Chipewyan's fortunes consistently dropped. For times were changing. A symbolic indicator of Fort Chipewyan's falling prestige came in 1939 when, except for one or two of them which were moved to new locations in the hamlet, all of the Hudson's Bay Company's old buildings, which in 1872 Chief Factor Roderick McFarlane had reconstructed so sturdily, were torn down and the site abandoned.

Two years later, in 1941, another bastion of the community fell when at the age of ninety-one Colin Fraser died. The most highly respected man in the whole North and probably the most wealthy too, his passing snapped the last link with the great fur trading past—with his father Colin Fraser the piper and with Sir George Simpson, who 120 years earlier had fought the Hudson's Bay Company's battle at Fort Chipewyan and won.

By about the time of Colin Fraser's death, several hundred Indians lived on the Chipewyan reserve and a similar number lived independently in the Peace-Athabasca Delta. By 1956 the few who lived in the Fort Chipewyan hamlet swelled its population to some three hundred. Though compared to the standard of living in the rest of the Province of Alberta theirs was deplorable, it was nevertheless better than it had been before the white traders had brought some of their inventions and conveniences to the area.

The writing was on the wall, however, and concerned governments, foreseeing the end of the fur trade, took steps aimed at helping the Indians make the transition to the modern white man's economy. Whether for good or evil these steps resulted in a rapid growth of Fort Chipewyan's population from 304 in 1956 to 717 five years later and to about 1,500 today. Its gain was at the expense of depopulating the Chipewyan Indian reserve and at the expense of moving the Cree families hitherto scattered about the Delta area into the hamlet as more or less permanent residents. Unfortunately, though its population increased, its economic base declined. Year by year the yield from commercial fishing and trapping became less and less. So while the population of Fort Chipewyan continued to increase, the gap between its indigenous earnings (that is, what the people can produce) and what it needs to consume grew. That growing gap was bridged by larger and larger loads of government subsidy.

Though in this modern age Fort Chipewyan's homes are lit by electricity and its people travel in and out from a splendid airport, its days of glory have long since gone. Hopefully the recent Peace-Athabasca Delta Project study will offer some solution to its problems and once more it will become a viable community.

There were times too when the people of Fort McMurray, seeing how the gods had averted their eyes from Fort Chipewyan, began to have misgivings about their own future. Starting in 1946, however, when the mines at Uranium City and Gunnar had come into being, the tonnages setting out from Waterways started to rise to new heights. McMurray had been saved by the bell—the dropping of the first atomic bomb—and continued to be saved for over a decade until about 1960 when the world demand for uranium fell off.

In the post-Second War era energy had become the symbol of material progress and the slogan on everyone's lips—energy in the form of electricity, coal, oil, gas and uranium—and though energy in the form of cliffs of oil sands stared the people of McMurray in the face, they could neither solve the riddle of how to utilize them nor find anyone else who could. It was all very disappointing and this lack of progress was reflected in the combined Waterways-McMurray population which during the war had been less than one thousand people and twenty years later stood at less than twelve hundred.

During and after the war the shortage of oil had sent many a scientist and geologist to McMurray to observe the oil sands, but invariably they came to look and then went home and nothing visible ever came of their looking. Then when other geologists in their wild scramble for oil probed intensively into the strata underlying the Edmonton area, out gushed Alberta's first really significant oil well, Leduc No. 1. It soon became merely the advance guard of thousands of other wells for strangely enough Alberta was found to be floating on oil. During the next twenty years, while the oil sands lay blistering in the sun, drillers and wells and pipelines swept north and west across Alberta and on and on into the Northwest Territories. The appetite of an oil-hungry world was being satisfied by conventional oil wells and once more McMurray's prospects wilted.

Then the far-off Mackenzie Highway started tampering with McMurray's monopoly of northern shipping. The Hudson's Bay Company sold its Mackenzie River Transport with its steamers, tugs and barges to the Northern Transportation Company and thenceforth in effect that company became the sole survivor of all the shipping outfits which had plied the Athabasca. For 135 years Hudson's Bay Company's craft had been docking at McMurray. Two-thirds of a century earlier that company had launched the Athabasca's first sternwheeler, the *Grahame*, followed by many a staunch successor, some of which had been diesel operated. Now the flags of the Hudson's Bay Company steamers came down for the last time. All the old links were snapping.

Over the years other links had snapped. During the mid-forties Christine Gordon—one of McMurray's most ardent supporters who had arrived some forty years earlier and had been a mainstay of the settlement for so long—died. In 1955 in a less personal way the people of McMurray heard of the death of Jim Cornwall, who by then was almost a legendary figure, the man of many nicknames, all of them indicating greatness as the pre-eminent devotee and developer of the North. He had been one of the first to try to make something of the oil sands. That, of course, was back in 1908, forty-seven years before when all McMurray folk had been young pioneers who had hoped to see their hamlet blossom into a city overnight.

Creating cities, however, had turned out to be a slow process—slow as the seepage of oil from the surrounding oil sand cliffs in December. And just as the years since Jim Cornwall had drilled his first wells had been years of hope deferred, so were the next ten after his death. During them, as opposed to some of the more hopeful years, no oil of any commercial kind had been produced. Not only that, but the Great Slave Lake Railway, completed in 1965, had stolen more of Waterways' shipping business. McMurray, sitting atop the biggest storehouse of oil in the free world —were its hopes to be postponed forever and ever?

CHAPTER SEVENTEEN
Bucket-Wheels

Fate favours the faithful. And eventually she rewarded McMurray's old-timers as well as the two scientists who had spent their lives searching for a solution to the problems of the oil sands.

Nevertheless, the battle to untangle their riddles took decades of devotion and in the end an immense accumulation of capital. Unfortunately we can skim only briefly over its highlights from the year 1913, when young S. C. Ells of the federal Department of Mines, first laid eyes on the sand cliffs. When that fall he decided to take a sizeable sample back to Edmonton and loaded it on a scow for the 250-mile upstream trip to Athabasca Landing, his initiation as a man of the North began.

When he was ready to begin having his forty-foot scow pulled at the end of five hundred feet of manilla rope, his twelve-man crew refused to move. Sergeant LaNauze got Ells out of that difficulty by striding down to the shore, seizing the line and shouting to the trackers in Cree till, somewhat ashamed of themselves, they took hold and the scow started upstream. Seven days later at Grand Rapids, with eighty-seven miles of ceaseless struggle behind them, three of them were laid up, one by a hernia, one by appendicitis and one by pneumonia. But because for another sixteen days Ells kept the men at their slaving task, the sands went through. For seventeen days in all it had rained. Three times the men went on strike and Ells coaxed them back to the line. On the last occasion they made the mistake of quitting not only before supper but at the foot of a long stretch of quiet water. Taking up the line, Ells persuaded two of the men to pull with him and, rather remarkably, inched the scow half a mile upstream. There, well in sight of the disaffected trackers, he and his loyal companions stopped and lit their cooking fire. Before they had finished eating, the rest of the crew, hungry and humble, joined them and the strike was over.

For all this toil he paid the men the going wage—$45 for the trip—and supplied each of them with tobacco and several pairs of moccasins. His outlay for these essentials cost him $38. His own salary at the time, the official rate for young graduate scientists, was $1,800 a year. When he turned his expense account in to Ottawa they quickly reimbursed him for the wages he had given his trackers but refused to pay the $38 the tobacco and moccasins had cost him. Thus he made one of the earliest of his many sacrifices in the cause of the oil sands.

The next year he made better progress, for his 1,200 one-hundred-pound bags of sands only travelled three miles in a scow and downstream at that, until they were unloaded into a shed at McMurray. In December twenty-three teams came across from Athabasca Landing, loaded up the sacks and took them over the winter trail to House River and on to the railway station at The Landing. In due course Ells saw them heated and hammered out into a piece of pavement near 82nd Street along Edmonton's old Fort Saskatchewan Trail where they served well for four or five decades. Moreover, at the request of the National Parks people, Ells chose a reservation of 580 acres near the mouth of the Horse River and about a mile and a half west of McMurray, from which it was planned to mine sands which could be used for paving in Jasper National Park. Having accomplished these things, he went off to fight in World War I.

On his return he hurried back to his sands and for a few years spent much of his time mapping the huge area they covered. By 1926 he had come to realize that the land around Tar Island, Mildred and Ruth lakes held rich development possibilities. All the while, of course, he worked very closely with Karl Clark, who like himself soon became a devotee at the oil sands' shrine.

By 1923, in association with S. M. Blair, Clark had begun operating his first primitive hot-water separation plant at the University of Alberta. Obtaining encouraging results, the pair decided to build a larger plant out at the E.D. & B.C. yards where they could receive batches of the sands direct from the AGW Railway. By 1929, having made further progress there, Clark moved the plant to Waterways.

Soon after his arrival in Alberta, Clark met Ells and, in spite of the fact that one was employed by the provincial and the other by the federal government, their intense interest in their work was a bond between them. While in 1926 Ells was opening up his quarry near the Horse River, he kept sending batches of sands to Clark and when in 1929 the provincial scientist moved his plant to the banks of the Clearwater River, he and Ells continued their helpful co-operation.

Meanwhile, in 1927 Ells sent a major shipment of sands, some 2,400 tons, to Jasper where far up the headwaters of the Athabasca River it was used to surface the old highway which connected the town with Jasper Park Lodge. This shipment, having descended about a mile of the Athabasca River at McMurray, was then towed up the Clearwater and loaded on the AGW.

Shortly after Clark re-erected his plant at Waterways, Ells started a new quarry directly across the Clearwater from it, opposite the mouth of the Hangingstone River and about a mile below the Waterways station. When, working co-operatively, the federal Mines Branch and the provincial Research Council connected the quarry and the plant by a crude tramway spanning the river, the two operated as a unit. Ells directed his efforts to trying to solve the problems of mining the very abrasive sands while Clark worked out answers to the puzzles of producing oil and a material which could be used for paving purposes. Seeking solutions to these many problems the pair continued their operations until 1936 when the Depression halted the work. In 1938 Clark accepted the post of Professor of Metallurgy at the University of Alberta, a position he held until his official retirement many years later. Although Ells and Clark had accumulated a great deal of experience and knowledge which was later to be most valuable, commercial development of the sands appeared as far away as ever.

For many years previous to the Depression as well as after it, enterprising men kept trying to fabricate and finance plants which would extract the oil from the sands. For years their individual or corporate names loomed large on McMurray's horizon. Amongst them were Thomas Draper, J. O. Absher and Max W. Ball and his Canadian Northern Oil Sands Products Ltd., which later became Abasand Oils Ltd. During its 1941 operating season Abasand produced 21,476 barrels of oil at a maximum rate of 200 barrels per day, but a fire in 1945 finished its career.

Perhaps the most promising attempt to overcome the problem of producing oil from the sands was the plant at Bitumount, some fifty miles downstream from McMurray and near the site of the old Pierre au Calumet fur-trade post. It passed through a number of stages and hands starting with those of A. W. Wheeler, who opened the Wheeler post office about 1922 and called his venture the Alcan Oil Company. The next year, a man whose devotion to the sands was to span the half century which ended with their successful development by Great Canadian Oil Sands Ltd., R. C. Fitzsimmons, took over Wheeler's leases and called the operation the International Bitumen Company at a new address known as Bitumount. From Fitzsimmons' hands in 1942 it passed to L. R. Champion and became Oil Sands Ltd. Under that management the Government of Alberta put up $500,000 to help construct a new plant. When by 1948 the venture had fallen short of realization, the province assumed sole ownership and a new plant was completed the next year, and for some months operated well. In doing so, under another devotee, W. E. Adkins, it demonstrated that Clark's hot-water process was technically feasible.

It remained to be seen, however, how technical feasibility could be translated into commercial practicability and how many millions of dollars it would take to make that jump. Thus far all told, it had taken maybe a million dollars spent by venturous men and interested governments and practically all that had been obtained was a process capable of doing the job. How much capital would it take sometime in the future to start the long-locked oil pulsing to markets through a pipeline?

So far, though many brilliant men had worked at the problem, the high cost of producing the oil kept it from being competitive with that from Alberta's hundreds of oil wells and McMurray had reaped precious little reward for all its optimism and its hopes. Not that these brillant men had not done their best. As S. C. Ells said when speaking of others, "They had all made major contributions to the solution of the problem"—all of them, Adkins, Ball, Clark, Cornwall, Fitzsimmons and Von Hammerstein.

Perhaps the best tribute was that of Max W. Ball who in his turn referring to Ells had said: ". . . for thirty-five years in the face of indifference and skepticism, he has been the courageous and unremitting advocate of the value and importance of the bituminous sand deposits."

Nevertheless, while sitting on top of the world's richest oil field, McMurray had not grown. In 1950 its population was still less than a thousand. Short in quantity those people may have been but they were long on quality. Indeed, on May 6, 1947, that quality had led them to incorporate as a village, which in December 1948 was proclaimed a town. Moreover, though filled with a sense of their town's destiny, they did not forget their proud past and made the fortunate decision to revert to their original name, Fort McMurray.

Fort McMurray's long-term destiny, if not as immediate as tomorrow's daylight, was definitely as certain. At the time of its incorporation, however, that destiny was still shrouded in uncertainty. With hundreds of recently drilled wells spouting oil all over southern Alberta, there was no incentive to try to produce the more costly oil from the sands. And yet underlying the town and underlying an area of 13,000 square miles all around it lay 300 billion barrels of marketable oil. Coupling that fact with the memory of the oil shortage during the recent war and the fear of similar shortages in the future made it imperative for governments and the large oil companies to start the sands producing. Undoubtedly many unsolved problems still strewed the path to that production but the time to find and overcome them was now, before the next oil crisis made it too late.

In 1950, with that in mind and while the provincial government still operated the Bitumount plant, it turned to S. M. Blair to make a report and to point the way to the future. By that time Blair, who had worked with Karl Clark in 1923, had become a recognized authority on similar problems. His report set the stage that was to lead to the next plateau, that of actual production. It advocated using Clark's hot-water method of separation and was an authoritative exposition of the many problems involved. It brought into focus the fact that the major ingredient in the formula for successful production would be large-scale operation—terrifically large-scale operation. To be economically competitive oil had to be produced not in terms of the two hundred barrels per day which Abasand was turning out but in terms of thousands of barrels per day. The only practical plant of the future would need not an investment of $500,000 but well on towards five hundred times that, say $250 million.

By that time the Bitumount operation had been sold to Can-Amera Oil Sands Development Ltd. and Royalite Oil Company jointly. In due course these two companies announced plans for a plant and a pipeline project costing $50 million. But, like so many others, these plans fell through.

At that point the Sun Oil Company came into the picture and in 1953 incorporated Great Canadian Oil Sands Limited (GCOS) which acquired the interests of Oil Sands Limited, the successor to Fitzsimmons' old International Bitumen Company. A year later, Sun Oil Company secured a 75 per cent interest in the Mildred-Ruth Lakes leases, about twenty miles north of Fort McMurray. When oil would flow from these leases, however, was still a question to be left for time to answer. Years, of course, counted for so little in the scale of time applied to the oil sands which had been some one hundred million reaching their present state. Nevertheless, one at a time, in their inexorable march, the years had been catching up with the sands' most devoted disciples. Sidney Clarke Ells had reached the age of sixty-five and had been retired. Then in 1954 Karl Clark, after thirty-four years of devotion to the sands, reached the age when all government employees are retired and pushed out to pasture.

Karl, however, refused to pasture passively but maintained his interest in the sands and placed his encyclopaedic knowledge and skill at the disposal of GCOS as a consultant. In 1960 Great Canadian Oil Sands Ltd. applied to the Alberta Oil and Gas Conservation Board for approval to go ahead and put it in a difficult position. On the one hand, a look into the future made it imperative to seize every opportunity to find a way to extract oil from the sands. On the other, Alberta was suffering from a glut of oil from conventional wells and any input from the sands would only worsen the situation. The Board's compromise was to permit GCOS to gear up to produce some 30,000 barrels and to insist that even that amount must not be thrown on the Alberta market but must go to outside purchasers.

Much still remained to be found out about a plant and a process which would obtain the oil economically. As further studies progressed, GCOS went to the Board once more explaining that its computers indicated that to produce oil which would be cheap enough to compete with that from conventional wells its operation would have to be on an even larger scale than had been anticipated and that economic production could be obtained only by turning out 45,000 barrels per day. At this point J. Howard Pew, owner of Sun Oil Company, cast his fortune and his company's future into the gamble. First, he undertook to cut down on the crude oil which the American Sun Oil Company imported from South America and to replace it with enough additional oil from Fort McMurray, so as not to disturb the Alberta market but yet to let the proposed plant gear up for an output of 45,000 barrels. Second, in spite of his colleagues' fears, he committed the Sun Oil Company's finances to the project. As a result, early in 1964 the Conservation Board issued a permit allowing the company to build a plant capable of producing at least 45,000 barrels per day.

At last Thomas Spence's eighty-six-year-old prophecy began coming true. At last, although in a somewhat altered form, the "miner's pick and shovel, his drill and his explosives" were indeed ready to force the sands to "give up their secrets of fabulous wealth." Moreover, the day of the first of his "wonderful bridges" had arrived. In the biggest gamble in its history the Sun Oil Company, through its subsidiary, GCOS, committed itself to expenditures involving a quarter of a billion dollars. Its gamble on the oil sands was to be the largest single private investment ever made up to that time in all of Canada's history. Eighty years after the Edmonton *Bulletin* had so gleefully reported forty miles of pipe lying at Calgary ready to ship north to bring out the oil from the sands, the forces of world finance had concentrated on the sands with the magic which was to unlock their secrets—money. Fort McMurray's day had come; money—which after all only means man-hours, much of which in this case was converted into petroleum engineering know-how from our southern neighbours—had come pouring in.

The story of how these man-hours concentrated into the form of pipes and fittings, belts and bucket-wheels, all conceived by world-wide specialists in technology and wrestled and welded into an oil separation plant in three years by a force of workmen of many skills is a remarkable one. At the peak of the construction period twenty-three hundred men —riveters and riggers, engineers and electricians, scientists and catskinners, plumbers and painters—were pitting their brawn and their brains against many odds on the job site. On September 30, 1967, the great jig-saw puzzle, the world's first commercial oil sands venture started turning out synthetic crude oil and piping it away to market. That day dignitaries from all over and specialists in many facets of the construction and oil industries gathered to rejoice that at last the oil sands had come into their own and that Fort McMurray had come into its kingdom. The bulk of those assembled at the plant opening were young workers, technicians or executives. Of the old men, many were staunch old-timers from Fort McMurray's earlier days.

The one old-timer who for forty-seven years had applied his keen scientific mind to solving the tar sand riddle was not there. For, the previous winter, at seventy-eight years of age, Karl Clark had died. Nevertheless, his dedication to the cause had permitted him to see his life's work crowned with success when in July 1964 he took part in the plant's ground-breaking ceremonies. Of the other old-timers, one was R. C. Fitzsimmons who some forty years earlier had first pitted his enterprise against the stubbornness of the sands. The other was J. Howard Pew, an old-timer whose life's course had been run in America's conventional oil fields far removed from the oil sands' cliffs.

Amongst the other dignitaries present was Russ Patrick, Alberta's Minister of Mines and Minerals, who for years had been involved in the intricacies of controlling oil production. He was one of the very few men present who knew the J. Howard Pew story. Indeed, he was the only outsider who had been present at Sun Oil Company's directors' meeting in Philadelphia when Mr. Pew had made the decision that allowed the oil sands' development to go ahead.

Prior to that time the recently incorporated GCOS had sub-leased part of the land which Sun Oil controlled and, as a result, along with the Canadian Pacific Railway, Canadian Oils and Abasand, Sun Oil shared in this new company. This group, although it was given certain valuable options and concessions, was after all a relatively small company. For a year or so, without success, it had tried to interest investors, Canadian and otherwise, in financing the risky gamble of the sands. All the investment brokers had shaken their heads; the risks were too great. Faced with this lack of confidence, GCOS officials had come to the point where financing their project appeared hopeless and they were preparing to throw up their hands, relinquish their options and forget about the whole venture.

Before that happened, however, Russ Patrick, in a last ditch effort to ensure the development of the sands, flew to Philadelphia to address a meeting of Sun Oil's directors. Some of them may have expected him to plead for the sands' development and undoubtedly he did so, but his pleading took the form of a challenge. He did not paint the path leading through the sands as the soft, easy road to success, but instead reiterated that the going would be tough for anyone who would pick up the gauntlet of the oil sands. As the mood of the meeting developed, he found himself aiming his remarks not at the chairman, Robert Dunlap, but at J. Howard Pew, the president. This white headed gentleman's whole life had been passed overcoming seemingly impossible obstacles until now in his old age he practically owned Sun Oil Company, and as well, in a totally different field, had put together a vast shipping enterprise—a man of great wealth, courage and determination.

When Patrick had finished, all eyes turned towards the head of the table to watch the old man rise with a new gleam in his eye as he set off to tilt with the greatest challenge in his career.

"Young fellow," he said in effect, looking at Patrick, who was never to forget his words, "you've caught me in a good mood. Today is my eighty-second birthday, and this morning on the course my golf score equalled my age. For many of those years I have met many a challenge, and at times lost, so I'm glad you didn't come here to try to soft-sell me, because that doesn't work.

"As I see the situation, perhaps Sun Oil has been remiss in its exploration program aimed at securing ample future supplies of oil for its integrated company operation and in not taking a more significant share in the sands and a share in their risks. Personally, the sands have always fascinated me but I have been so busy."

Then, after a pause, he continued: "And yet the years are catching up on me. When the world looks back it will soon forget that I built up the Sun Oil and put together my large shipping interests—maybe, however, it will not forget the man who provided the key to unlock the riddle of the oil sands—we'll go for it."

Having appalled his colleagues with that pronouncement, he started acting upon his decision immediately and, turning to his nephew and successor, he said: "That 10,000 barrels per day we get from Venezuela, we will replace that with oil from GCOS. And we'll take other measures."

Then, coming around the table to shake hands with Patrick, he repeated: "We'll go for it."

A hush settled over the room and Robert Dunlap rose to confirm the acceptance of the challenge but added that they were about to take on the greatest gamble any integrated oil company had ever faced.

Without Mr. Pew's intervention, which entailed casting his entire multi-million dollar fortune into the uncertain venture, one of the greatest risks ever entered upon, GCOS would not have been transformed from a hopeful infant to the giant which was to tackle the oil sands' problems head on. Pursuant to that, on September 30, 1967, this gathering had assembled at Tar Island to celebrate the opening of the great adventure. Not all pioneers wear work clothes.

When the participants returned from the plant opening to their hotels in Fort McMurray, they drove along the most northerly hard-surfaced road then in Alberta, the twenty-mile link connecting the plant to its dormitory city, Fort McMurray. Moreover, they drove over the newly built steel bridge across the Athabasca—one of the bridges of which Spence had dreamed.

But they were to sleep in a transformed Fort McMurray, a city springing from the two old villages of McMurray and Waterways and grown to hold eight thousand people. Paved streets, buildings like Walter Hill's new drug store costing well on towards half a million dollars, composite schools (one named after Karl Clark), shopping centres, splendid churches and quiet residential subdivisions spread for over three miles along its river flat.

By that time a highway had been chopped through the 150-mile forest from the direction of Lac La Biche because in 1964 the Alberta government had authorized an expenditure of $1,750,000 to begin work on it. Until this highway was opened, the cheapest, if not the most sublime, way to get to Fort McMurray was still by the vastly upgraded AGW. During the construction of the GCOS plant this railway, now known as the Northern Alberta, operated two passenger trains per week to the oil sands town, but now that the highway has been opened its service has fallen back to what it was for decades, a mixed train with a passenger coach tied on behind freight cars.

During plant construction days it forgot all its old youthful foolishness and buckled down to the heavy task of carrying in the thousands of tons needed. Perhaps its most telling test came when it was time to take delivery from the CPR of one of the major tanks for use in the new plant, a carbon dioxide absorber. It was 14 feet in diameter and 144 feet long, weighed 340,000 pounds and reached Edmonton on three special railway cars. For months the AGW officials had been preparing for the day when it would be entrusted to their care. They had specified that they would have to haul it during the winter when the muskegs would be frozen so that the road-bed could bear its weight.

Like many a lesser load borne in the good old days of its earlier decades, this load was to travel only during daylight hours. And as during the years when the AGW had been known as the Muskeg Special, the officials sent a track crew along with it. It was a long and an awkward load and getting it around some of the sharp curves of the road-bed posed problems. Now, on railways the sharper the curves in the track the more one rail is elevated above the other. That allows the train to speed around it without upsetting. When, however, the long tank was expected to crawl around, the difference in the elevation of the rails would tend to topple the awkward load. So at each of these risky places the road crew got out their shovels and bars and jacked up the lower rail till it was level with the other. Once the load passed beyond the curve they returned the rails to their normal position.

The refurbished AGW and the new highway to Edmonton were not the only means of transporting materials south. While the early stages of the work had been progressing at the GCOS plant site out at Tar Island, other crews had been building a 266-mile, sixteen-inch diameter pipeline to carry the plant's production out to civilization. At Edmonton it was to link up with the Inter-Provincial Pipe Lines which would whoosh Fort

McMurray's synthetic crude off to eastern Canada and the United States. This GCOS oil line had been built early in the life of the project so that until the plant got into operation it could be used in a reverse direction to take natural gas from the Edmonton area to supply fuel for the many construction processes. Once the project began producing synthetic "crude" oil, some of the by-products would be used to fuel the plant. When the storage tanks were full and the plant start-up completed, it was intended that the northern flow of fuel would cease and oil at a rate of 45,000 barrels per day would go coursing south.

But there was to be many a slip between the bucket-wheel cups and the storage tank lips, and disappointments and repeated discouragements dogged the plant operators. One of these headaches was the fuel for the project's power plant. Eventually a gas pipeline had to be built, this time south again but only some 125 miles long to bring in gas from the Lac La Biche field near the AGW station of Tweedie. This line gave the plant the necessary feed-stock gas to be turned into hydrogen for final upgrading of the naphtha, gas oil and kerosene that are later combined to make "synthetic crude." If GCOS officials begrudged the money they had to spend on this line, the Fort McMurray people blessed the day it was completed for to them in their severe climate it brought natural gas for heating. During those years many blessings came to Fort McMurray and for all of them they had to thank GCOS, whose tireless machines were tearing away at the sands and pouring their precious product into the oil pipeline.

For out at Tar Island the company's machines were indeed tearing away. The first step in the process was for a huge electric-power shovel to strip a large area of trees, muskeg and earth so as to expose the valuable sands. Standing seventy feet high, weighing four hundred tons, gobbling up fifteen cubic yards at a bite, this shovel which cost nearly one million dollars loaded a line of nine dump trucks which hauled the overburden away. Each truck could haul seventy-five tons, cost $85,000 to buy, and required six tires costing $9,000 per set. Once the fifty feet of overburden was removed, the bed of mineable sands being worked lay exposed, 150 feet deep and covering an area a quarter of a mile wide and nearly a mile long. The two gigantic bucket-wheel excavators which rip into the sands sit on their extensive caterpillar crawlers and tower 150 feet in the air. Their 30-foot diameter digging wheels armed with some ten buckets tipped with hardened steel which rip into the sands' bed operate on discharge booms which extend for 210 feet. Each excavator weighs 1,700 tons and by the time it was assembled on the site, cost $5.6 million. The eons-old tar sands will yield their riches profitably only to those who approach them with money. And GCOS came armed with that money and set each of its excavators to clawing out nearly one hundred tons of sand a minute—over 140,000 tons if they worked a full twenty-four-hour day. These wheels deliver sand to a fantastic set of conveyor belts, travelling at over 1,000 feet per minute, some of them 6 feet wide, some only 5 feet wide. Some of them are nearly a mile long and as the years go by and the mining surface recedes from the plant, will be extended to several miles. They in turn deliver the mined sands to a point 151 feet above ground level and dump them into the extraction plant. At this stage the mining has been done.

What happens to the sand and the oil from there on no layman can understand, but to start with some 6,000 tons per hour are mixed with steam and hot water—Karl Clark's process. The floating bitumen froth is skimmed off, diluted with naphtha and goes to storage tanks which hold 300,000 barrels, while the sand goes to the tailings pond in a manner which meets the demands of the Provincial Conservation Authorities. From the tanks the hard-won product goes to giant coker drums to extract 2,800 tons of coke a day, which goes to fuel the operation. Naphtha, kerosene and gas oil remain, from which 300 tons of sulphur a day are removed for environmental reasons. By separate lines, the naphtha, kerosene and gas oil are pumped to the outgoing 266-mile line. There, as they gush through the line buried under the vast forest, they blend for the first time to become Athabasca synthetic "crude" oil.

When this plant employing 1,500 people and turning out 53,000 barrels per day, is compared with its predecessors Abasand and Bitumount, only their bravery remains the same. Once upon a time Bitumount shipped a few tank cars of roofing tar, once upon a time in one season Abasand produced 21,476 barrels of oil; today with luck GCOS turns out 50,000 barrels a day. Once upon a time Abasand and Bitumount between them represented somewhat more than a million dollars invested. GCOS investment is some $300 million.

Long ago, plagued with difficulties, both Abasand and Bitumount lost money and went broke. GCOS, like them, has had its share of difficulties and like them it has consistently lost money—some $90 million since its official opening. During 1972, however, its output of oil rose to over eighteen million barrels and the company's loss for the year dropped to less than a million dollars. Hopefully, future years will offset these losses and increase that output. Only great know-how and infinite fortitude, combined with a near-bottomless cash barrel, could have pioneered as GCOS has done. Now that the continent is facing a shortage of energy, the company's outlook will improve. Hopefully, the late J. Howard Pew's courage will be justified.

The energy shortage will also hasten the day when other oil sand plants turn the first sods on their leases. For the portion of the oil sand deposits which the GCOS plant will mine is but a trifling part of the total area capable of yielding oil. Already Syncrude Canada Limited, a consortium of four companies, has started construction of another oil sands plant which it hopes to bring into production sometime in 1977. The company expects to spend $744 million on it. Beyond that, other consortiums have announced plans for more plants of about the same magnitude. Undoubtedly construction will start on these before the Syncrude operation begins producing. How many other such plants are waiting in the wings is something only time will reveal. The only certainty is that they will come into being.

Now that Syncrude is going ahead, Fort McMurray has to consider subdividing more land because long before five years are up the influx of additional workers will probably double its population. In the town's history nearly a hundred years of patience has finally paid off. No longer need its citizens worry about the Great Slave Lake Railway and what the

Mackenzie Highway might do to its water-borne traffic, a small but stable part of the town's industry.

For ninety years the people of Fort McMurray have looked north down their mighty river for the telltale smudge of approaching paddle wheels. Now as they look down that vista the reassuring plume of smoke rising from the GCOS plant twenty miles downstream tells them that the great bucket-wheels are still turning. But though these are providing Fort McMurray folk with all the wealth of modern material civilization, the splash of a thrashing paddle wheel takes them back in a twinkling to the romance of the old days of river captains, scowmen, voyageurs and dog drivers. And when on a fall morning the yelp of geese lifts their heads to watch great flocks which at daylight take flight from the Athabasca Delta marshes their thoughts turn back to the days of the great priests, Taché and Faraud, and the early explorers, Alexander Mackenzie, Peter Pond and Samuel Hearne. For though Fort McMurray has won through to success in the modern world, its heart strings still vibrate to its vivid memories of the men, Indian and white, who once sped up and down its great river, winding its way through the illimitable forest.

Occasionally a dreamer, escaping from the modern reality of paved streets, motorcycles and hamburger stands, strolls out to the tip of land that separates the Clearwater from the Athabasca. There in peace he can watch the quiet mingling of their waters.

Behind him and on his right slides the placid Clearwater with its memories of fur-trade canoes and York boats and of Peter Pond, Turnor, Fidler and Mackenzie, the men who set the white man's seal on this vast, forested page of northeastern Alberta. For down the Clearwater came the bold men who started all this activity.

To the left, surging in from the west, comes the Athabasca, eager to reveal to any dreamer its memories of Shot and his scowmen, Bishop Faraud and his nuns and lay brothers, all exulting at having run the rapids. And following them closely come other devoted men: Cornwall, Von Hammerstein, Clark and Ells, rocking with the ripple of the river but fixing their eyes on the oil-soaked cliffs.

To the right, the mingled waters point the way to Fort Chipewyan, Fort Simpson and the Arctic. Hovering over them are the spirits of dog teams and runners and Mounties receding into the North, the sternwheelers dissolving into the middle distance under the disappearing dots of intrepid bush pilots leading the way to mineral claims.

But these are mere visions revealed only to dreamers dipping nostalgically into the past. Persisting through these visions, however, is that distant down river smudge—the faint smoke which indicates to the world that at GCOS J. Howard Pew's bucket-wheels are still turning and that McMurray's oil is still surging south to fuel a hungry world.

Index

185

Stewart & Bannerman, 90.
Sun Oil Co., 176-79.
Sutherland, Angus, 156, 161.
Sutherland, John, 94, 124.
Swain, Thomas, 27, 28.
Sykes, Harry, 146, 147.

Taché, Rev. Father Alexander,
   66-69, 72, 73.
Tay, John W., 156.
Taylor Brothers, 118.
Taylor, Miss Elizabeth, 119.
Tête Jaune, the Iroquois, 48.
The Swan, 4.
Thibault, Rev. Father J. B., 66.
Thomas, Thomas, Jr., 33, 35.
Thompson, David, 15, 23, 29, 31.
Thorne, Sgt. "Nitchie," 129, 134,
   146, 147, 152, 157-59.
Todd, Dr. William, 35, 36, 47.
Tourand, J., 90.
Tremblé, Duncan, 98, 99.
Trotter, Cpl., 130.
Turnor, Philip, 9, 12-14, 17-19, 24.
Tyrrell, J. W., 101.

Upee, Tommy, 90.
Uranium City (Sask.), 167.

Velgue, M., 109.
Vermilion Chutes, 51, 89, 114,
   117, 120, 125, 128, 130, 153, 156.
Von Hammerstein, A., 142, 143,
   162, 175.

Waden, Etienne, 12, 14.
Wallwork, Jim, 110, 111.
Walter, John, 87.
Waterways: town of, 138, 151,
   152, 157, 159, 161-66, 172,
   174, 179.
Western Canada Airways, 164.
Wheeler, A. W., 175.
Whitley, Raynor, 118, 121, 122.
Williscraft, E. J., 153.
Wilson, W. D., 130.
Wood, Leslie, 121.

Wood Buffalo Park, 137, 163.
Woods, J. H., 116.
Wylie, William, 120.

Yale, John, 35.
Young, Campbell, 129.
Young, Harrison, 106.
Young, Bishop Richard, 91, 119.